After Liberalism

ESSAYS IN SEARCH OF FREEDOM, VIRTUE, AND ORDER

Edited by

William D. Gairdner, Ph. D.

Stoddart

Published in 1998 by Stoddart Publishing Co. Limited
34 Lesmill Road, Toronto, Canada M3B 2T6
180 Varick Street, 9th Floor, New York, New York, USA 10014

ORDERING INFORMATION

Distributed in Canada by General Distribution Services Limited
34 Lesmill road, Toronto, Canada M3B 2T6
Toll-free tel. for Ontario and Quebec 1-800-387-0141
Toll-free tel. for all other proivinces and territories 1-800-287-0172
Fax (416) 445-5967
Email Customer.Service@ccmailgw.genpub.com

Distributed in the US by General Distribution Services Inc.
85 River Rock Drive, Suite 202, Buffalo, New York, USA 14207
Toll-free tel. 1-800-805-1083
Toll-free fax 1-800-481-6207
Email gdsinc@genpub.com

02 01 00 99 98   1 2 3 4 5

Cataloging in Publication Data

Main entry under title:
After liberalism: essays in search of freedom, virtue and order

ISBN 0-7737-3071-0

1. Conservatism — Canada.
I. Gairdner, William D. (William Douglas), 1940–

JA84.C3A37 1998   320.52'0971   97-932740-7

Jacket design: Pekoe Jones
Text design: Tannice Goddard

Printed and bound in Canada

CONTENTS

INTRODUCTION

The word is out that modern "liberalism" is very sick; maybe even dying by its own hand. What began as an effort to protect individuals from undue authority has through a weird internal logic somehow become the voice of big government. At the same time it is accused of elevating the ideal of the autonomous individual above all else and thus producing a hedonistic, self-contradictory, morally stuporous society that even die-hard supporters didn't want and can no longer define or defend. The disappointed won't admit to being "conservatives" yet — Heaven forbid! — but out of raw embarrassment a lot of them are quietly becoming non-liberals. Point being, they would cheerfully drop the wimpy liberal something if they could just find something better. This book aims to point them in the right direction. It is a distinctly unwimpy book.

Meanwhile, those who have consciously taken a position against modern liberalism and dare to call themselves "conservative" (however heavily qualified) cannot afford to be smug. For even modern conservatism has no public moral or philosophical presence whatsoever outside the minds of a few nostalgic academics, columnists, or party hacks. It is wimpy, too.

So as an antidote to both liberal and conservative wimpiness, I want to embark on a restoration project, to discuss what the word *conservative* means, not as a squishy punching-bag political label, but in its full and rightful sense. So I'll use the term *true conservative* to make the case for an identifiable transhistorical human temperament that is at war with the radical temperament wherever the latter arises.

I am aware of the many objections to this exercise, and also of the argument that modern political conservatism only came into being with the eighteenth-century philosopher David Hume.[1] But I argue that the underlying human attitude has been around a lot longer. Like, since forever. Aristotle, to take the most famous example, was a prototypical conservative in most of the senses I wish to clarify. The distinctly conservative temperament was also felt everywhere in the community life of the Middle Ages, and again in debates against the social, moral, and political radicals of the English Civil Wars of the seventeenth century. Significantly for our time, it was ringingly heard under various labels in the founding debates that resulted in the American as well as Canadian constitutions, deeply influenced as these both were by the conservative principles of such as Edmund Burke.[2]

Having said this, I don't want all the fine writers gathered in this book to think I am going to present them as historical relics. On the contrary, much of their conservatism, seen in the light of the failure of conviction in our time, seems refreshingly *avant-garde*! By their insight and passion they sail boldly on an ocean of the uncommitted. And yet, although I am certain they would all leap to defend themselves against a too-easy label of any kind and would prefer to define the term themselves before conceding to it, the word *conservative* is used in half the essay titles and in the body of most. I suspect they all might agree with enough of the ideas, principles, and assumptions I will describe to say they at least share a distinct intellectual kinship.

Space being at a premium, what follows seeks to gain in feeling and understanding what must be sacrificed in the historical details. Only the most common and, I hope, least contentious points can be sketched out. First comes a description of the conservative concept of human nature, then the view of politics and government that necessarily flows from this, followed by the conservative complaint about radicalism of all kinds and a word about why conservatives defend certain key political, social, and economic institutions and moral beliefs.

HUMAN NATURE AND THE SELF

The Liberal View — The cleavage between the modern liberal and the true conservative notion of human nature and the self is as wide as the Grand Canyon. For the former, Man is naturally good and is ultimately perfectible by human means and reason alone, with no particular help needed from God, transcendent moral standards, or, for that matter, the next-door neighbour. Human failings and ignorance are ultimately said to be rooted not in the individual but in badly flawed human societies. That is why "progressive" regimes are needed to engineer human perfection. Voltaire said if we want good laws the best way to get them is to throw out all existing ones and start over. That is the radical formula for earthly happiness.

The Conservative View — For the true conservative, however, this is a prideful, catastrophic idea that paved the way for the mild despotism of gigantic welfare states and became the operating premise of all totalitarian regimes: if you can manage to produce the good society, you can produce good human beings. But the truth is the opposite. By definition, only God can be perfect. Man is by nature not so much evil as he is a flawed and by definition imperfect creation with a great capacity for good or evil. He suffers a constant inner warfare between reason and impulse. And so it follows that the governments he creates can only be imperfect, too. Even worse, they may do great evil because they are the only human institution with a monopoly on force. It is thus no surprise to a true conservative, it is axiomatic, actually, that the twentieth century, the most "progressive" of all, was also the bloodiest and cruellest in history. Obviously, more than our own naked untutored reason is required. To find the good and avoid the bad we also need the wisdom of the ages, to be found in tradition, wise customs, honoured beliefs, religion, and venerable moral standards.

How Is Freedom Used? — The true conservative has always been vitally interested in personal freedom, of course, because we cannot be moral agents, cannot choose between good and bad, unless we are free. But he is far more interested in knowing exactly what it is we wish to use our freedom for than in abstract freedom itself — a beguiling concept used mostly as a self-serving personal or political rationale. Indeed, he would argue that abstract freedom cannot exist because freedom is always for something concrete and particular. And for what? In contrast to the modern liberal theory of individualism as described by such as John Stuart Mill, he argues that the consequences of all our actions extend far beyond our own noses. Precisely by our personal freedoms and choices, we add to or subtract from the quality of life not only for ourselves but also for our families, our friends, and our communities, and most often in ways not at first apparent. That is why the true conservative says we are first of all social, interdependent beings. Free, but also bound. And because human community can only arise from some prevailing unity, society always has a natural and logical primacy over the individual. What is needed is the freedom to bind ourselves to proper ends.

Man More Than Atoms — Flowing from this social ontology is the true conservative's refusal to accept the depressing materialist and mechanical idea — an idea essential to the secular and political aims of pure liberal philosophy — that we are mere atoms, genes, or quanta. Even a conservative with no fixed religion or church will generally believe that there is something of the sacred in the constitution of the universe. For certain, he will say that to comprehend human life and society we need to know how the mere parts form a living, organic whole. This means understanding that what is pre-rational in life and society is as powerful and significant as the rational. And most important for politics, he will see clearly that without some grounding in a transcendent source, the liberal claim that all morality and law are merely man-made automatically reduces life to a contest of political wills. If the conservative has to choose between God and Nietzsche he will choose the former.

The Search for Absolutes — Accordingly, the true conservative will seek out fixed truths, laws, and moral standards not as inventions of the Self (that all-purpose liberal grab-bag for the surrogate soul) but as enduring things discoverable outside us that must then be incorporated into daily life. All religions have done this in a remarkably consistent way, as did the classical "pagan" virtues rendered by the likes of Cicero. For at bottom such concepts as truth, courage, loyalty, justice, prudence, duty, and love, or treason, cheating, and lying do not alter with the ages. Our difficulty in discerning or honouring standards is no proof of their absence, or relativity, but rather of our weakness. From this it follows that a true conservative is sensitive to the role of moral choice and standards in the formation not only of personal character, but especially of community. He refuses to hide behind the myth of the autonomous individual, or to believe that a collection of such individuals, each with a private moral agenda, who merely agree at most not to harm each other but otherwise may disagree on all things moral, could possibly constitute a thriving society.

In Defence of Inequality — He is also prepared to defend the full range of natural differences that arise from the free expression of talent and effort in each human being, and thus will refuse in principle to forcibly equalize society. He generally seeks local solutions to human problems rather than any homogenizing state action. He is naturally anti-egalitarian, and finds poisonous and immoral the idea of forcibly levelling society, of trying to raise the weak by weakening the strong. He believes that the only truly equal societies are to be found in prisons, and that levellers who gain sufficient power will always turn the whole of society into a prison. He is not surprised that freedom sprouts social and economic inequality, nor is he worried about it as long as all are governed under the same rule of law, and decency and charitable instincts are encouraged everywhere, especially at home and in local communities. He believes that healing society begins with healing oneself and helping one's neighbour, and that if all followed this logic, most of the larger social grievances and crises would end. The modern liberal rush to government as a solution to social problems he deems an insidious and morally evasive device that infantilizes human beings by making them dependent, thus destroying the fabric of community.

IDEAS, POLITICS, AND SOCIETY
Perfectible Man: Perfect Democracy — Sufficient scrutiny will reveal that different political systems are shaped utterly by different concepts of

human nature, as outlined above. The bloody Jacobins of revolutionary France, a most visible example, forcibly structured their entire regime to reflect Rousseau's idea that evil comes from outside man, who is inherently good, even if temporarily ignorant. This is the still beating heart of modern liberalism, however expressed. The formula says that if one man is good, a million must be better. That is why such optimistic radicals will always call for more direct democracy in all things, for the abolition or electoral control of any appointed upper house that might block the pure voice of the people (which they see as the voice of God: *Vox Populi, Vox Dei*), and will want every government official continuously subject to re-election or dismissal by the people. (In polities with an existing radical egalitarian superstructure, we find an inversion of this paradigm in the form of conservative populists using radical techniques to achieve conservative social and economic ends. The Reform Party of Canada is an example.)

Imperfect Man: Qualified Democracy — Such a radical scheme is enough to deeply frighten the true conservative, who sees it as encouraging mob rule, bitter factionalism, and oppression of the minority, with all the typical vices in attendance. The conservative is moved by the exactly contrary persuasion: all government must be structured to protect man from his own worst proclivities. One man's cruelty is bad enough — multiplied by millions it produces tyranny. Because we know there is a wide range of abilities and intelligence, virtues and vices, the raw will of the people as a whole needs to be "filtered" by the experience and prudence of the best and wisest among us. This demand in turn arises from the prior idea that difficult standards of good actually exist and must be sought by those best suited to find them. The democratic *representative* as a trustee of the people's will? Fine. But as a mere *delegate* of that will? A surefire recipe for factionalism.

In addition to filtering, there must be sufficient checks and balances to frustrate abuses of power and encourage moral virtue, high character, and the development of wise institutions and laws. For the only difference between a tyrannical leader and a tyrannical majority is that the latter is worse. You can ostracize or assassinate a single tyrant, but never a tyrannical majority. The true conservative thus tends to prefer a system of government with a judicious mixture of monarchical/presidential, constitutional, aristocratic, and democratic elements in a formula sufficiently complicated and self-checking to restrain the ultimate political vice from which the people cannot escape, which is unlimited power.

The Struggle Continues — All political debate in North America has been and continues to be shaped by the struggle between such conflicting views: Man the Perfectible vs. Man the Flawed; Utopian vision vs. Realist vision; Rousseau vs. Burke; Radical Democracy vs. Parliamentary Democracy; Secular values vs. Judeo-Christian values; the Court vs. Parliament; and so it goes. Which leads to the problem of differing conceptions of order.

Organization Requires Order — The conservative knows that even the simplest form of organization is impossible without order, whether in the home, school, corporation, association, committee, sports team, or army, and all order requires rules, command, and obedience, however formal or informal. But where will order come from? The answer is that if a society is to remain free, it must either produce the many voluntary forms of legitimate authority, rank, duty, and obligation itself from non-government sources such as mentioned above, or these myriad foci of order will soon be absorbed by a single and very power-hungry coercive source — the state. The true conservative has thus most often stood for a judicious balance between freedom and order, and for an authoritative but never authoritarian government that understands the free and proper role of duty and obligation in cementing a free society.

Welfare State an Aberration — He faults the comprehensive regulatory welfare state as a political and moral aberration that far exceeds the proper duties of government. For it becomes powerful either intentionally or willy-nilly by entering into a deadly war against natural society, eventually taking over the latter's organic, traditional forms of authority and community, and of course much of its income to accomplish this. Although attracted to some of the tenets of pure libertarianism, he also faults it for weakening resistance to that welfare state, by championing an atomistic philosophy that celebrates the priority of the individual over social and moral obligation.

The Real Voice of the People — For all these reasons and more, the true conservative listens deeply to the lessons of history as he strives to protect enduring political, moral, and social institutions. He is moved by "the voice of the people," of course, but in a far different way from the radical. He is attuned, to borrow G. K. Chesterton's fine phrase, to "the democracy of the dead," though this might be even better described as "the democracy of the living dead." Namely, all that has been thought, felt, and passed down to us, that lives on in the concrete forms, customs, habits, principles, and symbols of the best of our ancestors. When the conservative acts to change a thing, it is with the knowledge that circumstances will soon alter yet again. So he must change with prudence, not merely for his own time, but with due respect for the future generations to which he feels we must all be responsible.

Social Contract a Myth — He thus despises the radically anti-social belief that society and political life may be based on a mere *contract*. Locke's solitary "individual" in some "state of nature," lecturing the trees and the little rabbits on his "right" to freedom, is absurd and childish. The conservative does not see abstract individuals. He sees a certain quiet village carpenter, a curmudgeonly pharmacist, an unappreciative sister-in-law, an ailing but courageous mother. Abstract individualism is as denaturing and dehumanizing a concept as abstract freedom. By its very nature contract delegitimizes all government by making authority and order conditional and ephemeral, a set of momentary commitments that may be reversed or ripped up tomorrow by the most powerful faction of the day. Contract as a basis for society is a formula for permanent social revolution.

Charters Most Vulnerable to Political Manipulation — Worst of all, the idea of contract as a basis for society usually ends up in a list of abstract terms and "rights" much like Canada's Charter of Rights and Freedoms. The people often think such a list is a guarantee, never asking who is to provide these rights besides their neighbours. Because written constitutions cannot be self-interpreting, they soon become instruments for political and social engineering in the hands of radicals empowered to interpret them (those who win the struggle of political will): namely a tyrant, a shadowy "human rights tribunal," a Supreme Court — or, as Robespierre was astonished to see just before they took off his head, a Committee of Public Safety. To this alternative, the conservative prefers a transgenerational unwritten constitution more like the common law, a constitution so deeply embedded in the hearts, minds, practice, and experience of all society that it cannot be written down in any one place. England, whence have flowed so many of our concrete common-law rights, has never had written constitution (as yet). The true conservative cherishes something more like this compact (Burke again) between the dead, the living, and the yet to be born — a set of inherited customs, experiences, and actionable (as distinct from abstract) concrete rights, which comprise the terms of a truly vital and historically embedded constitution that conserves the best that has been said and done. Freedom is not a right but an achievement, something acquired and refined over many generations that has become the practical and unconscious reflex of an entire society, very difficult for tyrannical leaders or majorities to root out. The concrete and actionable common-law writ of *habeas corpus*, for example, which prevents police from detaining a person without warrant, and is historically derived from centuries of English legal practice, is worth any number of glorious-sounding abstract paper constitutions. Few constitutions have ever sounded as fine as France's Declaration of the Rights of Man and the Citizen, or the Constitution of the former Soviet Union — and few regimes were as cruel and bloody.

COMPLAINTS ABOUT RADICALISM

No Change for Its Own Sake — For all these reasons, the conservative, while he is not, as his enemies like to think, opposed to change, is certainly opposed to radical change for its own sake. At a minimum, he sets a high standard: *the burden of proof is on the innovator.* For a good society is like a delicate spider's web, an intricate and wholly connected creation that is hard to create, easy to wipe away. Unless the virtues of a proposal can be overwhelmingly demonstrated as superior to what is customary, then it is always better to go with the true than the new.

More to Reality Than Appearance — Further to this, in the same way that the conservative looks beyond the present voice of the people to hear the voice of the ages, he likes to peer through the surface of things present to perceive their real, deeper meaning. Just because we do not "consciously" understand the function of a ceremony, a myth, a symbol, an institution, or tradition, is no good reason to eliminate it. It could mean, rather, not that the tradition is useless, but that we have been useless in comprehending it. The deepest meanings of what we do and signify are often somewhat obscure, if not often unconscious, to hasty reflection. At the least, the fact of their endurance over a great span of time suggests they have a hold over us in ways often mysterious, and ought to be upheld for that reason alone. The true conservative is wary of reacting to anything too soon, or basing his reaction on the mere appearance of things, which he senses is always a trap. Culture in this very broad sense, conscious and unconscious, serves as an invisible armour to keep the state of nature and its primitive manifestations at bay. It is our way of protecting ourselves from ourselves.

Unintended Consequences — Finally, while the radical tendency, based in fervour and zeal, always yields to impulse and grasps reflexively at the first ideal "solution," the conservative watches policy after policy founder on predictable if unintended consequences, as often as not producing perverse moral, social, and economic effects opposite from those intended. Liberals pity unwed mothers, for example, and so pay them more to support each child, and then are anguished and uncomprehending when this results in more illegitimate children. The conservative says sufficient reflection would have predicted such a result — there have always been better means to prevent such effects. However, these means demand that politicians and their policy wonks give up the liberal understanding of human nature. This, most liberals cannot do, for it would mean surrendering the ideological basis underpinning all their other beliefs.

FAVOURITE INSTITUTIONS

To summarize, for the true conservative there is a connected stream of virtues, standards, and institutions that must be distinguished and pro-tected. At the base of things is the freedom to act as a *free moral agent*, adding to or subtracting from the fabric of *society as a whole*. (As distinct from increasingly taking cradle-to-grave moral direction and economic security from governments, or acting merely with regard to oneself alone.) Next in importance is the freedom to form and sustain vital *voluntary associations*, especially a *natural family*, defined as *a married mother and father living together with their dependent children*, an institution crucial for the protection and nurture of each new generation. (In contrast to the liberal notion of the family as something defined by the weekend live-ins.) Next are required the economic institutions and laws supporting *free markets* and *private property*, through which free persons and their families may work hard to create a good living and secure future. (In contrast to the welter of government regulation, suffocating taxation, and control of enterprise beyond normal laws against force and fraud.) Not least are the reasonable freedoms *to think and to speak within the bounds of decency*, also *to worship* a higher source of morality than the state itself, and here below to be treated *equally under a rule of law*, and not of men. (In contrast to a modern liberal regime that preaches moral "neutrality" yet is deeply zealous to control speech and thought with multifarious codes and punishments, and as deeply mired in myriad forms of arbitrary governance that impose laws and programs utterly contrary to our ancient customs.)

The feast of essays in this book begins with Janet Ajzenstat's arresting constitutional scholarship in which she challenges many misconceptions concerning the founding and present status of Canada. In a gracious and easy style she points out that the country we live in has from the beginning been endangered by political thinking energetically opposed to our tradition of parliamentary democracy. What is new at present, she tells us, is the intolerance of the sort of political give-and-take that has for generations been the earmark of a healthy liberal democracy ("liberal" here used, I think, in the earlier, more classical sense before the word got connected with the party of statism). Today, she warns, parliamentary democracy, most of all the idea of parliamentary democracy, is in crisis, reeling before the widespread belief that "the institutions of liberal democracy are not compatible with justice." She convincingly demonstrates that Canada's founders, as supporters of a tolerant system in which good government was defined in terms of security for dissent, were profoundly conservative in ways we would do well to remember and imitate.

Ajzenstat's historical perspective is followed by F. L. Morton's just as bracing and detailed, indeed, quite disturbing, account of what has happened to liberal democracy at the hands of the law — or should I say what is taken to be the law — of our 1982 Charter of Rights and Freedoms. In exposing a series of "myths" about the Charter that dominate the public mind, Morton gives us a piece that should be read aloud before the Supreme Court. He demonstrates that contrary to what is believed and was originally expected, the Charter does not protect basic rights and freedoms; ordinary citizens cannot easily avail themselves of Charter protection; it does not enhance liberty or limit government action, nor does it prevent the tyranny of the majority; and worse, by its very existence it establishes judicial supremacy over Parliament and therefore over the people. The fox is controlling the chickens, but no one is controlling the fox. Morton proposes a number of ways to do so.

Of my own essay I will only say that it explores the tension between two strong concepts — democracy and the family — of which many citizens, including many conservatives, are passionately fond, and which they proudly defend. Hence the perceived offensiveness of my title, "Democracy Against the Family," and the disturbed reaction I have often noticed when people first hear it. They react as if such a conflict were impossible. Regrettably, it is not.

Allan Carlson, our first guest American writer, has a wide reputation for his use of penetrating and bold arguments studded with hard research results to embarrass virtually every leftist social program that has been tried, just about wherever it has been tried. There is fascinating historical material here about the "family wage" legislation of a few generations ago, about the intricate complexities this "cultural" (as distinct from government) attempt at family justice and protection brought about, and how it fared well compared with today's government policies. Especially scary are his explanations of how in America, federally subsidized mortgages for single-parent and divorced families virtually came to sustain a housing industry that "needed" high divorce rates to survive; how the feminist gender wars evolved into a choice for unmarried mothers between "private or public patriarchy"; and not least, how the opposing demographics of the "Youth State" and the "Elder State" imply a kind of social war for resources between generations.

From here we move to the business of putting old heads on young bodies. I am pleased to say it would be difficult to find another nonideological essay that so thoroughly and calmly rebuts and disputes every aspect of the liberal educator's canon. "A Conservative Education" by veteran educator Mark Holmes provides a sound formula, or rather a sound conservative way, to educate based on a grounding in order, in substantive content, in the organic classroom, in a true values community, in leadership, and in many other things that need to remembered and practised. What he has to say holds hope for any parent whose children have survived, or should I say suffered, through that manifestly inadequate experience called the "education system."

The barrier that separates the present from the past, and all the forgetting this implies in the anti-conservatism of a modern liberal society, where information and knowledge have come to mean the same thing, is manifest in Peter Stockland's wide-ranging essay, "Contact Conservatism," which is next. With a deft hand he juxtaposes the modern fever for immediate raw information against the still immensity of real meaning, and shows how we have suffered as a civilization from — in one of Peter's memorable formulations — "the triumph of the disembodied present over the substantial past."

In "Who's Right, Who's Left, and What's Left Over," Michael Walker is clearly enjoying himself as he exposes the inadequate and self-serving nature of contemporary political terminology. Some of it is not so humorous. Our notion of a placid and politically tolerant Canada is mightily disturbed by accounts of ridicule, bombings, and death threats

at his home and place of work. But the stories of label-switching according to whose oxen has just been gored are instructive, to say the least,
and give a Swiftian sense of how ludicrous are the media and their
mavens when riding their own hobby-horses. Readers will enjoy testing
themselves on his World's Smallest Political Quiz.

Another dose of realism follows from Tom Flanagan and Stephen
Harper, who give a short lesson on the travails, not so much of conservatism, as of conservative party politics in Canada for most of this
century. We gain insight into how a political competition held under our
first-past-the-post system tends to produce an outcome-bias, and how
conservative wins have generally been due to "throw-them-out" coalitions. The distinction between "economic" and "social" conservatives
is explored here, as well as the split in theory and practice between
populism ("democratic monism") and traditionalism (Burkean "trustee"
conservatism). Of great interest is how a change to something like a
"preferential ballot" system would help create conservative clout in
Canada and greatly alter the political landscape.

Canada's landscape may, after all, be altered against the will of the vast
majority of the population by a very small number of the people — say,
by my estimate, somewhere around 12 percent of the Canadian population needed to win a Quebec referendum on secession. The latent
conservatism of Scott Reid's essay, "The Quebec Question: Debt Division
and the Rule of Law," lies in its persuasive appeal to prudence, the rule of
law, and impartiality as means to avoid chaos and potential violence in the
event of a "Yes" vote in Quebec. Reid fingers the apportionment of debt
between Canada and a departing Quebec as a problem akin to a boundary dispute. He describes how a special international five-member Court
of Arbitration, established through binding legislation by both parties in
advance, could be properly structured to avoid repudiation both of the
debt and of the arbitration itself, and thus could peacefully settle this
nation's most potentially inflammatory situation in advance.

Our book closes with two essays that return us to the moral ground
with which true conservatism has historically been most deeply concerned. That is not because all true conservatives are moralizers, but

rather because they see keenly that all social, political, and, yes, even raw economic policies rest at bottom on preferences, and these in turn rest on some more deeply planted moral axiom. On some preference for the way the world ought to be. This appeal to the future, to how we ought to behave tomorrow, next year, or indeed for life, is inherent in human freedom. It is part of the struggle for self-transcendence that forms the basis of community. So it is better to ferret those axioms out than to pretend they do not exist. Or, as liberals do, to pretend that all axioms may happily coexist, even if in direct conflict.

Michael Coren certainly grasps the nettle on such matters, and expresses an emotional defence of "social conservatism" that demarcates it as clearly as we need from libertarianism and neoconservatism. He is persuasive that one cannot be a true conservative without being "social", and I suspect he would agree that the term itself is somewhat tautological. What is especially enjoyable here is how after laying out the conservative view, or feeling, or position on a variety of topics such as homosexual rights, the family, and abortion (this last, I believe, the most obvious and unbreachable divide between economic and social conservatives), he nicely forces a confrontation with the so-called economic conservative. He does this by showing how in many instances past (slavery) and present (lap-dancing), the "free market" and its economic wonders can produce the economic good of some, but through its rotten spillover effects, the morally bad for all. Eco-nomic freedom, he writes, "does not necessarily guarantee a good and fair society and is not an end in itself — nor, in a moral vacuum is it even a means to an end."

We end our *tour d'horizon* of the conservative landscape with the second of our two guest American writers, Jay Budziszewski. I have never met Jay except by e-mail, the occasion for contacting him and inviting him to participate having been the prior enjoyment of several of his arresting and challenging essays. I was struck by the moral courage, insight, and lucidity — I might even say the daring — of what he had to say, especially given that he is saying it as a professing Christian to a smug and condescending modern liberal culture. The hungry lions of the philistine legions rage and claw away, and Jay is down there in the pit with his intellectual and moral weapons driving them back. His essay on conscience in this collection makes the case that the natural moral law is permanently "written on the heart," and that resistance or evasion or repression of conscience does not so much weaken as divert, so that by a series of moral self-deceptions, we end up going from doing bad, to doing far worse, in a diversionary and compensatory downward spiral. In essence, we get hunted down, and humbled, by the truth.

With great pleasure I close with a few words of appreciation: to my wife and children for their constant support and their understanding of the writer's woes and satisfactions; to Don Bastian of Stoddart Publishing, for his continued and so capable assistance and advice; and not least, to the Canadian writers and our American friends whose work is gathered in this book. They made this editor's job a rewarding one.

NOTES

1 A very useful modern anthology with instructive supporting text and notes that has proved a refresher for this Introduction is Jerry Z. Muller, *Conservatism: An Anthology of Social and Political Thought from David Hume to the Present* (Princeton, NJ: Princeton University Press, 1997).

2 See especially the highly readable and informative book by Christopher Moore, *1867: How the Fathers Made a Deal* (Toronto: McClelland and Stewart, 1997).

THE CONSERVATISM OF THE CANADIAN FOUNDERS

JANET AJZENSTAT

In the Charlottetown Referendum debates of 1992 both sides came close to repudiating parliamentary democracy. Both suggested that the present constitution is unacceptable, that it is holding Canada back, perpetuating old injustices and preventing obvious remedies.[1] The Yes side (the leaders of Canada's eleven governments and the Territories, leaders of the opposition parties at the federal level, the national aboriginal organizations, and numerous other important political constituencies) were backing the most massive program of constitutional reform Canada has ever seen. The No side (prominently represented by the Reform party, the Bloc Québécois, and the National Action Committee on the Status of Women) maintained that the proposed reforms did not go far enough. It was not revolutionaries on the fringe but the elites of the Canadian mainstream who were recommending a revolutionary overhaul of the Canadian political system! Despite their differences on particular issues, the Yes and the No sides were in complete agreement that the constitutional status quo was intolerable.[2] "Status quo" became a term of abuse. Only a new constitution, a new founding, would remedy Canada's ills.

A generation ago Canadians were proud of their constitution — proud in modest Canadian fashion. They took it for granted that it is good to live in a parliamentary liberal democracy. Today, we see ill-defined discontent, impatience with parliamentary institutions, disdain for politics and politicians, and a readiness to press ahead with radical change in defiance of constitutional procedure.[3] How did mild-mannered Canadians get into such a tizzy?

Not all political discontent is suspect in liberal democracies; far from it. Liberal democrats are proud that their constitution allows, indeed honours, expressions of dissatisfaction with laws and the conduct of public officials. Democracies thrive on discontent of this kind. Electoral politics and representative government require it. The assumption is that the airing of disagreements and debate about alternative policies are the welcome consequence of political freedom and encourage development of better laws. But what we have been seeing in recent years is more than dissatisfaction with particular laws and policies. It is dissatisfaction with the very idea of liberal democracy itself. General grumbling about politics is not new in Canada. What is new is discontent with the régime. What is new is the idea that the institutions of liberal democracy are not compatible with justice.

Popular discontent of this kind is epidemic in the Western world and comparative studies reveal aspects of the phenomenon that cannot be fully explored here.[4] But each nation has its own story and Canada's story is not the least interesting. The peculiar feature of Canadian discontent is that, paradoxical as it may seem, it is often couched in terms of an appeal to conservatism. The contention is that historically Canada is a conservative nation; the Fathers of Confederation are said to have held conservative values difficult to reconcile with liberal democracy.[5] From such a premise it is only a step to the idea that Canada needs a new constitution to reflect our supposed anti-liberalism. But advocates of this position seldom recommend a return to conservatism. For the most part they value conservatism only because they believe it contains the seeds of a powerful argument against liberal democracy. The important thing in their view is that Canada should reject liberal democracy. They picture a Canada boldly advancing into a new age, beyond both liberalism and conservatism.[6]

I argue here that the premise of this argument is false and the conclusion unacceptable. There is in fact no essential opposition between Canadian conservatism and liberal democracy. On the contrary, Canadian conservatives have been liberal democracy's ardent champions from the very beginning. It was the proudest act of the Conservative Fathers of Confederation to entrench in the Constitution Act of 1867 (the old British North America Act) the principles and institutions of parliamentary liberal democracy. The idea that an antiliberal conservatism lies at the heart of the Canadian political identity, and that the founders' conservatism detracted from their support for liberal democracy, is an invention, a myth, the product of the false hopes and political dreams of the 1960s.

If Canada is to avoid the perils of political dissatisfaction, what it needs today above all is to revive traditional Canadian conservative confidence in liberal democracy. The liberal democratic constitution, born of a period of marked political upheaval, offers an unequalled formula for accommodating and moderating political discontent.

Few of Canada's political philosophers look on liberal democracy with unqualified favour. George Grant, Gad Horowitz, Charles Taylor, C. B. Macpherson, and James Tully: all are profoundly critical of liberal democratic institutions and practices. They argue that Canada's electoral and legislative systems do not promote fruitful and effective political participation; that the rule of law fosters a selfish individualism that thwarts collective action; and that in general liberalism ignores the communal character of human identity.[7] The contention *in toto* is that liberal democracy precludes human flourishing. Grant and Horowitz are the premier teachers in this tradition of antiliberalism.

The idea that Canadians should be wary of liberal democracy because Canada is inherently a "tory" nation originated with the publication of

Grant's *Lament for a Nation* in 1965. It is now a staple of political science and Canadian studies courses. Few students graduate without being told that what is distinctive and precious about the Canadian political way of life is that the Canadian founding, in contrast to the American, contains an element of political thought hostile to liberal democracy. It is not clear whether we should think of Grant's anti-liberalism as a direct cause of today's political discontent. We can say he has given Canadians a language in which to express their discontent. One comes across his arguments constantly in the media and in the political statements of educated Canadians.

Grant admits that liberal democracy comprises one aspect of the Canadian political tradition. He even suggests that the liberal constitutionalism of the American founders like Hamilton and Madison has considerable merit.[8] But it is an essential part of his teaching that liberal democracy of the kind Madison recommended is a thing of the past. He believes that liberalism in both the United States and Canada has undergone a transformation; it has become, or is becoming, an intolerable and, in a deep sense, inhuman regime. Madisonian liberalism contained at least a residual notion of human dignity; twentieth-century liberal democracy devalues all idea of human worth.[9]

The part of Grant's and Horowitz's argument that made such an impact in the 1960s was the idea that Canadian political history, in contrast to the U.S., contained a saving element in the form of "toryism."[10] The suggestion is that tory ideas of truest blue were brought to Canada by the United Empire Loyalists in the late eighteenth century and left an indelible conservative stamp on the Canadian way of thinking until well into the twentieth. Toryism may never have been more than a subordinate strand of thought in Canadian history but it was supposedly the essential and defining element.

The conservatism or toryism that Grant describes as an aspect of our history more closely resembles a justification of feudalism than it does a modern political ideology. In contrast to liberal democracy, with its emphasis on individualism, political equality, and human dignity, Grant's toryism depends on notions of collective good, and on concepts of honour and virtue that legitimate a social hierarchy. It posits the direct influence of religion in political affairs. Fear of hell, not the populace, should restrain political rulers; social elites properly define the common good according to their understanding of God's will.

Grant is not arguing that conservatives should encourage a climate of moral and religious belief as support for liberal institutions. Certainly he does not suggest that Canadians can ever recapture their happy liberal-tory past.[11] At the heart of his political thought is the idea that liberal democracy has become monstrously inhuman; liberal democracy is not a regime Grantian "conservatives" should be prepared to endorse in any degree. The picture of Canadian toryism in *Lament* functions chiefly as a position from which Grant can argue the deficiencies of Canadian liberal democracy.

No one reading Grant can fail to benefit from his analysis of moral and religious issues; a profound vision of our relation to God informs his political writing. But admirable as it is, or perhaps exactly because it is so elevated, this glorious moral teaching turns to lead when translated into a prescription for Canadian politics. Grant's toryism is a world away from the kind of conservatism that counsels prudence, restraint in political affairs, and patient toleration of opposing views. It is wildly imprudent, idealistic, mille narian. It bears no resemblance to the political philosophy of the Conservative parties that have played such a distinguished role in Canadian political history. It is extraordinary that *Lament for a Nation* has been so successful in persuading Canadians that the Grantian definition of conservatism is the true definition, the Canadian one!

Grant deeply believes people become morally worse by living in a liberal democracy. The argument of *Lament* is heightened to an almost unbearable pitch by the idea that Canadian politics is part of the great, eternal battle between human good and evil. It recounts the particular events of the Diefenbaker era against the broad sweep of history's philosophical and religious ideas: Canada *sub specie aeternitatis*. On one level the argument is that Canada as a nation founded by conservatives might have been in a position to resist the worst effects of liberal democracy;

in contrast to the United States, always treated by Grant as an irredeemably liberal democratic nation, Canada might have retained, into the twentieth century and beyond, ideas of political virtue.

But Grant is ambiguous on the subject of historical progress and human agency. Although he sometimes seems to suggest that political efforts can change history's course for the better, elsewhere he takes a fatalistic position: liberalism inevitably degenerates; even good regimes inevitably go to hell in a handbasket. The ambiguity merely contributes to the excitement of *Lament*. If we had been better Canadians, tried harder, been more appreciative of our conservative heritage, could we have fended off the crude and selfish liberal individualism of American politics? Could we have prevented Canada's fall into the maw of the evil empire to the south? Grant gives no conclusive answer.

Lament does not recommend a course of political action. One laments, one grieves, but there is no concrete remedy. In contrast, Gad Horowitz, and after him the economic nationalists, offer a clear-cut, well-defined political program.[12] They believe it is possible to combat the influence of American liberalism and to build a new Canada that will capture the collectivist elements of the old toryism while discarding such outmoded notions as social hierarchy and the influence of established religion.

Horowitz's definition of toryism, not incompatible with Grant's, is formulated in terms derived from the American scholar Louis Hartz.[13] According to Hartz, the political thought of the modern period reveals a necessary progression from feudal toryism, essentially collectivist and hierarchical in character, to liberalism, which is individualist and egalitarian, and thus to socialism, which is collectivist and egalitarian. What interests Horowitz especially in this model is the idea that nations with a tradition of toryism are hospitable to socialism. Tory collectivism in the past leads to the emergence of socialist collectivism in the future. Hartz contended that the emergence of true socialism is virtually impossible in nations like the United States that have no history of toryism. Horowitz takes the next step: since Canada has at least a trace of toryism in its past, it should be able to support a degree of socialism. The article in which Horowitz argues that Canadian political history

cons → collective good

liberalism – individual autonomy?

cannot be understood except in terms of an inevitable progression towards socialism is said to be the most widely read essay in the field of Canadian political thought.[14]

Together Grant and Horowitz have the effect of a one-two punch: Grant teaches discontent with existing institutions, Horowitz, a utopian fervour for new forms of rule. Grant suggests that liberal democracy is destroying Canada; Horowitz promises a new Canada, distinguished by its capacity to move beyond liberal democracy.

Until recently, the account of Canada's past presented by Grant and Horowitz went almost unchallenged.[15] But their approach to the documentary history is open to criticism. The fact is that their thesis rests almost entirely on abstract political philosophy. They profess to explain Canadian history in terms of Loyalist conservatism and the founders' philosophy, but they do not themselves read the Loyalist declarations or the Confederation debates.

Recent scholarship finds no support for Grant and Horowitz in the historical record.[16] There is no Grantian toryism in Loyalist thought and certainly none in the Confederation debates. The new scholarship reveals instead a stirring debate between *liberal democrats*, including the Conservatives of 1867, and *radical democrats*, such as William Lyon Mackenzie and Louis Joseph Papineau and their followers. The conservatism of Macdonald and Cartier is demonstrated by their defence of liberal democracy against an ideology of radical democracy. Indeed the arguments of the 1867 Conservatives against radical democracy mirror almost exactly the arguments against the excesses of democracy famously associated with Americans like Madison. In brief, the Conservatives argue that radical democracy of the kind endorsed by Mackenzie and Papineau threatens political freedom by entrenching in office a party representing a permanent majority. In the Conservative view, radical democracy leads to one-party government and democratic despotism.

As the institutions of 1867 testify, the liberal democrats were victors in this great ninteenth-century battle.[17] When we think of the good old days in Canada, when we lament the passing of something fine, it is liberal democracy that should come to mind, not Grant's "conservatism."

Until sometime in the 1960s, Canadians lived, more or less contentedly, in decent, moderate fashion, with the institutions and practices of liberal democracy. The tory Canada that Grant describes is a Canada that never was. Grant invented the Canada he taught us to lament.

Scholars today call the ideology of radical democracy that flourished in British North America at the time of the 1837-38 Rebellions "civic republicanism" or "civic humanism."[18] Previously, historians either ignored this strand of radical thought or interpreted it as a variety of liberalism. The greatest benefit of the new scholarship, I would argue, is that by retrieving civic republicanism it reveals the essential opposition between radical democracy and liberal democracy, making it possible to articulate the defence of liberal democracy in the arguments of the 1867 Conservatives.

Civic republicanism resembles toryism insofar as it plays down the notion of the individual and emphasizes community. But in contrast to the hierarchical ideology Grant and Horowitz profess to find in Canadian political history, civic republicanism is scrupulously egalitarian, embracing even the idea of material equality. It offers a vision of the simple and virtuous life; the revolutionaries of the 1830s believed pursuit of commercial objectives, private or public, was proof of moral and political corruption.[19] Above all, they argued for government by "the people." They rejected British parliamentary institutions in favour of forms of government in which the "people's party" would govern directly from the popular house.

Consider Papineau's argument. In the 1830s he was leader of the party that spoke for the majority of the populace in Lower Canada. His political competitors were the appointed officials more or less permanently ensconced in the Executive Council and upper legislative house. Elections came and went, but the party winning the majority of seats in the popular chamber remained excluded from power. Papineau thought of the problem in terms of an opposition between Aristocracy, with a capital "A," and Democracy, with a capital "D." His party stood for Democracy, officialdom for Aristocracy.[20] Democracy with a capital "D" was the wave of the future. Aristocracy was an ideology of the benighted past. When he and his party were at last elevated to power, Democracy would have triumphed. The argument is perhaps understandable, given his situation. The trouble is that at the crucial point in his career, the period of the Rebellions, there is nothing to suggest that Papineau believed his party would ever be called on to relinquish office. Allowing the opposition to return to power would be tantamount to returning to the dark ages. His analysis simply does not allow him to think in terms of respect for a parliamentary opposition, or for the game of political "ins" and "outs" liberal democrats believe so crucial to political freedom.

The liberal democrats in Lower Canada argued that the clique in the upper chamber, far from being aristocrats, were merely petty, greedy men taking advantage of defective political institutions. The liberal democratic remedy called for correcting the institutions, and in particular for introducing the principle of responsible government.[21] But radical democrats were wary of responsible government. They preferred schemes to transfer the powers of government from the Executive Council to the Legislative Assembly. At times they were prepared to accept an elective Executive Council.[22] The more ambitious proposal was to make the Council a mere administrative tool of the Assembly, entirely subordinate to the people's chamber. In either case their objective was government by the people's party in the people's house: Democracy.

In the 1830s it was not obvious that the liberal democrats would win the day. But with the defeat of the rebels in 1837-38, the radical democratic vision goes into decline. The struggle for responsible government is successful, and by the 1860s no one can doubt that the new constitution will entrench the principles of the parliamentary system. Nevertheless, memories of the old battle linger. In the 1860s the Conservatives must still couch the defence of parliamentary democracy in terms of its difference from Democracy.

Admittedly the language in which Macdonald and Cartier defend liberal democracy is open to misinterpretation. They declare their absolute opposition to "purely democratic institutions."[23] They defend the "monarchical principle" of government. They express doubts about the further extension of the franchise. How easy it has been to interpret these statements as expressions of disdain for liberal democracy, or lingering affection for old forms of hierarchy. But when we understand that the Conservatives were defining their position in opposition to radical democracy, the true import of these statements is revealed.

"In all countries," says Macdonald, "the rights of the majority take care of themselves." It is "only in countries like England enjoying constitutional liberty, and safe from the tyranny of a single despot or of an unbridled democracy, that the rights of minorities are regarded."[24] The "great test of constitutional freedom," he argues, is that "the rights of the minority are respected." Today we usually think of minorities in terms of class or ethnicity. Macdonald speaks of "the" minority. Just as "the" majority in liberal democratic theory refers to the part of the populace supporting the party in office, "the" minority refers to the losers, the party or parties out of office. Macdonald first describes two forms of tyranny, the tyranny of a single despot, and the tyranny of unbridled democracy, and contrasts both with a system in which political losers are "regarded" (honoured). He virtually *defines* good government in terms of security for political opposition and dissent.

Papineau argues for the rights of the majority, "the people," the winners; he disdains the idea of political opposition. Macdonald defends the rights of the minority, the political losers; he elevates the idea of opposition. Papineau believes radical democracy is the necessary next step in the evolution of politics, liberating the voice of the people. Macdonald and Cartier see it as the royal road to democratic tyranny; it will "liberate" popular leaders to enslave the people they profess to speak for.

In a parliamentary democracy, security for the opposition depends on the principle of responsible government, the requirement that Ministers of the Crown maintain the support of the majority in the popular house. Canadians sometimes allow themselves, carelessly, to speak as if responsible government "fused" Cabinet and Commons. Such a description blinds us to the distinction between Cabinet and Commons that liberal democrats like Macdonald believe all-important. Although the governs, it represents only a party, a part, "the" majority: the majority the day. It is the House of Commons that represents the whole of the populace. The Commons, however, does not govern. In a parliamentary liberal democracy the business of government is not conducted from the floor of the House of Commons.

This distinction between Cabinet and Commons reminds the party in office that it is there on sufferance; an adverse vote can turn it out. (No true liberal democrat believes it is anything but salutary to keep political leaders uneasy.) And it means what is just as important, that political opposition in the Commons is there by right; it cannot be permanently silenced. The constitutional distinction between Cabinet and Commons is what enables parliamentary debate; it is what guarantees respect for expressions of political dissent, and political dissatisfaction.

Macdonald's reference to the two forms of tyranny sums up in a phrase the whole history of liberal democracy. It was born in the struggle against the autocratic rulers of the seventeenth century, and was nearly destroyed by the democratic excesses of the French Revolution. The contrast between the Glorious Revolution of 1688 and the French Revolution had been the stuff of political debate in the British North American colonies from early in the century; Macdonald's rhetoric would have been perfectly clear to his listeners. Parliamentary liberal democracy would keep the new country safe from the tyranny of a single despot, and the tyranny of unbridled democracy: safe from the Stuarts, safe from the Papineaus.

In a longer essay it would be possible to show just how closely the arguments of the Conservatives in the 1860s resemble those of American thinkers like Madison. Canadian scholars are familiar with the opposition to radical democracy in the founding documents of the United States. The pity is that they so seldom look for it in the Confederation debates. No doubt the reluctance to find a defence of liberal democracy in 1867 reflects a peculiarly Canadian desire to interpret Canadian political history in ways that distinguish us from our neighbours. Canadians are always looking for new ways to say that Canada differs from the U.S. But when the argument is that the peculiar excellence, the special value of our political way of life, lies in difference, hope of understanding Canadian political history and present institutions flies out the window. There is more insight to be gained by looking for principles and experiences common to the two countries. History shows more parallels than differences. Dissatisfaction with liberal democracy now flourishes in the U.S. as much as in Canada. Americans historians now play up civic republican elements in their political past. Indeed they sometimes appear to be arguing that liberal democracy played no role at all in the American founding.[25]

The 1867 Conservatives feared a regime in which the political opposition was ignored, and dissent smothered. The Canadian problem today is rather different. Dissent is overwhelming us, dissent of the kind that calls in question the value of liberal democratic institutions. Our problem is to moderate discontent while still guaranteeing effective dissent.

Liberal democrats have two overriding fears; they envisage two evil futures. The first fear is that a single leader, a "single despot," will emerge, suppressing dissent and opposition. The second is that dissent will become unmanageable, fragmenting the polity and leading to a breakdown of public order, and perhaps even to civil war. In the first case there is too little effective dissent, in the second there is too much, and it is only too effective.

The evils are related. Macdonald's term "unbridled democracy" could describe a system in which the intransigent dissent arising from the *demos* erodes support for responsible leaders, or one in which a despot rides to power on the basis of such great popular appeal that the few dissenting voices are silenced. Perhaps the one scenario follows from the other. When prudent leadership fails and civil disorder threatens, the popular despot appears as saviour. At any rate, in both scenarios, the one in which there is too little dissent and the one in which there is too much, political prudence and moderation vanish; exciting and wholly immoderate political passions rule the day.

Paradoxical as it may seem, liberal democracy poses the same institutional remedy for both threats. I have already argued that parliamentary institutions are designed to honour and secure political dissent. The question now is how those same institutions also *moderate* dissent.

The argument is that if dissenters have a fair chance to seize the reins of government peaceably they will play by parliamentary rules. They will keep up the kind of dissent necessary to establish their credibility with the electorate but refrain from carrying it to the point where it threatens the rules on which their hope of attaining office rests. Thus if all is working well, the same institutions promote dissent, protecting us from the despot, and also moderate it, protecting us from civil war. For Joseph Howe, campaigner for parliamentary democracy in opposition to the civic republicans, the best way of dealing with potential despots like Papineau and Mackenzie was to enable them to come to power under the rules of responsible government.[26]

It may seem a tall order. The very fact of dissent is supposed to foster moderation. Debate in the electoral and parliamentary arenas generates considerable heat and noise; then a vote is taken and the opposition agrees to live with a result that only a short time before they professed to believe intolerable. Of course although the dissenters must live with the results of an adverse vote, they are not expected to give up the fight. There will be another election, another vote, another chance. Politics is about compromise, give and take — and living with distasteful results. The political institutions of liberal democracy require the exercise of political moderation, and also provide lessons in moderation.

The signal characteristic of the present political discontent in Western nations is that living with distasteful political results has little appeal. Today's opponents of liberal democracy are as intransigent as the radical democrats of Canadian history. Like the radical democrats they want to inject into politics a richer idea of community and public virtue, and a more immediate sense of the people's will. If they differ from the radicals of old it is that they are more enamoured of change and have more ambitious political programs. They want immediate remedies: ending violence against women, eradicating child poverty, saving the environment. No liberal democrat is going to object to such aims. What is objectionable is the impatience, the demand for immediate results, and the intolerance of dissent and debate about alternative programs for achieving these objectives. Nothing indicates Canadians' present confusion about constitutional reform more than that, in the attempt to deal with such insistent demands, we are proposing to jettison the institutions of liberal democracy that are supremely designed to moderate intransigence without suppressing all expression of discontent.

It is an additional irony that we so often justify this rejection of liberal democracy by an appeal to Canadian conservatism. The truth is that the solid heart of Canadian conservatism has always supported liberal democracy. The conservatism of Macdonald and his colleagues lies exactly in their refusal to adopt the exciting innovations proposed by the radical democrats. They were founding a new nation, but they refused to adopt a new political regime. They spoke glowingly of the prospects before the new Confederation but did not turn their backs on the traditions of parliamentary democracy.

We have never needed the conservatism of the founders more.

NOTES

1 According to Thomas Courchene, the Referendum vote said "in no uncertain terms" that "the conceptions and traditions which had dominated Canadian governance during the past 125 years were no longer appropriate for the Canada of today." Thomas J. Courchene, "The Meaning of No: A Political Era Dies," *The Globe and Mail*, October 27, 1992, p. A1.

2 The defence of parliamentary government in the Beaudoin-Edwards report was a notable exception. *The Process for Amending the Constitution of Canada. Report of the Special Joint Committee of the Senate and House of Commons*, June 20, 1991.

3 Evidence of popular dissatisfaction with existing institutions is supremely evident in the *Citizens' Forum on Canada's Future: Report to the People and Government of Canada* (the Spicer Report) (Ottawa: Supply and Services, 1991). "One of the strongest messages the Forum received from participants was that they have lost their faith in the political process and their political leaders" (Spicer Report, p. 96). And see "The People's Verdict," *Maclean's*, July 1, 1991.

— 30 —

4   Neil Nevitte, "New Politics," in Mark O. Dickerson, Thomas Flanagan, and Neil Nevitte, eds., *Introductory Readings in Government and Politics*, third edition (Scarborough, ON: Nelson, 1991), pp. 161-70. Jean Bethke Elshtain, *Democracy on Trial* (Concord, ON: Anansi, CBC Massey Lectures Series, 1993).

5   George Grant, *Lament for a Nation: The Defeat of Canadian Nationalism* (Toronto: McClelland and Stewart, 1965; reprinted many times by Carleton University Press in the Carleton Library series).

6   Gad Horowitz, "Conservatism, Liberalism, and Socialism in Canada: An Interpretation," *Canadian Journal of Economics and Political Science* 32:1 (1966).

7   George Grant, *Lament for a Nation*. Gad Horowitz, "Conservatism, Liberalism, and Socialism in Canada." C. B. Macpherson, *The Life and Times of Liberal Democracy* (Oxford: Oxford University Press, 1977). Charles Taylor, *The Malaise of Modernity* (Concord, ON: Anansi, CBC Massey Lectures Series, 1991). James Tully, *Strange Multiplicities: Constitutionalism in an Age of Diversity* (Cambridge: Cambridge University Press, 1995).

8   Grant, *Lament*, chap. 5.

9   Grant, "Faith and the Multiversity," in George Grant, *Technology and Justice* (Toronto: Anansi, 1986).

10 Grant, *Lament*, chap. 6.

11 Samuel Ajzenstat, "The Place of Abortion in George Grant's Thought," in Yusaf K. Umar, ed., *George Grant and the Future of Canada* (Calgary: University of Calgary Press, 1992).

12 "Liberalism" in this argument and elsewhere refers to the political philosophy of constitutional liberal democracy; it does not refer to the statist doctrine sometimes called "liberalism" in popular circles. Horowitz and the economic nationalists are strenuously in favour of big government, and the extension of the regulatory and welfare state. In popular terms, they are "liberals," perhaps Canada's most famous. Among the best-known economic nationalists are James Laxer, Kari Levitt, Ian Lumsden, W. H. Pope, Abraham Rotstein, Phillipe Syke, and John W. Warnock.

13 Louis Hartz, *The Founding of New Societies: Studies in the History of the United States, Latin America, South Africa, Canada and Australia* (New York: Harcourt, Brace and World, 1964).

14 H. D. Forbes, "Hartz-Horowitz at Twenty: Nationalism, Toryism, and Socialism in Canada and the United States," *Canadian Journal of Political Science* 21:4 (1988). That the Horowitz thesis retains its hold is suggested by its use in Paul M. Sniderman, Joseph F. Fletcher, Peter H. Russell, and Philip E. Tetlock, *The Clash of Rights: Liberty, Equality and Legitimacy in Pluralist Democracy* (New Haven, Connecticut, 1996), where it is accepted as the authoritative account of Canada's origins despite the fact that the study's own survey data do not bear it out.

15 The notable exception is Kenneth McRae, "The Structure of Canadian History," chap. 7 in Louis Hartz, ed., *The Founding of New Societies*.

16 Peter J. Smith, "The Ideological Origins of Canadian Confederation," *Canadian Journal of Political Science* 20:1 (1987); Janet Ajzenstat and Peter J. Smith, eds., *Canada's Origins: Liberal, Tory, or Republican?* (Ottawa: Carleton University Press, 1995). *Canada's Origins* reprints a number of articles illustrating the new scholarship, including Smith's "Ideological Origins."

17 For the idea that aspects of radical democracy survive in the provincial rights movement, see Robert C. Vipond, *Liberty and Community: Canadian Federalism and the Failure of the Constitution* (Albany, NY: State University of New York Press, 1991); and Paul Romney, "The Nature and Scope of Provincial Autonomy: Sir Oliver Mowat, the Quebec Resolutions, and the Construction of the British North America Act," *Canadian Journal of Political Science* 25:1 (1992). For a comparison of civic republicanism and later populist movements in the Canadian west, see David Laycock's introduction to his *Populism and Democratic Thought in the Canadian Prairies, 1910 to 1945* (Toronto: University of Toronto Press, 1990).

18 Smith, "The Ideological Origins of Canadian Confederation."

19 Louis-Georges Harvey, "The First Distinct Society: French Canada, America, and the Constitution of 1791," in Ajzenstat and Smith, eds., *Canada's Origins*.

20 See the correspondence between Papineau and John Arthur Roebuck, Lower Canada's spokesman in Britain, especially Papineau to Roebuck, October, 1835 (Public Archives of Canada, Roebuck Papers 1:4), and Roebuck to Papineau, September, 1836 (Roebuck Papers 2:xi).

21 See the articles by Etienne Parent, a staunch liberal democrat, in the journal Le Canadien, especially February 18, 1824, and June 19, 1833.

22 John Arthur Roebuck, *Existing Difficulties in the Government of the Canadas* (London: C. and W. Reynell, 1836).

23 See the addresses by Macdonald and Cartier on Confederation in the Canadian parliament in 1865. W. P. M. Kennedy, ed., *Statutes, Treaties and Documents of the Canadian Constitution, 1713-1929* (Toronto: Oxford University Press, 1930), CLXXIII.

24 W. P. M. Kennedy, *Statutes, Treaties and Documents,* p. 569. This passage comes towards the end of Macdonald's great speech of February 6, 1865.

25 Michael Sandel, "The Political Theory of the Procedural Republic," in Allan C. Hutchinson and Patrick Monahan, eds., *The Rule of Law: Ideal or Ideology?* (Toronto: Carswell, 1987).

26 See the fourth of Joseph Howe's four public letters to Lord John Russell, September 1839, in W. P. M. Kennedy, *Statutes, Treaties and Documents,* CVI-CIX.

THE CHARTER OF RIGHTS: MYTH AND REALITY

F. L. MORTON

On April 16, 1997, the fifteenth anniversary of the Charter of Rights and Freedoms, Canadians were treated to a barrage of self-congratulatory pronouncements on how the Charter had made Canada a freer and more democratic society. "Thank God for the Charter," declared the Chief Justice of Canada, whose modest evaluation was reported on the front page of *The Ottawa Citizen*. In the more somber *Globe and Mail*, Jeffrey Simpson gravely pronounced that "the Charter has sunk deep roots in Canada's psyche." He was backed by recent opinion polls showing that 85 percent of Canadians thought that the Charter was a "good thing."

In truth, there are two Charters: the mythical Charter and the real-world Charter. Canadians love the former because they don't know the latter. Canadians don't know the reality, because it is conducted in a rare dialect — Charterese — of a foreign language — legalese. Those who practise the dark arts of the Charter — lawyers, judges, and Charter-based interest groups — have a vested interest in obscuring the reality and perpetuating the myth. The myth is constitutional supremacy and the rule of law. The reality has become judicial supremacy and the rule of lawyers. This new jurocracy has given wealth to lawyers, power to judges, and influence to a new breed of rights-advocacy groups. Rather than being offended by their loss of power to the courts, many re-election-minded politicians have welcomed the development as a convenient way to avoid controversial issues. Why would any of the beneficiaries want to spoil a good thing? Indeed, why not "thank God for the Charter"!

The purpose of this essay is to spoil this "good thing" by pulling back the veil of legalisms and revealing the real world of Canadian jurocracy that has been constructed out of the Charter. The preservation of Canadian democracy requires no less, for this new politics of rights has undermined the accountability of governments to citizens; damaged the independence of the judiciary; and weakened the social and moral fabric of Canadian society, the only lasting foundations of a free people.

The Charter mythology is simple and compelling. It can be broken down into eight myths: (1) The Charter protects the basic rights and freedoms of Canadian citizens. (2) When a government violates one of these rights, a citizen can go to the courts for protection. (3) The Charter protects individual liberty by promoting the practice of "limited government." (4) The Charter is necessary to prevent the problem of the "tyranny of the majority." (5) The Courts are more willing than legislatures to protect minorities. (6) The Charter establishes constitutional supremacy, not judicial supremacy. (7) Courts protect rights while legislatures broker interests. (8) Judges are impartial in their interpretation of the Charter.

MYTH #1
THE CHARTER PROTECTS THE BASIC RIGHTS AND FREEDOMS OF CANADIAN CITIZENS.

The basic rights and freedoms of Canadians were already well protected before the adoption of the Charter in 1982. While certainly not perfect, the human rights record of Canada was as good as any of the other twenty or so democracies in the world and immeasurably better than the 100 other dictatorships and "people's republics" that then constituted the rest of the United Nations. The proof is the hundred thousand immigrants a year who "voted with their feet" and chose Canada over their homelands.

As Peter Russell observed at the time, the principal effect of the Charter is institutional. The Charter did not create new rights, but a *new procedure for making decisions about rights-claims*, a procedure in which courts now play an authoritative role.[1] The relevant question is not, "Does the Charter make a difference?" It is, "Do courts make a difference?"

Courts do make a difference in the interest group activity of "rights claiming" (see Myth #5), but not in stopping true tyranny. When the core meaning of a right has been violated by government policy, judicial review will almost never be effective. Concerted government attack on the core meaning of a fundamental right is the very definition of tyranny, but courts are normally too weak to oppose the tyranny of the majority or the tyranny of a single despot.

The architect of the American system of checks and balances, James Madison, argued against the addition of a bill of rights (akin to our Charter) to the U.S. Constitution for precisely this reason. He wrote: "Experience proves the inefficacy of a bill of rights on those occasions when its control is most needed." History has repeatedly proven Madison right. Rights can be well protected without a bill of rights, and wholly unprotected with one.

The American Bill of Rights did nothing to impede the anti-Communist hysteria in the United States during the 1950s. During this same period, Canada and England, without any rights document, showed much more respect for freedom of speech and association. Similarly, the U.S. Constitution's "guarantee" of the equal protection of the laws did not prevent race segregation laws in the American South. Indeed, the Supreme Court's misinterpretation of "separate but equal" in its 1896 *Plessy* v. *Ferguson* decision provided the constitutional foundation for racial apartheid.

This pattern is not an American idiosyncrasy. In Canada during the 1890s, judicial attempts to protect the constitutional rights of Franco-manitobans were ignored by a provincial government bent on extinguishing the linguistic and education rights of French Catholics. In South Africa, early judicial attempts to oppose apartheid policies were ignored by political authorities. In Uganda, Idi Amin ordered his secret police to shoot the judges when the Supreme Court began to intervene to stop his persecution of political opponents. They did. No wonder Alexander Hamilton, another one of the American Founders, observed that the judiciary, armed with "neither the sword nor the purse," is "the least dangerous branch of government."

To conclude, while a bill of rights certainly stimulates rights litigation (see Myth #7), it has almost nothing to do with *protecting* rights. The truth of the matter is found in Judge Learned Hand's observation: "Liberty lies in the hearts of men and women; when it dies there, no constitution, no law, no court can save it. While it lies there, it needs no constitution, no law, no court to save it."

MYTH #2
WHEN A GOVERNMENT VIOLATES ONE OF THESE RIGHTS, A CITIZEN CAN GO TO THE COURTS FOR PROTECTION.

Costs pose a formidable barrier to Charter litigation by individual citizens. To take a case to the Supreme Court in the 1990s costs a minimum of $90,000. For this reason, our ancestors were understandably sceptical about placing primary responsibility for settling rights-claims with judges. In the United States, where this model became the norm after World War II, the price of access has meant that most rights litigation is conducted by institutional players that can afford it — corporations, labour unions, and interest groups.

Ottawa purported to respond to this problem by creating the Court Challenges Program (CCP), which provides funding for Charter litigation by citizens. Unfortunately, this funding is restricted to interest groups that Ottawa favours. Initially, only "official language minorities" qualified. Anglophones in Quebec and francophone groups in the rest of Canada have funded their language rights litigation through the CCP. These litigation grants are in addition to their operating grants from the federal Bilingualism Program, which typically account for over 90 percent of these groups' annual budgets.

In 1985, the CCP was amended to extend funding to section 15 equality rights litigation and given another $9-million. While open to all citizens in theory, the screening committee that vets applications was immediately captured by partisans of the so-called "equality-seeking" groups. The results have been predictable. The leading recipient has been the feminist litigation organization, the Legal Education and Action Fund (LEAF). Other recipients include the gay rights advocacy group Equality for Gays and Lesbians Everywhere (EGALE), the Canadian Council for Refugees, Canadian Council of Churches, and so forth. The few individual litigants who received CCP funding were raising policy issues of interest to gay rights[2] and feminist[3] groups.

Meanwhile, applications for funding by non-liberal groups — such as Kids First or the National Citizens' Coalition — were rejected. In the Borowski appeal on the rights of the unborn before the Supreme Court of Canada, CCP funded the pro-choice intervention of feminist LEAF but rejected a request by REAL Women, a pro-life women's group. The true extent of the CCP's ideological bias is difficult to document, since it refuses to release the names of rejected applicants.

The Supreme Court itself has made it difficult for individual Canadians to influence Charter litigation. A recent study by Brodie found that the least successful applicants for intervener status before the Supreme Court have been individuals. The study also found that the most successful intervener applicants were LEAF and the Canadian Civil Liberties Association (CCLA). Indeed, the Court has never rejected any of LEAF's seventeen applications to intervene. LEAF has appeared before the Supreme Court in more Charter cases than several provincial governments! Brodie concluded that "the fact that individuals are amongst the least welcome interveners at the Court demonstrates how much legal politics is for organized interests."[4]

In its 1991 *Lavigne* decision, the Supreme Court created a new and much more serious financial deterrent to individual use of the Charter.[5] Merve Lavigne, a college teacher in Ontario, objected to portions of his mandatory union dues being used by the Ontario Public Servants and Employees Union to support left-wing political causes that he opposed. These included support for the Nicaragua Sandanistas, striking British coal miners, and the Palestine Liberation Organization. With the financial backing of the National Citizens Coalition, Lavigne brought a "freedom of association" challenge to Ontario labour legislation. Predictably, the major labour unions — such as the Ontario Federation of Labour and the Canadian Labour Congress — intervened to oppose Lavigne. The trial court ruled in favour of Lavigne in 1986, but this was reversed on appeal by the Supreme Court of Canada in 1991. The Supreme Court then took the unprecedented step of assigning the legal bills of all the labour union interveners — over $600,000 — to Lavigne, and indirectly, the NCC.

The Court has never used this punitive measure against liberal interest group litigators, and for good reason. If Charter claimants were automatically responsible for the legal costs of interveners, no one would dare risk bringing a Charter claim that offended powerful interests. The threat of massive interventions — and thus liability for massive legal costs — would force any but the wealthiest of litigants to withdraw their claim.

There is only one way that most Canadians can get tax payers' dollars to pay for their Charter litigation: to break the law and then get caught. Then — if you are poor enough — you qualify for legal aid. Nothing has fueled the Charter litigation like legal aid. Three out of every four Charter cases involves criminal law. Tax payers currently pay approximately $700 million a year for legal aid. This is double what legal aid cost in 1988, which in turn was double the cost for 1982, the year the Charter was adopted — a neat 200 percent increase in only fifteen years.[6]

To conclude, while the average Canadian is unlikely ever to go to court to claim protection for Charter rights, we have the privilege of paying millions of dollars a year for interest groups and criminals to do the same. Trudeau's promotion of the Charter as the "people's package" may have been good salesmanship but it was hardly accurate.

MYTH #3
THE CHARTER PROTECTS INDIVIDUAL LIBERTY BY PROMOTING THE PRACTICE OF "LIMITED GOVERNMENT."

"More freedom through less government" has indeed been the historical purpose of bills of rights. Unfortunately, Canada's experience with the Charter of Rights has proven to be an exception to this tradition. Rather than protecting citizens against excessive state regulation and bureaucracy, the Charter has actually contributed to their growth. The explanation of this is to be found in the purposes of the so-called "Father of the Charter," Pierre Trudeau, the judges he appointed, and the coalition of interest groups he financed.

The creation of the Charter during 1980-81 was a top-down exercise in statecraft, not a bottom-up populist effort to restrict state power. Trudeau viewed the Charter as an instrument to extend his policy of national bilingualism to primary and secondary education — policy areas otherwise beyond the jurisdictional reach of the federal government. The Charter enabled Trudeau to achieve this objective indirectly by making education services for "official language minority groups" (OLMGs) a constitutional right and vesting authority to enforce that right in the Supreme Court. The Court — a bilingual, Cabinet-appointed body — in effect became the new national school board. The Court Challenges Program was created to ensure that OLMGs would be able to afford to litigate their new "rights."[7]

To overcome provincial opposition to his Charter project, Trudeau recruited allies from individuals and groups associated with federal and provincial law reform commissions, human rights commissions, OLMGs, and feminist, aboriginal, and "multicultural" groups. What is less well known is that this "Charter coalition" consisted almost entirely of state-sponsored clientele groups, created and funded by the first

Trudeau government. Trudeau translated his "just society" campaign slogans from his 1968 election into a raft of new "citizenship" programs that funded the creation of francophone, multicultural-ethnic, feminist, aboriginal, and youth groups.[8] In a similar vein, the Trudeau government created the federal Law Reform Commission, the Canadian Human Rights Commission, and launched a national legal aid program.

Prior to Trudeau, the voluntary sector protected its autonomy from the state by relying on its own members for financial support. Ottawa's lead role in the formation and funding of these groups marked the abandonment of this "classical liberal model" that had governed state-society relations until then.[9] By the late 1970s, the government agencies that administered these programs were effectively taken over by the very interest groups they had helped to create. The purposes of these programs was transformed from "citizenship" to "social justice" via the discourse of "rights."[10] The coalition that successfully fought to add the Charter to the constitution represented the marriage of these state-funded "equality-seekers" with Trudeau's belief in expanded bilingualism as the key to national unity. Elsewhere I have designated this coalition as the "Court Party," since their common denominator is the desire to expand judicial power.[11]

Given such a genesis, it is hardly surprising that the Charter has done more to expand the scope of Canada's government than to shrink it.

The Court Challenges Program, originally limited to funding minority language rights litigation, was expanded to include equality rights litigation in 1985. Imbued with the Trudeau "social justice" policy vision, CCP administrators have given litigation grants to "equality seekers" who want more, not fewer, government services and regulations.

Unorthodox state involvement in rights litigation is also evident in how governments have chosen to participate in Charter cases. Ottawa and Ontario have frequently intervened to *support* OLMG and feminist rights-claims against other governments. The last two Attorneys General of Ontario sided with feminist and gay-rights legal challenges *against their own governments' legislation*. This evidence further contradicts the standard portrayal of rights litigation as pitting the private sector against the public, and individual liberty against over-reaching governments.

Trudeau did not leave the implementation of his pet project to chance. In 1973 he broke the convention of seniority to appoint an activist junior member of the Court — Bora Laskin — as the new Chief Justice. In 1980, with the battle to adopt the Charter in full swing, Trudeau appointed the former chairman of the federal Law Reform Commission — Antonio Lamer — to the Court. In 1982, one month before the Charter took effect, Trudeau appointed Bertha Wilson, the first woman ever to serve on the Supreme Court.

Wilson quickly established herself as an outspoken feminist advocate and the most activist member of the Court. In a 1990 ruling, Wilson explicitly rejected what she described as the "doctrine of . . . 'constitutionalism' . . . according to [which] states are a necessary evil."[12] According to Wilson, the equation of constitutionalism with "limited government" is an American idiosyncrasy that "is no longer valid in Canada, if indeed it ever was." The Canadian experience, Wilson declared, "shows . . . that freedom has often required the intervention and protection of government against private action." While Wilson may represent the extreme on this issue, the Supreme Court's sympathy for equality claims suggests that she is not isolated.

Consistent with Wilson's views, the Supreme Court has sanctioned "affirmative judicial remedies": the authority of judges to order the extension of government benefit programs to new categories of recipients.[13] Following the Supreme Court's lead,[14] numerous courts have ordered provinces to extend or expand French-language education services. The Ontario Court of Appeal has ordered the addition of homosexual spouses to the province's benefit programs, a policy change that is estimated to cost tens of millions of dollars.[15]

The most extravagant form of judge-ordered state expansion occurred when a trial judge found that Alberta's decision *not* to add sexual orientation in its anti-discrimination statute violated the equality guarantees of the Charter. As a remedy, she ordered that the statute be read as *extending* its protection to homosexuals.[16] By this logic, a government's failure to take legislative action may be deemed unconstitutional and judges are authorized to order government to take action. Regardless of one's position on the gay-rights issue, this is a complete reversal of the "state-limiting" logic of constitutional rights. Notwithstanding this, it has been widely praised by the "advocacy scholarship" that now dominates Canadian law reviews.[17]

Inspired by this same logic, a group known as the Anti-Poverty Coalition — with the financial backing of the Court Challenges Program — has encouraged the launching of Charter challenges to the budget cuts of the "neo-conservative" Harris government in Ontario.

These efforts to use the Charter (i.e., the courts) to protect the welfare state against cutbacks are beginning to succeed. In September 1997 an Ontario Divisional Court judge ruled that the Harris government's cancellation of future pay-equity increases for women provincial employees violated the Charter. The pay-equity law had been enacted by the Rae government in 1993 to pay off its public sector unions supporters, and was part of the NDP's 50 month/$50 billion dollar deficit legacy. This judicial ruling will cost Ontario tax-payers $418-million if it is upheld on appeal, according to The Globe and Mail (Sept. 9, 1997, p. A1). The following month, in Eldridge v. British Columbia, Oct. 9, 1997, the Supreme Court ruled that the failure of British Columbia to provide sign language interpreters for deaf patients in B.C. hospitals constituted discrimination against the physically handicapped. While the costs to provide such service in this particular hospital are modest (around $150,000 annually), the principle behind the ruling could end up costing all governments billions. As in Vriend, the Court has said that the failure of a government to provide a service constitutes discrimination. By this logic, all governments now have a positive constitutional obligation to "remove barriers" to people with disabilities. In the immediate context, this ruling invites all handicapped groups — the blind, the speech impaired, the mentally impaired, as well as the deaf — to sue all public institutions — not just hospitals but schools, universities, and all other public bureaucracies — that do not provide the additional services or equipment necessary for handicapped persons to achieve "equal service."

Read together, these cases stand for the proposition that the Charter can be used to order the expansion of the welfare state but forbids any cutbacks of entitlements or social programs. To the extent that the courts accept this view, it may not make any difference if the NDP ever wins another election! They will be able to achieve what they want through the courts, anyway.

Consistent with these developments, the Supreme Court has generally preferred equality claims over liberty claims when the two collide. Under section 1 of the Charter, the Supreme Court has made itself the arbiter of the "reasonableness" of any limitation on rights. National columnist Andrew Coyne has aptly described this perversion of traditional legal logic as, "Give me liberty or give me an excuse." The Court's preferred excuse for restricting liberty has quickly become "equality."

In its two most important free-speech decisions, the Supreme Court upheld criminal code sanctions on "hate-speech"[18] and obscenity.[19] The Court ruled that these restrictions on liberty are justified because their purpose is to protect the equality interests of "historically disadvantaged groups" — ethnic minorities and women. Using the same logic, the Court upheld restrictions on television advertising aimed at children.[20] In its *Lavigne* ruling (discussed above), one of the Court's justifications for upholding the involuntary contribution of union dues for political causes was that it promoted the equality of "workers." This type of reasoning has been encouraged and then applauded by a new genre of advocacy scholarship in the law schools, which would reduce the entire Charter to the single criterion of helping "historically disadvantaged groups."[21]

In sum, the Canadian Charter has not been a liberty-enhancing institution, if by "liberty" one means restricting the size and scope of government. Both in its inception and in its development, the Charter has done more to expand the Canadian state than to restrict it.

This interpretation is unorthodox, but it is more consistent with the other Trudeau legacy — the largest expansion of the state in Canada's history. Why would the architect of Canada's modern welfare state suddenly become a champion of individual liberty against the state?

Rather, why not view the Charter as the culmination of a subculture of state-sponsored social engineering that was already thriving in Trudeau's Ottawa of the 1970s?

MYTH #4
THE CHARTER IS NECESSARY TO PREVENT THE PROBLEM OF THE "TYRANNY OF THE MAJORITY."

The ease with which this concept, "the tyranny of the majority," is now bandied about is a measure of how deeply disaffected Canadians have become with our own traditions of parliamentary democracy and "responsible government." Earlier generations of Canadians thought that parliamentary democracy was perfectly compatible with the protection of fundamental rights and liberties. Indeed, they thought the two were complementary. What has happened to change this?

If politics is the art of the half-truth, the new bogey-man of "majority tyranny" is a classic example of how a half-truth can be spun into a lie. The half-truth is the premise — hardly new — that in a democracy, electoral majorities can use their political clout to deprive minority groups of their fundamental rights and freedoms. The lie is that this accurately describes what has occurred in Canada. As noted already, Canada was a liberal democracy before the Charter and would still be one if the Charter were abolished.

The plausibility of the false conclusion from the true premise comes from the deliberate confusion of political loss with majority tyranny. Charter apologists have invented a category of so-called "historically disadvantaged groups" and then persuaded us that every time one of these groups loses a policy dispute, their political loss is evidence of the tyranny of the majority.

This preposterous argument is a recipe for the end of democracy and responsible government as we know it. Every government decision entails a policy loss for some "minority," and in a pluralistic society such as Canada we are all minorities. Canadians are divided by an infinite myriad of overlapping cleavages — language, income, geography, occupation, race, gender, age, geography, religion, marital status, immigration. Still further divisions occur on the basis of policy issues — the size and generosity of the welfare state, abortion, gun-registration, environment, and so on, infinitely. There is no "natural majority." Consider the results of the 1997 federal election. The new Liberal government received only 38 percent of the popular vote. The rest was divided between four different parties, each of which represents another coalition of minorities. Governing majorities are a temporary construct of the electoral system. They are shifting coalitions of minorities that are patched together from one election to the next. Indeed, the real challenge for successful democracies is not to protect minorities but to create sustainable majorities. A quick check of the history books reveals that very few societies have been able to achieve this.

Such diversity is the traditional liberal solution to the age-old problem of "majority faction." By protecting individual liberty, liberalism encourages a "multiplicity of factions," such that it becomes impossible to assemble an electoral majority except through broad coalitions. Of necessity, building coalitions requires compromises, which in turn imparts a moderating character to the political process. The coalition building required to build an electoral majority is inhospitable to extremist views and groups. It also means that virtually no interest gets what it wants, including the members of the winning majority coalition. Typically, they have already made concessions to become part of the coalition.

Charter-based rights-advocacy groups are characterized by their lack of patience with this process. They claim that their history of being "underprivileged" gives them the privilege of being exempt from the democratic discipline of coalition building. A successful democracy both requires and generates a spirit of moderation in its citizens. Yet the most distinguishing characteristic of the rights-advocacy groups is their lack of political moderation. This is reflected in and encouraged by their rights talk. Rights talk unduly inflates the moral seriousness of political disputes and makes rights-claimers less willing to compromise. This is the attraction of the courts: courts do not require compromise. If the court accepts your rights claim, the judge *orders* the other party to comply.

To conclude, democracy's vulnerability to the tyranny of a majority must be taken seriously. But it must not be trivialized so that every political loss becomes a pretext for going to the courts for redress. The latter tendency creates the equally serious threat of the tyranny of the minority exercised through the courts. In a democracy, over the long term, the governors must remain accountable to the governed. Government by judges — jurocracy — fails this test. As G. K. Chesterton observed, what good are all the other rights if the people lack the most important right — the right to choose their governors?

MYTH #5
THE COURTS ARE MORE WILLING THAN LEGISLATURES TO PROTECT MINORITIES.

It is somewhere between comic and frightening the rapidity with which the American myth of the benign judiciary has insinuated itself into post-Charter Canadian orthodoxy. In the United States, the "heroic Court" myth at least had some recent grounding in the Supreme Court's leading role in striking down the race segregation laws in the American South. (We can overlook for the moment that this same Court created the constitutional justification for racial apartheid in its 1896 ruling that upheld the "separate but equal" treatment of the races.) In Canada, however, there is almost no historical support for the theory of an intrinsically benign judiciary. Indeed, there is much to contradict it.

The same Supreme Court that feminists today hail as the champion of women's rights routinely upheld much more egregious practices of sex discrimination only a decade earlier. In 1974, the Supreme Court upheld a section of the Indian Act that stripped native women of their Indian status if they married a non-Indian but imposed no similar penalty on Indian men who married non-native women.[22] The Supreme Court also sent Henry Morgentaler to jail for violating Canada's abortion law, and refused to recognize a wife's non-monetary contributions to family assets upon divorce.[23] Against this background, it is not surprising that some feminist leaders initially opposed Trudeau's Charter initiative because it would put more power in the hands of judges!

Judicial disinterest in the causes of underdogs was not limited to women. Several generations of Canadian scholars have interpreted the Judicial Committee of the Privy Council's (JCPC) decentralist federalism jurisprudence as cloaking a deeper business-class antipathy to the regulatory and redistributive policies of the modern welfare state.[24] The Supreme Court also turned a blind eye to the well-founded legal claims of French-speaking Catholic school boards in Manitoba and Ontario. Nor did Canadian Aboriginals find any relief in the Canadians courts prior to the 1970s. In sum, there are numerous examples of Canadian courts ignoring and even contributing to the misfortunes of disadvantaged groups or individuals.

A clearer picture of the political predilections of judges comes from assessing courts by the same criteria as other institutions of government. Sustained rights litigation in appellate courts privileges certain political resources. Since these resources are not evenly distributed, some societal interests benefit more than others from the legalization of politics. These resources include organizational strength, money, and access to legal expertise. Political scientists describe interests that possess a sufficient amount of these resources to use the courts on a continuing basis as "repeat players" and predict that they will be more successful than "one-shot" litigants. Canada's Charter experience fits this model perfectly. The two most frequent interest group interveners before the Supreme Court — LEAF and the CCLA — have also been two of the most successful.

Courts also privilege political interests with socio-economic connections to the legal profession, and the educated classes more generally. The correlation between education and income means that rights claiming tends to privilege the more affluent segments of a society. From Bentham onwards, the class bias of judicial policy-making has been a long-standing criticism of those on the left in the English-speaking democracies.

The class bias of judicial policy-making takes on a different political significance in postmaterialist[25] societies such as contemporary Canada. Until recently, greater wealth and education were associated with conservative opposition to the redistributive policies of the left.

However, in postwar Western democracies, the most dynamic agent of social change has been not Marx's industrial proletariat but a new "oppositionist intelligentsia," drawn from and supported by the more educated, more affluent strata of society.

The new "knowledge class," having experienced unprecedented levels of material comfort and security, has become more concerned with non-economic and social issues: "a clean environment, a better culture, equal status for women and minorities, the quality of education, international relations, greater democratization, and a more permissive morality, particularly as affecting familial and sexual issues."[26] This postmaterialist agenda describes almost perfectly the issue areas in which the Supreme Court has been most active since the adoption of the Charter.

Two less-noted institutional biases of the courts are urban-rural and centre-periphery. The urban-rural bias follows from the modern connection between the legal profession and universities. In the rare instances that law schools are not located in cities, they are still urban in culture. There is a decided urban-rural cleavage on many of the social issues that now dominate the rights agenda in Canada. Transferring these policy decisions into the courts has privileged the more liberal-urban views on issues such as abortion, bilingualism, multiculturalism, feminism, gay rights, aboriginal rights, and environmentalism. It is not by accident, for example, that three-quarters of all gay-rights litigation is initiated in Toronto, or that Toronto-based judges have been so receptive to these claims. Via Charter litigation, the urban subculture of the Annex is transformed into the new national norm.

In a related manner, hierarchical appellate court structures privilege political interests that occupy the centre of national government over those at the periphery. In federal states such as Canada (and the U.S.), an activist national court of appeal has the opportunity to help interests that are unpopular locally but that have the sympathy of national political elites and the judges they appoint.

In the U.S., for example, the federal courts were able to protect Black Americans against hostile state governments in the South. But this occurred only as Black voters (in Northern states) displaced southern

Whites as a more important member of the post-1932 Democratic New Deal Coalition. Similarly in Canada, the courts did little to help francophone minorities protect their educational and religious rights until the Trudeau Liberals made expanded bilingualism a national priority and then entrenched it in the Charter. It was not a coincidence that the Liberals' renewed interest in assisting francophones outside of Quebec coincided with the new separatist threat to one of the Liberals' most important constituencies, English-speaking Quebecers. Since the 1970s, the Supreme Court has actively implemented the policy of national bilingualism, intervening to aid francophone minorities in English-speaking provinces and the anglophone minority in Quebec.[27]

The courts' opportunity to protect dispersed minorities and actually doing it are two different things. In both Canada and the U.S., the minorities aided by the national courts were at the time important constituencies of the governing national coalition. At different times under different political configurations, the respective courts have ignored or even contributed to the political misfortunes of these same interests.

To conclude, courts are not necessarily the protectors of minorities. Like other institutions, courts privilege certain resources and, by extension, certain constituencies. In discretionary matters such as rights claiming, the influence of the courts — both in degree and direction — tend to reflect the interests and power of these constituencies. Other things being equal, the transfer of policy decisions to the courts tends to favour interests that are more educated, more affluent, more urban, and more at the centre of the extended nation-state. Whether or not protection for minorities (and which minorities!) is on the courts' agenda is a matter of historical contingency.

MYTH #6
THE CHARTER ESTABLISHES CONSTITUTIONAL SUPREMACY NOT JUDICIAL SUPREMACY.

There is nothing to prevent constitutional supremacy from degenerating into judicial supremacy, because the Charter is not self-interpreting.

Judges may use their interpretive discretion to give a meaning to the Charter that was not intended. If this occurs, the judges, instead of enforcing what the constitution requires, are simply imposing their own policy preference. Instead of enforcing the law, the judges are making it.

This is the paradox of constitutional law: the only restraint on the judges is their own sense of self-restraint. Unfortunately, the Supreme Court judges have shown no such self-restraint in their interpretation of the Charter. From the outset, they have invoked the metaphor of the constitution as a "living tree" to justify judicial revision of the original intended meaning. There is some logic to this "updating" technique when interpreting constitutional texts that are hundreds of years old, such as the 1867 BNA Act or the U.S. Constitution of 1787. It is absurd, however, to adopt the "living tree" approach to interpreting a document on which the ink is barely dry. The Charter hardly needed "judicial updating" in the first decade after it was adopted. Unfortunately, this is what the Supreme Court chose to do. Several examples tell the story.

Section 15 of the Charter declares: "*Every individual* has the right to equality before and under the law, the equal protection of the law," etc. (emphasis added). In *Andrews* (1989) the Court ignored this wording and ruled that section 15 protects only groups — not all groups but only "historically disadvantaged" groups — against discrimination by the state. This notorious perversion of the meaning of section 15 automatically eliminates all Canadian males of European descent from ever claiming the protection of section 15 against discriminatory government policy. A lower court judge subsequently used the *Andrews* precedent to deny relief from an admittedly discriminatory section of the Income Tax Act to a "two-parent family with a full-time stay-at-home parent," on the grounds that there was no history of government discrimination against such families! Thanks to the Supreme Court, only the "historically underprivileged" now have the privilege of protection against contemporary government discrimination.

Section 15 enumerates a list of prohibited grounds of discrimination: race, sex, religion, and so on. This list does not include "sexual orientation." This exclusion was not by accident. Those who framed the text of the Charter during 1980-81 rejected numerous requests to insert sexual orientation into the Charter while it was being negotiated. In its 1995 ruling in *Egan*,[28] the Supreme Court blithely ignored the framers' intent and added "sexual orientation" to the list of prohibited kinds of discrimination.

Section 35 does not protect "aboriginal rights" but *"existing* aboriginal rights" (emphasis added). The adjective "existing" was added at the insistence of a group of provincial premiers, led by Alberta's Premier Peter Lougheed, who sought to impose some scope on an already nebulous and ill-defined concept. In its 1990 *Sparrow* decision,[29] the Court completely eviscerated the meaning of "existing," thereby opening up the entire corpus of provincial regulation of Indian activities to constitutional challenge.

Similar examples could be endlessly multiplied. By refusing to give Charter rights their originally intended meaning, the Court has turned Canada's experiment with constitutional supremacy into judicial supremacy. In doing so, it has robbed the Charter of its integrity. The Supreme Court's disregard for the framers' intent has reduced the Charter to the legal equivalent of a lump of wax, waiting to be shaped by the policy whims of each new generation of judges.

Curiously, rather than being criticized for its corruption of the Charter, the Supreme Court has been praised by legal academics for its "progressive" interpretation of the Charter. Once again, the double standard is in play. Imagine the cries of outrage if the Court had decided to "discover" protection for property rights or the rights of the unborn in the text of the Charter. What would be the response if the Court decided to protect the "liberty" of law-abiding gun-owners or grain-growers? Suddenly the law professors would rediscover the virtues of "judicial fidelity to framers' intent" and majority-rule democracy.

The left-wing bias of the university-based "Charter experts" is predictable. More troubling, however, has been the deafening silence of the rest of Canada's judges. Happily, this conspiracy of silence was recently broken by Justice John Wesley McClung of the Alberta Court of Appeal. Justice McClung declared that judges must stop "repealing and even amending legislation under the cloak of merely interpreting it." If this trend is not stopped, McClung warned, Canadians will face a future "spectre of crusading . . . ideologically determined . . . constitutionally hyper-active . . . rights restive . . . legisceptical judges pronouncing [on] all our emerging . . . laws . . . according to their own values; judicial appetites, too, grow with the eating."[30]

MYTH #7
COURTS PROTECT RIGHTS WHILE LEGISLATURES BROKER INTERESTS.

This is another corollary to the law-politics distinction discussed in the preceding proposition. Just as the motives of judges are presumed to differ from those of legislators, so the object of their actions — rights — differs from the object of legislative struggle — competing interests. Once again, what is distinct in theory turns out to be similar in practice.

When a government violates the core meaning of a right, judges are usually unable or unwilling to stop such tyranny. In Canada, there are few if any recent examples of government violations of core rights. All the rights litigation generated by the adoption of the Charter has been stimulated not by government tyranny but by uncertainty over the peripheral meaning of rights. While the core meaning of a right is widely agreed on, its outer-limits are inherently contestable.

For example, freedom of religion clearly prohibits governments from punishing individuals for their religious beliefs (or non-beliefs). It is much less clear whether it makes behaviour based on religious belief immune from otherwise valid policies with a secular purpose — i.e., a common day of rest or the prohibition of polygamy. Freedom of speech clearly protects the right of individuals to criticize government policy and leaders. But does it also protect the obscene publications of pornography entrepreneurs like Larry Flynt? Equal protection of the laws clearly prohibits government from targeting an ethnic or racial group for punitive treatment. But does a government policy that has an unintended, indirect, but negative effect on such a group — for example, strict firearms regulations on aboriginals — constitute illegal discrimination?

Rights claiming arises in this nether region. A (wealthy) individual, a corporation or a (well-funded) interest group can try to prioritize its policy goal by claiming that it falls within the outer contours of a right; that is, they can re-articulate their policy claim as a rights claim. This dynamic has stimulated the "legalization of politics" in Canada since 1982.

Charter litigation has had almost nothing to do with the basic freedoms that have made Canada one the world's oldest liberal democracies. The Supreme Court has rejected two-thirds of the approximately 300 Charter claims it has heard. If these cases truly engaged the core meaning of our traditional rights, we would now be living under a tyranny!

Indeed, by this logic, Canadians would be twice as "free" if the Court had decided every one of its Charter decisions exactly the opposite. This would mean 200 victorious Charter claims, and only 100 losses. Imagine if this were indeed an option. Would it be widely embraced? Hardly! The coterie of left-wing interest groups that have benefited from the Supreme Court's misinterpretations of the Charter would protest vehemently; such a reversal would deprive them of a number of significant policy victories.

This hypothetical case underscores what is typically at stake in Charter litigation are partisan attempts to skip over the democratic electoral-legislative process and to gain policy advantage by exploiting the ambiguity of the peripheral meaning of traditional rights. Charter cases are primarily about policy issues with rights consequences, not rights issues with policy consequences. The Charter has not given Canadians an alternative to interest group politics, but an extension of such politics.

MYTH #8
JUDGES ARE IMPARTIAL IN THEIR INTERPRETATION OF THE CHARTER.

This is another corollary to the law-politics distinction implicit in the preceding two myths. The norm of judicial impartiality in constitutional interpretation is illustrated by the concept of "neutral principles" — the rule that judges should interpret and enforce a right regardless of its beneficiaries. Under this norm, all religious sects are entitled to the same religious freedoms; freedom of speech means the same for groups of every political stripe; and equal protection of the laws means that no ethnic or racial group can be singled out for either more favourable or less favourable treatment by government.

As indicated in preceding sections, however, the Supreme Court has been anything but "neutral" in its application and development of the Charter. According to the courts, the right to freedom of religion prohibits government policy from accommodating the beliefs of Christians, but requires it to accommodate the beliefs of non-Christians. Sunday-closing laws are declared unconstitutional, but Sikhs must be exempted from RCMP dress regulations. Freedom of expression does not prevent government prohibition of "traditional" pornography, but does protect pornography targeted at gay and lesbian markets. Individual Canadians have been deprived of the protection against government discrimination unless they belong to a "historically disadvantaged group." The most glaring example of this double standard was the Supreme Court's assignment of punitive legal costs in *Lavigne*. (See above.) This precedent has already forced another teacher to withdraw her Charter challenge to mandatory union membership in British Columbia. No similar assignment of interveners' legal costs has ever been made to any other individual or interest group!

In an earlier era, such judicial favouritism would have been criticized as "result-oriented" jurisprudence — a concept that denotes judges reshaping their interpretation of a right to ensure that the "right side" wins. Remarkably, rather than being criticized, the Court's result-oriented approach to the Charter has been encouraged and applauded by Charter gurus in the law schools. Somewhat ingeniously, they have sought to dignify (or hide) this corruption of principle by christening it as a new principle: "contextuality."

Contextuality, we are told, directs the judges to pay attention to the power relationships implicit in a legal dispute and to balance these by favouring the interest of the weaker party. The standard forms of this new secular version of "the last shall be first, and the first shall be last" are now well known: women's claims are to be preferred over men's; non-Europeans over Europeans; homosexuals over heterosexuals; the disabled over the able-bodied; the poor over the not-so-poor (i.e., the middle-class); labour over management.

There are, however, some curious variations in the application of contextuality. The claims of the criminally accused are to be preferred to those of their accusers, except in rape cases. The claims of the young should be preferred to those of the old, except for the unborn. The claims of "visible minority" immigrants trump those of the two "Founding Nations," but "First Nations" are *über alles*. More comic versions of contextuality can be found in the earnest arguments for the "doubly disadvantaged": the Native woman, the black homosexual, and so forth. The effect of contextuality, Anthony Peacock has pointed out, has been to transform the Charter from a "Citizens' Constitution" into a "Victims' Constitution."[31]

As noted earlier, this political favouritism becomes particularly virulent at the section 1 "reasonable limitation" stage of Charter reasoning, where many commentators have urged the Court to accept government promotion of equality as automatically qualifying as "a reasonable limitation" on all Charter rights.[32] Under the judicial recipe of "Give me liberty or give me an excuse," this proposal would indeed transform the Charter into a black hole of freedom for "ordinary" Canadians.

CONCLUSION: WHAT IS TO BE DONE?

The rise of the new jurocracy has already eroded Canada's tradition of constitutional democracy and will do still more damage if it is not challenged. The project of the Victims' Constitution invented by the Court Party propagandists must be challenged and overthrown. In its place, Canadians must rediscover the Citizens' Constitution the Charter was supposed to be. We must reclaim the Charter as a foundational document for the practice and preservation of liberal democracy in Canada. While not an easy task, it is not impossible. Unlike less fortunate nations, Canada has a liberal democratic tradition to fall back on.

It is basically a question of undoing the damage of the last fifteen years. The problem is not the Charter itself, but the jurocracy that has grown around the Charter.

The project to reclaim the Charter must proceed on two levels: ideas and actions. The growth of the jurocracy is testimony to the proposition that "ideas matter" — in this case, false ideas. The web of egalitarian deceits that props up the Victims' Constitution must be challenged and swept aside. The friends of liberal democracy must rearticulate the true meaning of constitutional rights. This understanding must be one that respects the preponderance of the elected branches of government in matters of public policy; that places liberty on an equal footing with equality; and that reasserts the primacy of judicial impartiality in preserving the rule of law.

We must relearn that constitutional democracy is more than a configuration of institutions and procedures that "check and balance" one another. Constitutional democracy is as much a social project as a political and economic project. A society that seeks to enjoy more liberty through less government must cultivate citizens whose conduct does not require government intervention to prevent harm to others (crime) or harm to self. The practice and preservation of limited government presupposes citizens who are morally self-restrained and self-dependent; individuals who are mindful not just of their rights but also of their responsibilities. Since the "limited" nature of liberal democracy restricts government from shaping the character of its citizens directly, legislators and judges must learn to do so indirectly by respecting those mediating institutions that transform the "me" into the "we" in the habits of the heart: the family, religion, local self-government, and the other voluntary associations that constitute "civil society."

Joining the battle of ideas will not suffice. Today, the friends of liberal democracy are a minority in the law schools and universities. The partisans of jurocracy occupy the ivory towers, and they have no intention of voluntarily relinquishing this advantage. The battle for ideas is a medium- to long-term project. More immediate practical responses are required. I propose four:

- Defund the Court Party.
- Resurrect the section 33 legislative override.
- Adopt a form of parliamentary review of rights issues.
- Reform the judicial appointments process.

While there are other practical reforms that may be desirable,[33] the virtue of my four recommendations is that they are all politically achievable and would have immediate results.

Indeed, the first — to defund the Charter-based interest-group litigators — could be done tomorrow. Media whining notwithstanding, this should not be a hard sell. It is absurd that Ottawa should hand over tax dollars to groups who turn around and use them to attack the "bourgeois prejudices" of middle-class tax payers who elected the government in the first place. Most of the rights-advocacy groups depend on Ottawa for 90 percent of their budgets. Pull the plug, and their ability to act on the political stage — especially to litigate — will be severely curtailed. Abolishing these subsidies can hardly be deemed unfair, since it simply puts these groups on the same playing field as all others: go to your own supporters for financial contributions.

The section 33 legislative override power must be resurrected and used before it becomes defunct. Section 33 of the Charter allows a government to resurrect a law that a judge has declared invalid by re-enacting it with a new clause stating that the law shall take effect "notwithstanding" the Charter; i.e., notwithstanding the judge's mistaken interpretation of the Charter. Section 33 is as important as any other section of the Charter. It was demanded by Premiers Lougheed, Lyon, and Blakeney in 1981 to defend the century old Canadian tradition of "responsible government" against any future imperial judiciary. Little did they know that such a monster would arise so soon! Section 33 is the most readily available weapon with which to fight policy making by judicial decree. It rests on a simple and irrefutable argument: that judges are fallible. They can and do make mistakes.

Scott Reid has made an insightful proposal to make the use of section 33 more politically palatable: a government could put any use of the override before the voters in a referendum.[34] His proposal would not require any amendment to the Constitution. It is also consistent with policies already in place in Alberta and British Columbia that require any amendments to the Constitution to be ratified by the people in a referendum. When judges misinterpret the Charter to give prisoners the right to vote, they have amended its original meaning. Why not put such amendments-from-the-bench to the test of a referendum also?

The third reform, recently suggested by Janet Hiebert, is to adopt a form of parliamentary review of rights issues as part of the legislative process.[35] Under this reform, a parliamentary committee would scrutinize government bills for possible infringement of rights after first reading. The committee would hold public hearings that would allow concerned groups and individuals to criticize (or support) proposed policy. If the committee is persuaded that changes are desirable to better respect rights concerns, it could recommend amendments to government bills. If the government rejects the committee's recommendations, opposition parties and the press would have the opportunity to chastise the government and alert the voters. Unlike the current practice, this would stimulate rather than preclude parliamentary and public debate about rights issues.

This is not a radical idea. Australia and New Zealand already have such procedures. Parliamentary review would complement, not replace, the Charter. Dissatisfied groups could still bring legal challenges to laws that they perceive to violate the Charter. In certain instances, a group's Charter challenge might even be strengthened by use of the committee's report. However, parliamentary review would challenge the myth that only judges are capable of assessing rights concerns and would break the courts' growing monopoly on Charter interpretation. Such review would facilitate more informed government defence of challenged legislation in Court, since Crown lawyers could use the reports of the committee. Finally, it would facilitate the use of the section 33 override in instances where the courts make a wrong or unacceptable interpretation of the Charter. Governments could point to committee reports to justify their choice of policy design. In short, adopting a legislative-rights review

process would restore elected governments to the status of equal partners with courts. The result would be not just a fairer but a more
competent process for resolving rights concerns.

Judicial appointments are the fourth area of practical action.
Parliamentary hearings for nominees to the Supreme Court of Canada
would inject some accountability into a government's choice of judicial
appointments. It would also serve to educate the public about the new
role of judges under the Charter. Canadians must learn that the Charter
interpreted by judges of the Bertha Wilson school will mean something
very different from the Charter interpreted by the John Wesley
McClungs of the Canadian bar.

A second desirable reform in this area would be to transfer responsibility for the appointment of provincial superior court judges from
Ottawa to provincial governments. This has been a long-standing interest of many provinces and is not a radical step. It would, however, require
an amendment to the Constitution. Its benefit is that it would connect
court of appeal judges to provincial governments, thereby introducing
greater accountability on the part of the appointers and increased
sympathy for provincial "distinctiveness" on the part of the appointees.
This pool of provincial judges would continue to be the primary recruit-
ing grounds for Supreme Court of Canada appointments.

I realize that these proposals pose a dilemma for many Canadians.
Our instinctive respect for the rule of law makes us wary of practices
that appear to conflict with judicial independence. But the Charter has
introduced a new game with new rules. The other side — the partisans
of jurocracy — are already playing by these rules. The longer the true
friends of constitutional democracy wait, the further behind we fall.

NOTES

1   Peter H. Russell, "The Effect of the Charter of Rights on the Policy-Making Role of the
    Canadian Courts" in *Canadian Public Administration* (1982), p. 25.
2   *A.-G. Canada v. Mossop*, [1993] 1 S.C.R. 554.
3   *Schacter v. Canada*, [1992] 2 S.C.R. 679.

4   Ian Ross Brodie, *Interest Groups and the Supreme Court of Canada*. Ph.D. thesis, University of Calgary, 1997, p. 53.

5   *Lavigne* v. *Ontario Public Service Employees Union* (1991), 81 D.L.R. (4th) 545 (SCC).

6   Roughly half of legal aid goes to criminal trials. See Paul Brantingham and Stephen T. Easton, "The Crime Bill: Who Pays and How Much?" in *Fraser Forum* (1996), p. 28.

7   See Christopher P. Manfredi, "Constitutional Rights and Interest Advocacy: Litigating Educational Reform in Canada and the United States" in F. Leslie Seidle, *Equity and Community: The Charter, Interest Advocacy and Representation* (Montreal: Institute for Research on Public Policy, 1993), pp. 91-117.

8   See Leslie A. Pal, *Interests of State: The Politics of Language, Multiculturalism and Feminism in Canada* (Montreal/Kingston: McGill-Queen's University Press, 1993), chap. 5.

9   *Ibid.*, p. 104.

10 *Ibid.*, p. 144.

11 See F. L. Morton and Rainer Knopff, "The Supreme Court as the Vanguard of the Intelligentsia: The Charter Movement as Post-Materialist Politics" in Janet Ajzenstat, ed., *Two Hundred Years of Canadian Constitutionalism* (Ottawa: Canadian Study of Parliament Group, 1993); also F. L. Morton, "The Charter Revolution and the Court Party" in Patrick Monahan and Marie Finkelstein, eds., *The Impact of the Charter on the Public Policy Process* (North York, ON: York University Centre for Public Law and Public Policy, 1993); and Knopff and Morton, "Canada's Court Party" in Anthony A. Peacock, *Rethinking the Constitution: Perspectives on Canadian Constitutional Reform, Interpretation and Theory* (Toronto: Oxford University Press, 1996), pp. 63-87.

12 *McKinney* v. *University of Guelph; Harrison and Connell* v. *University of British Columbia,* [1990] 1 S.C.R. 927.

13 *Schacter* v. *Canada* (1992), 93 D.L.R. (4th) 1.

14 *Mahé* v. *Alberta,* [1990] 1 S.C.R. 342.

15 *Leshner* v. *A.-G. Ontario* (1992), 16 C.H.R.R. D/184.

16 *Vriend* v. *Alberta,* (1996) 132 D.L.R. (4th) 595 (Alta. C.A.).

17 See *Constitutional Forum* 7:4 (1996).

18 *R.* v. *Keegstra,* [1990] 3 S.C.R. 697.

19 *R.* v. *Butler,* [1992] 1 S.C.R. 452.

20 *Irwin Toy Ltd.* v. *Quebec,* [1989] 1 S.C.R. 927.

21 Troy Riddell, *The Development of Section 1 of the Charter of Rights and Freedoms: A Study in Constitutional Politics*. M.A. thesis, University of Calgary (1994), pp. 79-89.

22 *A.-G. Canada* v. *Lavell and Bedard,* [1974] S.C.R. 1349.

23 *Murdoch* v. *Murdoch* (1977), 26 R.F.L. 11; [1977] 1 W.W.W. 16 (Alta. S.C.).

24 J. R. Mallory, "The Courts and the Sovereignty of the Canadian Parliament" in *Canadian Journal of Economics and Political Science* (1944) 10: pp. 165-78.

25 "Postmaterialist" denotes the point at which a society becomes sufficiently affluent that many of its citizens cease to be concerned with satisfying primary needs (food, shelter, clothing, military security, and so forth) and focus instead on quality of life and so-called social-justice issues. Postmaterialist values are most prevalent among the more educated,

wealthier, and urban members of such a society. Those who work in non-manual, service sector industries (e.g., education, media, law, administration, financial services) are also more likely to have postmaterialist values than those who work in the agricultural and manufacturing sectors.

26 Martin Seymour Lipset, "The Industrial Proletariat and the Intelligentsia in a Comparative Perspective," chap. 5 in *Consensus and Conflict* (New Brunswick and Oxford: Transaction Books, 1995), pp. 187, 196.

27 See Manfredi, "Litigating Education Reform" and F. L. Morton, "The Effect of the Charter of Rights on Canadian Federalism" in *Publius: The Journal of Federalism* 25:3 (1995), pp. 173-88.

28 *Egan* v. *Canada*, [1985] 2 S.C.R. 513.

29 *R.* v. *Sparrow* [1990] 1 S.C.R. 1075.

30 *Vriend* v. *Alberta*, (1996) 132 D.L.R. (4th) 595, at 619.

31 Anthony A. Peacock, "Strange Brew: Tocqueville, Rights and the Technology of Equality" in Peacock, ed., *Rethinking the Constitution*, p. 123.

32 Charter interpretation proceeds in two stages. First the judge inquires whether the right in question has been restricted. At this stage, the burden of proof is on the rights claimant. If the judge is not persuaded that a right has been restricted, the claim fails and the case is closed. If a rights restriction is found, the inquiry moves to a second stage. The burden of proof now shifts to the government to prove that the restriction is "reasonable." This operationalization of section 1 is known as the "Oakes test," after the Supreme Court's 1987 ruling in *R.* v. *Oakes*. It is another example of the Supreme Court interpreting a clause of the Charter in a manner that contradicts the intent of the Framers and making it much easier for "official minorities" to win their Charter claims.

33 Quebec's demand for constitutional recognition as a "distinct society" also presents an opportunity to rein in judicial power, but one that requires an amendment to the Constitution. One solution would be to combine recognition of Quebec as a distinct society with an amendment that makes the Court's Charter interpretations "advisory" (but not legally binding) on provincial governments. This would give Quebec the symbolic distinction it desires, while giving all provincial governments the "equal" shelter against court-imposed public policy.

34 Scott Reid, "Penumbras for the People: Placing Judicial Supremacy under Popular Control" in Peacock, ed., *Rethinking the Constitution*, pp. 186-213.

35 Janet Hiebert, "'Righting' Policy through Parliamentary Rather than Judicial Means" (paper presented at 1997 annual meeting of the Canadian Political Science Association, St. John's, NF, June 8-10).

DEMOCRACY AGAINST
THE FAMILY

WILLIAM D. GAIRDNER

The first time this writer became deeply alarmed about democracy and the family was after hearing a talk show host say that "the family" ought to be defined as "any four people seen together on Donahue."

That got a hearty laugh. But after that came the disturbing realization — even for the host — that many of the callers thought this was a great idea. "We should all be free to live as we please," they said. *"That's what democracy is all about!"*

Something was deeply wrong with such a claim, for it seemed to confuse democracy with freedom, classical liberalism with its antithetical modern variety, and all three with libertinism.

For the purpose of defending procreational society, the natural family must surely be defined as a married mother and father living together with their dependent children. Despite the protestations of hip anthropologists and urban libertarians, this basic unit has been and still is a primordial fact of life in the West, if not for the vast majority of mankind in all of history.[1]

In poll after poll the people say family is central to their existence and constitutes their most important duties. Yet a bit of historical research reveals the unsettling truth that there has always been hostility, implied or expressed, between the state and this ordinary idea of the private family throughout the history of the West. (No one questions that this hostility exists in overtly totalitarian states.)

But if it is true that the people are bonded to family, and that democracy expresses the people's wishes, then how could a democratic state be anti-family? The mere suggestion seems bizarre. Yet it is becoming clear that democracy is no exception to the rule. For underlying all forms of government, each in its own way, is a bitter conflict, however well camouflaged, between private and public demands. As the sociologist Robert Nisbet points out, the state and the family seek opposing forms of allegiance; the two seem to wax and wane inversely to each other.[2]

In the broader sense this is not news. We were fairly and eloquently warned over a century ago by Alexis de Tocqueville in *Democracy in America* that modern democracy under which individuals hewed mostly to their private selves would serve as a sweet vehicle for the rise of statism, for a "mild tyranny"; that masses of individuals who surrender their faith in transcendent social bonds and purposes for the freedom of individual autonomy become ripe for takeover by government. Moral authority and social order must originate and arise from somewhere, and if not from religion, family, community, and civil society, then it will descend with destructive and highly ideological vigour from government.

What is quite new, however, is that we are already far beyond simple hostility. We have moved in a brief space of time — a mere generation or so — from an unintentional to a deliberate quasi-official demolition of civil society and the natural family in the name of four little "hurrah" words: rights, freedom, choice, and equality. At present there is little hope of resisting or reversing this process because even conservatives, for whom the family ought to be sacred, find themselves defenceless against such language. As a people we seem to have forgotten what our founders knew so well: that claims asserted in the name of democracy may or may not be good ones. If they are good, the process may be useful. But if they are bad, bad will follow. The democratic process itself is neutral with respect to the good.

FROM AN ORGANIC TO A RADICAL VIEW OF SOCIETY

Before discussing a number of individual conflicts that contribute to the tension between democracy and the family, we must examine the ongoing struggle between the *organic* and the *radical* views of the status, or position, of "society" (as distinct from the position of government, or state power) in the broader scheme of human life. Just to clarify these distinctions: throughout history, government or the state (where such exists) is that institution which holds a monopoly on force. From the point of view of those subject to its power it is *involuntary*.

In contrast, what we call "society" or "civil society" is the opposite, and however authoritative, has no such monopoly. Society must direct its members through the millions of associations of which it is comprised by *voluntary* moral authority whose tools are reward and stigma. We may go straight to jail if we refuse to pay taxes to the government. But if we refuse to obey our mother, a teacher, our boss, or the local priest, we go to our room, to the corner, to the employer next door, or perhaps to confession. But never to jail.

In the classical Athenian and even the New World forms of democracy, society was always held to be at the centre of life, and a producer, or rather an absolute origin both of the individual and of government; the latter was seen at best as a kind of delegated defender of the mostly unwritten social constitution. This was an organic concept which said that the individual is impossible without society and is naturally obedient, to government by law and to society by convention and morality.[3]

Most scholars refer to civil society as comprised of "intermediate associations." But this language itself seems to be a capitulation, for it places these associations in a subordinate position between government at the top and the undifferentiated mass of autonomous individuals at the bottom. That is the modern liberal view, and result, of such thinking.

CIVIL SOCIETY AT THE CENTRE

From the organic perspective, however, the truth is otherwise. The institutions of civil society — especially the natural family — are not intermediate to anything. They are "originating" institutions without which neither individuals nor governments would be possible.[4] In this respect, it is misleading to speak of "the people," when we ought really to speak of "society." For buried in the former phrase is the assumption of a mass of selfish disconnected wills seeking individual ends, while the latter invokes the ideal of some common higher end.

Some quipster has said, "If you don't know where you're going, you'll end up somewhere else." This is true of societies. They are always heading somewhere, towards some end, even when not aware of their direction. The job of the perceptive analyst is to determine what those ends are even when they are denied.

The larger question, however, is whether the democratic process or logic has a direction of its own in which societies become trapped, even against their better judgment, by virtue of a general unquestioning acquiescence to that logic. For in the much larger picture, and for reasons forever debated, I think we can say that modern democracy is a uni-directional phenomenon, beginning organically and transforming over time into a radical form with no apparent exceptions to this rule. When they have huge tax harvests to spend, democracies may travel from organic to radical with amazing speed. Canada and Sweden are examples.[5] Both were transformed from deeply conservative to extremely radical in less than half a century.

THE STATE AT THE CENTRE

After only one or two generations, all modern democratic societies have indeed been forcibly relegated to intermediacy, their bonds and normal forms of custom, tradition, authority, and obligation diminished. We have ended up with a radical tripartite structure: the provider state at the top as master and authority; civil society, especially the family, in the middle as a re-positioned and intentionally weakened servant to this provider; and finally, at the bottom, millions of increasingly isolated individuals (tax-slaves, really: citizens forced to give and to receive) lined up for equal "rights" and benefits dished out by the state.

Some will say that this is the eventual condition of all societies. But that is not so. In ancient Athens, for example, even in its most radical democratic period — a radicalism quite tame by modern social measures — the *graphe paranomon* law was invoked and used dozens of times each year to severely punish anyone who proposed a decree or law that attacked the traditions of Athenian society. Legislators could be punished retroactively for a law that turned out to be bad even after a majority of the people had accepted it. In short, preservation of society remained uppermost.

Although this modern process of re-positioning society was vigorously restrained both on the continent and in the New World until this century by classical liberal beliefs in freedom from the state, and of course by the strength of religion, much of the autonomism and subsequent atomization of society that has resulted was fully intended and has been carried out in the West under the flag of democracy.[6] This was made possible largely by the transformation of classical liberalism into its modern statist form, a transformation made smoother by the decline of the essentially religious idea of transcendent moral standards and laws that normally serve as a restraint on governments.

Part of the masking problem in North America is that we tend to equate democracy with classical liberalism, a philosophy of freedom defending the individual against coercive powers. But these two are quite separate phenomena. It is possible to have a great deal of liberalism with no democracy whatever, and a great deal of democracy (voting, participation of the people, and so on) with no true liberalism. For the fact is, no monarch in history has enjoyed anything close to the regulatory, policing, or taxing powers common to ordinary leaders and their cabinets in modern democracies. As Nisbet again put it, even "the theory of divine right, as pressed by the seventeenth-century monarchs, never extended to the point of the dissolution of traditional society." And again, to make the distinction, "liberalism is basically a conception of freedom from the state. Democracy is a theory of power, and is not intrinsically predicated upon any notion of the immunity of society from the state."[7] This point, commonly understood by most Europeans, is less well understood by North Americans, who tend to lump true liberalism and democracy together.

CONFLICT #1: INDIVIDUAL VS. SOCIETY

All this is essential background to resolving the first mini-conflict, which properly takes the form of a question: Which shall be first, the individual, or society? In forming policy, should we think first of the good of society, or of the individual and his or her rights? Clearly, it is impossible even to imagine the good of society if the operating assumption is that no such agreement is possible or permissible. From ancient times until quite recently in the West, there was no debate, for "ancient political theory held that the purpose of politics was to cultivate the virtue, or moral excellence of citizens."[8] But today even many conservatives accept the modern liberal belief that the state and its courts should establish no more than a neutral procedural framework within which the good life is for each individual to decide, and none of society's affair.

In Canada this notion has become something like a principle of law as uttered by Madam Justice Bertha Wilson who, in the 1988 Morgentaler decision that set aside Canada's abortion law, pronounced, astonishingly, that "the state will respect choices made by individuals and, to the greatest extent possible, *will avoid subordinating those choices to any one conception of the good life*" (italics mine). This is plainly dishonest, for the massive criminal codes and thousands of laws and regulations so typical of modern democracies have perhaps only this subordinative ambition in common. It is also a recipe for a moral scattergram.

The same topsy-turvy vision was uttered in a 1992 newspaper interview with the Honourable Antonio Lamer, Chief Justice of the Supreme Court of Canada. He held forth, rather inelegantly, "You know I don't think society is an end in itself. I think a person is the most important thing. Anything else is there to assist the person to fulfil one's [sic] life . . .

everything else is subordinate. Even collectivities." This is but a judicial foreshadowing of the thesis presented here: that in modern democracies true sovereignty now resides in the individual, and in the people only as a diminished, often empty convention.

But surely the most bombastic instance of such contemporary individualist fetishism is the loftily oblivious opinion formulated by the U.S. Supreme Court in *Casey* v. *Planned Parenthood* (also an abortion-rights case). The court declared without the slightest self-consciousness that "at the heart of liberty is the right to define one's own concept of existence, of meaning, of the universe, and of the mystery of human life." This is very pleasing hippie-talk. But such a judicially conferred *right to define* all meaning, and by direct implication all morality, will ultimately mean a single individual has a right to claim and impose views on and actions against society and, ironically, its courts. It is striking that not so long ago anyone professing such a belief would have fit perfectly the description of a psychotic (and I suggest should still do so).

MODERN LIBERALISM FAR FROM NEUTRAL

It is surely a mystery why so many moderns accept the terms of such a stunted and inbred conversation. For it is a monstrous distortion of the truth to say that modern liberalism and its courts are neutral as to the ends of society. Few states in history have been more resolute about ends than the modern liberal state, which quite obviously encourages moral neutrality in individuals only for its own strategic reasons — to gain its political, economic, and social objectives. Radical egalitarianism, economic redistributionism, progressivism, secular humanism, the whole underlying theory of the welfare state — each of these core components of modern liberalism requires a *resolute belief in specific ends* based on particular assumptions about value, and a widespread faith (I say "faith" because so many of these policies have proven problematic, and have produced contrary results) in the desirability of those ends.

Those of the opposite persuasion, who used to be known as "conservatives," will not be able to restore the priority of society and its rightful sovereignty until they expose the liberal political and judicial ploy of moral neutrality.

CONFLICT #2: HIERARCHY VS. EGALITARIANISM

Flowing from this conflict over the proper role of society and its ends is a second conflict, between the *hierarchical* and the *egalitarian* views of moral authority. The first says that the moral orderings of society flow from some high standard of the good, and of right behaviour, downward by degrees to lower forms. Until recent times the good began in God, then was expressed in His natural law, and finally in ordinary moral commands, the shalls and shall-nots of society without which the people quickly hit bottom. Most civilizations rest not only on clear moral rankings, but also on infinite gradations within them. This contrasts with the egalitarian objective to remove all forms of status and moral or social gradation.

Consider the subject of love. Egalitarian moderns seduced by the dogma of internal truth regularly cite "love" as justification for a whole range of behaviours. A recent *Globe and Mail* editorial typified this widespread and morally somnolent attitude when it declared, ever so hip, that "most Canadians accept the fundamental goodness of love between adults, whatever its sexual expression" (June 28, 1997). Yet much of the moral work of the West for two millennia has been devoted precisely to teaching hierarchical distinctions between the various kinds and degrees of love, categorically rejecting the lower forms as dangerous and deceptive, and encouraging the higher. Ready examples of the lower sort are self-love, adultery, gluttony, and pedophilia.

In every aspect of ordinary life, too, established civilizations value rank, gradation, distinction, status, authority, and especially *hierarchies of duty and obligation;* graded ladders up which all may climb if they have the talent and will, and nets comprised of local family, religious, and community groups to discipline or succour those who struggle. Such moral hierarchies constitute a spontaneous social order unique to the roots and history of each particular society. In their absence, as chaos closes in, the most common historical alternative has been a state order imposed by force.

A vision of this natural order was most elegantly and powerfully articulated by Shakespeare's Ulysses in *Troilus and Cressida* (I.III.101-124), and is a timeless marvel of concision and insight:

O, when degree is shak'd,
(Which is the ladder to all high designs)
Then enterprise is sick. How could communities,
Degrees in schools, and brotherhoods in cities,
Peaceful commerce from dividable shores,
The primogenity, and due of birth,
Prerogative of age, crowns, sceptres, laurels,
(But by degree) stand in authentic place?
Take but degree away, untune that string,
And hark what discord follows: each thing meets
In mere oppugnancy. The bounded waters
Should lift their bosoms higher than the shores,
And make a sop of all this solid globe:
Strength should be lord of imbecility,
And the rude son should strike his father dead:
Force should be right, or rather, right and wrong
(Between whose endless jar, Justice resides)
Should lose their names, and so should Justice too.
Then everything includes itself in power,
Power into will, will into appetite,
And appetite (an universal wolf,
So doubly seconded with will and power),
Must make perforce an universal prey
And last, eat up himself.

In these few lines lies an outline of the pathology of the modern world, all political science, and the most profound and prophetic conservative warning against egalitarian subversion.

WILL IT BE STANDARDS OR VALUES?

The modern liberal reflex of outrage at such rank and gradation springs from the fact that even the simplest moral standards automatically invite judgment enforced by stigma, and above all emphasize not the equality of persons and their behaviours but their subtle differences and distinctions. Today we are informed this is not in the democratic spirit. That we should not speak of standards, but of a diversity of "values."

Indeed, the democratic equation now insists that because all values are chosen by people of equal worth and rights, all values must be equal in rank. To insist otherwise is to "impose" your values on mine. However, neither the family nor society as a whole can survive as moral communities without a multitude of positive discriminations in the form of rewards and stigma required to defend some common conception of the good *which it is the ongoing job of society to elaborate and articulate.*

The liberal call for "tolerance," for example, is not in itself a good; it is a declaration that everything self-chosen is good; therefore nothing can be bad (except, of course, "intolerance"). Accordingly, as the notion of individual rights predominates, the idea of virtue as a common good and social objective must fall. Enter social disorder and the state, which then seizes the opportunity to rebalance disorder through standards of egalitarian correctness that will ensure the broadest reach for its power. Vast welfare spending, economic relief for morally gutted cities, sanctions and support for illegitimacy, state-funded abortion, easy divorce, liberalization of drug use, so-called human rights tribunals, mandatory attitude-adjustment courses for non-conforming professors and judges . . . these are just a few examples. There's nothing "neutral" about it. The common consequence of all such policies, however, is the atomization and subordination of natural society.

So the question, Shall we have family at the centre of a good society?, hangs on our prior decision whether we want to encourage virtue in citizens, whether to argue for *standards*, and the social hierarchy this entails, or merely *values*. Policy will flow accordingly.

The dilemma for those calling themselves "conservative" in any original sense of a term that implies conserving what is good, is that they must then publicly frown on some behaviours and favour others. Yet so to act is immediately to invite a highly emotional confrontation in the democratic language of rights, freedom, choice, and equality. Predictably, and understandably, most conservatives back down. Everybody backs down.

CONFLICT #3: TWO VIEWS OF SELF

Why? Likely because we want to be nice. We fear attacking the very self of another person. And this leads to the third mini-conflict, one between two visions of the self that underly modern times, both profoundly theological, both nicely captured in the mutually exclusive metaphors of *the glass house* and *the onion*.

The first imagines each of us as selves enclosed in a structure made of hundreds of panes of opaque glass. In this vision, the truth of the universe, the locus of reality, is *external*, and each time we achieve knowledge or insight one of those panes of glass breaks, allowing a fuller glimpse of the world beyond. The goal of earthly life is to strive for transcendent general truth to disabuse the self of inner and outer illusion, thus to improve one's character by breaking as many panes as possible, hoping to end with a luminous vision of the circumambient universe. We seek a mystical union with the truth outside ourselves, to become one with it.

The onion metaphor imagines that ultimate truth is already located *internally*, where it must first be discovered then authentically *expressed*. If we just peel back enough layers of false authority laid down by society, religion, family, and so on, we will eventually find a unique, unadulterated self, shining, true, and beautiful. This rests necessarily on the idea that all truth and value are relative, particular, and above all personal. The ultimate objective is to achieve a mystical unity with this true self, a self that serves as a vulgar secular surrogate for the old-fashioned soul. This image of the self as trapped and restricted by the bodily, material, and moral world in successive layers of false authority is profoundly rooted in the West and has vast moral and political implications, as we shall see. For it seems clear that the political heritage of the West, though commonly presented as a triumph of reason against the darkness of religion and ignorance, is in fact far more deeply theological even in its "rational" forms than is typically recognized, and this is certainly so in regard to Western concepts of the self.

GNOSTIC ROOTS OF THE SOVEREIGN SELF

The earliest and most powerful notion that the truth of existence is hidden internally as a form of immanent insight that needs only to be awakened through self-revelation was powerfully articulated in ancient gnosticism[9] (from the Greek *gnosis*, for *knowledge* or *insight*). This religion was enormously popular in much of the ancient world and has surfaced periodically in history as the great "alternative" conception of the cosmos. It spread outward for a thousand years after the birth of Christ in the form of "Manicheanism" (after its founder, Mani, born in Persia, A.D. 216) both west to Spain and eastward to China to become "a universal religion of revelation" once equal to Buddhism, Christianity and Islam.[10] It survived thus until the twelfth century, at which time it became the object of Mongol oppression in the East, and of purges by the medieval Catholic Inquisition in France and Italy.[11]

Politically, gnosticism found revolutionary expression in modern times chiefly through the misunderstood democratic bent of Rousseau in France, and through the subsequent Jacobin thinking he spawned everywhere with its radical idea that democracy must be grounded in the natural goodness, wisdom, and "general will" of "the people." Its German roots grew in the soil of the Romantic movement spaded by such as the poet Herder who celebrated ideas of personal and cultural expression and "national genius" that soon after helped produce hyper-nationalism and fascistic pride and politics.

CONTRASTING SOLUTIONS

By labelling gnosticism an "alternative conception of the cosmos," I mean to say that all civilizations seem to rely on a particular foundational solution to the puzzle of the co-existence of God with evil, and everything afterward unfolds accordingly. Thus the first step in understanding any civilization is to decipher its theological solution to this problem.

The Christian solution took the form of a theory of original sin grounded in the Edenic story of Adam and Eve who brought punishment upon themselves — and all future history — by disobeying God. This first half of the Christian solution succeeds wonderfully in absolving God of any responsibility for evil. Man fell by misuse of his own free will.

The second half of the Christian solution proceeds to offer salvation in the afterlife for the price of faith in Jesus Christ in the here and now. What is achieved by the two-phase Christian solution, and elementally so, is both *the absolution of God for worldly evil*, as well as *the preservation of his creation as something good*, despite the evil in it.

Gnostics, however, firmly take the opposing view, and on this difference hangs much of the complexity and tension of Western civilization. They argue that the Christian solution is a deception. To take the world's evil upon ourselves is a grossly demeaning act. For the true God, they say, is so good and pure He would never have permitted evil in His creation; He so loves his creatures He would never allow them to suffer. Therefore this evil world must have been created not by the true God, who is all but unknowable, but by a lesser, impostor god. Worldly creation was the result of a trickery by which men and their souls have been trapped here below.

Now here is a fascinating alternative "logic" that not only manages *to absolve God of responsibility for evil, but man as well*. Evil is the fault of a lesser god. Man is clean. This gnostic solution to the foundational problem of worldly evil relates directly to the ancient as well as modern problem of the self and its connection to God, as follows.

In the basic gnostic myth portions of the light or "spark" of divinity from the true God are believed to have fallen into this world, and rest latent in humans who must strive to discover it within. Thus the gnostic route to spiritual salvation is not through acknowledgment of personal sin and faith in Christ, but rather through *insight into one's own divinity* embodied in the spark or remnant of the true God. Insight, awareness of the light within, is our only possible connection with the true God.

The gnostic solution offers immediate spiritual salvation and a divinity-connection through self-awakening now. Furthermore, when the gnostic dies his soul alone joins the true God for eternity. There is no need first to repent, then die, then await a Judgment Day for the resurrection of the body. In fact, for gnostics the mere suggestion of bodily resurrection is offensive because the repugnant appetites, demands, and restrictions of the body are the most aggravating expression of the evil materiality of this imprisoning world.[12]

Christianity is seen as a pathetic alternative solution because it offers tortuous self-condemnation for evil that is not our fault, then an impossible moral and spiritual discipline, and finally conditional salvation on the installment plan.

What makes the gnostic solution so attractive to the materialistic and sensually repressive West is not merely that it vigorously denies inherent sinfulness in human beings, but that it much more boldly actually asserts a potential divine spark that may be awakened by self-recognition. Peel back the onion and see for yourself. This is the theological background to the rise of radical secular "selfism" and its syncretic pagan form in New Age philosophy that boasts of the divine within persons.[13] It is also the theological root of all modern notions of sovereignty and "rights talk."

DIVINE SELVES, DIVINE PEOPLE

Such a view of the self is both deeply anti-authoritarian and a critical repudiation of the Christian understanding of human nature on which democracy, especially in the New World, has until recently been firmly grounded. The new view went public during the French Revolution from the mouths of frantic Jacobin leaders who fancied themselves an elect class of interpreters of the (sacred) will of the people, than which there could be no higher law. The Jacobins expressed a confidence in the inner goodness of the people not shared in the least by the Christian constitution-makers of the New World.[14] For the latter, it was precisely the fallenness of Man that required checks, balances, and separation of powers in constitutions lest the whole people become tyrannized by the democratically expressed will of a simple majority. That had been the fate of the ancient democracies. But fallen individuals can only produce fallen polities. So checking human nature with modern constitutional devices would produce more true freedom for all than allowing that nature a full expression could ever do.[15]

MODERN LAW AND DEMOCRACY REJECT THE CHRISTIAN VIEW OF THE SELF

It is fair to say that the history of modern constitutional and legal revisionism is a record of the progressive repudiation of this pessimistic (but I think realistic) view in favour of the exceedingly optimistic (but unrealistic) gnostic idea that goodness is resident within the self and ought to be expressed as fully as possible. Flowing from this latter assumption is a secondary one: that *any higher law operant in this world must be repudiated.* In other words, divine man, political man, must be unfettered, must have a self unchecked from within or without, in a world deemed infinitely improvable by the unimpeded actions of lawmakers and judges.[16]

The prototypical modern voice celebrating a self obedient only to its own inner truth can be heard virtually ripping through the Puritan resistance in America in the poet Walt Whitman's arresting essay "Democratic Vistas" (1871). There Whitman speaks of "perfect individualism" and of "fusing" citizens in democratic unity, even (get ready) in "cosmic democracy." The tip-off to his modernity comes when he says, "What is independence? Freedom from all laws or bonds except those of one's own being," which leads to "the main thing . . . the democratic, the popular, on which all the superstructures of the future are to permanently rest."[17]

In modern times we encounter everywhere this same indignant claim of a right to seek out and fulfil personal desires and appetites as a kind of sacred internal obligation prior to all external obligations or conventions. For democratic Walt, the self is sovereign in the moral realm —

there is no higher external law, just as in democratic theory the collection of selves is sovereign. As early as the fifteenth century we began to hear the rallying cry of democrats and levellers, *Vox populi, Vox Dei,* "the voice of the people is the voice of God."

THE DESCENT OF SOVEREIGNTY

This suggests that over the past few centuries there has been a steady *descent of sovereignty.* First, radical democrats attacked the sovereignty of God, then of kings and Divine Right, then of aristocrats, then of all property and status qualifications for the franchise, and so on — until as part of "the people" even condemned murderers now get to vote. Yet despite this descent, the modern democratic ethos always until recently remained subordinate to some transcendent ideal of higher law, some definable idea of religious or social virtue, some collective good. No doubt this ideal arose from the Christian view of sin and the fallen self — that is, from the recognized need for some common vision of the good to contain errant humanity.

Even throughout that decorous revolt against authority known as classical liberalism, this controlling vision survived. Locke, Mill, Smith, and Burke were all devout Christians. Contrary to the standard "liberal history lesson,"[18] the freedoms they vouchsafed derived not from the rationalist tradition but from medieval Christian ideas. Certainly the American and Canadian founding fathers saw quickly that democracy could not survive without an immense and continuing effort of moral self-control based in the people themselves and grounded in religious belief. As Burke warned, some control is always needed, and the less we have within, the more is needed without.

But here we are. Secularism and materialism now hold nearly complete sway. Ironically, we now stare upon the amazing spectacle of the people and their cherished standards and culture being attacked in the name of *individuals and their rights.* The idea of sovereignty in our time has descended straight through the collectivity known as "the people," in whose name the theory of democracy originally stood, and now resides in individuals, who exert it *against the people as the lone remaining authority and impediment to individual freedom and self-expression*. Thus, not only has society been atomized and diminished, but so, too, has our ordinary conception of sovereignty and collective will. Alas, it will be impossible to restore organic society until we first restore a more realistic understanding of the self that includes its social and moral obligations, and I fear this will require a spiritual revolution beyond anyone's immediate imagining.

HOW RADICAL DEMOCRACY DESTROYS COMMUNITY

However, no imagination is required to see the destructive workings of modern democratic ideology as it attacks the very organic society it once nurtured. For the very notions of rank, moral and social hierarchy, the sense of privilege — especially the "insider/ outsider" or what some call the "friend/enemy" distinction — all these earmarks of spontaneous social order are repugnant to democratic thinking.[19] This suggests (and this is my most subversive point, an unavoidable conclusion that has surprised even me) that *the democratic impulse is in the very long run inherently contrary to the impulse for true community*.

That is because all social groups rely on a common four-step process to recruit and bind their members as insiders within specific expectations and limits. In other words, all forms of genuine human community are boundary-phenomena. They require a willingness among members to *sacrifice* self-interest to the group (a plain example is the Rotary International motto: "Service Above Self"). For internal control and order they require *subordination* to the group's authority and rules; for loyalty they demand some process or ceremony of *commitment*, whether by a solemn vow, a contract, or a ritual; and finally, when all this is done, as reward they reserve *privileges* and a special status for accepted members *that must be rigorously denied to all outsiders*.

These four steps are the very dynamic of human bonding, and of course represent the very crisis of egalitarian socialism, because true community can only be realized through some natural order that creates binding distinctions and rank. (Ironically, hard-core egalitarians see non-egalitarians as unenlightened, inferior outsiders.[20]) In short, it appears we may have equality and no community, or community and no equality, but not both: equality and community are asymptotic functions.

This means that as democracies move from their organic to their final radical form, there will always arise a kind of creeping civil war over moral standards due to democracy's imperative to eliminate all distinction and especially privilege, of which the natural family is historically the most glaring and persistent source and example.

When faced with two such conflicting ideals deeply held by the people, the ploy of all modern democratic states — shakened loose by egalitarian logic from any higher standard of the good and too cowardly to defend traditional society (for fear of attack upon democratic grounds) — has been to remove the offending privileged legal status of the family . . . but not its benefits. These it simply showers on all claimants alike, thus converting formerly exclusive policies that secured commitment and obligation from citizens to the family and to a procreative society, into general welfare rights that release them from and dissolve any such commitment.

THE FIVE RADICALISMS
Such democratic fundamentalism operates chiefly through five radical movements, each of which is aimed at the destruction of a specific *order* crucial to the survival of the natural family and civil society. Each realm of order is grounded in a hierarchy of obligation and authority, moral standards, an external view of truth and the self's relation to it, and a crucial insider/outsider distinction.

RADICAL FEMINISM
Radical feminism seeks to overthrow the *biological order* by negating all gender differences and the social and familial consequences that arise naturally from these. For such feminists the simplistic demand for "free-

dom of choice" supersedes all other claims.[21] Feminism of this sort is likely the most vitriolic and socially damaging of all assaults on the larger social order, and certainly the most fanciful — as well as most successful in its re-ordering, however temporary, of almost every social, political, and legal aspect of modern society. That it even imagines that such programs as "universal day care" will "free" all women, even the rich (as if they needed freeing!), from their biology is a sign of how deeply ideological, even theological and puritanical, this vision must be. At the extreme it is a dream of "liberating" women from the "rape" of male sexual demands and the "slavery" imposed by their own children.

The theology, so to speak, behind radical feminism is rooted in the ancient gnostic religion's detestation of the biological division of humanity into two genders, which it saw as a source of fundamental disunity in the cosmos. As a protest and bid for unity, the sexual ideal of gnosticism therefore was bisexuality as a kind of genital affirmative action.[22] Most gnostics also spurned fornication and especially procreation on the grounds that to marry and have children was to succumb to and perpetuate worldliness and the unfortunate sexual bifurcation of biological life. Not incidentally, these are also the theological roots of vegetarianism, for to eat any animal life is to perpetuate the biological order. Modern socialist-style academic utopians jump on this sexual unity bandwagon by promoting androgyny as the social ideal, the very means of "freeing" all humanity from divisive and oppressive heterosexuality.

It is only in the context of this demand for a *right to freedom*, then, that we can begin to understand these and other wacky-seeming anti-family statements such as the U.S. "declaration of feminism" (1971), which pronounced that "the end of the institution of marriage is a necessary condition for the liberation of women." This is basic freedom language, one of the four cornerstones of the democratic movement. It is used against the family conceived as a prison house so that women can be equal (another cornerstone). Such warfare against the biological order is very old. It could be heard in declining third-century Rome, mired as it was in divorce and broken families, in the cry for autonomy of then fashionable feminists whose motto was "live your own life."[23]

In our time it is shrieked from the pages of diatribes such as *The Dialectic of Sex* by the very angry feminist Shulamith Firestone, who warns (accurately from her perspective) of "the tyranny of biology." The tired intellectual grandmother of such anti-nature nonsense was Jean-Paul Sartre's mistress Simone de Beauvoir, who stated that although women are in fact free, "they should not be allowed to choose" the traditional role of mother and wife.[24]

RADICAL ABORTIONISM

By direct extension from the above, the radical abortion movement seeks to overthrow the *order of love* and to replace it with an order of death whose natural extension is euthanasia. (When administered to children some call abortion "pediatric euthanasia.") Once again we encounter the ancient imagery of slavery and entrapment. Radicals know full well that without the right to kill their unborn children, women may be "trapped" in motherhood and hence in the natural family by their own appetites, by their bodies, or by the bodies of their babies. Section 7 of Canada's Charter of Rights and Freedoms has supplied this killing right under the aegis of "security of the person" (with no mention of the security of their children). The U.S. equivalent was invoked in the name of an imaginary "right to privacy." In both countries unelected judges have "found" these rights in constitutional documents where they are not mentioned.

The first deeply shocking image that drove home to me the radical freedom politics underlying such ambitions was a pro-abortion poster that blared "ABORT GOD!" This angry placard seemed a primordial symbol of human protest against the existence, even the mere idea, of any controlling moral standard, from God on down. To such a mind, control of any kind or degree means less freedom.

That is why abortion has been advocated as a right by freedom fighters since ancient times. In his *Republic*, a template for the perfect state where individuals would be maximally free because maximally obedient to his Philosopher Kings and their perfect laws, Plato urged infanticide and eugenics (race purification by combining infanticide with directed mate-selection and licensed child-bearing), and advocated taking children from their parents at birth to be raised in state omnicare centres. This was an absolute requirement for the creation of the good state. *True freedom and equality* between the sexes was deemed impossible without such a program. It still is.

Rousseau, who described himself as "a child of Plato," urged the same destruction of the natural family (the main source of inequity, he argued) and of all biological distinctions between the sexes. He so longed to fulfil his own ideals he gave up his own five children (by a broken-hearted mistress of 30 years whom he steadfastly refused to honour with marriage) to orphanages where they surely died. Marx and Engels simply echoed this austere program, and every attempt was made to carry it out under communism.

Which brings us to the connection between abortion and Nietzsche. Here was a man who argued that as God is dead, all moral systems are just rationalizations for the will to power, thus all morality is an artifact. His ideas reinforced the notion of moving beyond ordinary good and evil by exerting personal will and control over the material world. As Canada's George Grant put it, "It is the very heart of fascism to think that what matters is not what is true, but what one holds to be true."

But his charge holds as well against the pure democratic state, the soft tyranny in which what matters is not what is true, but what all the people hold to be true. That is why U.S. Senator Huey Long said long ago that "when fascism comes to America it will come in the name of democracy." He meant the word *democracy* would serve as a mask to hide the triumph of the collective will over truth.

Anyone searching for examples need go no farther than the local public shool where under the guise of Moral Values Education (MVE) young children are taught that all values are personally determined, that "self-esteem" is more important than estimable actions, that general moral beliefs are condemnable as "impositions" on others, and generally that personal liberation matters most in all things: free the imperial self within! In matters of reproduction the unborn child is objectified as a fetus/thing which (not "who") exists as a potential impediment to the mother's freedom, an interference with her right to "have sovereignty" and "control" over her own body.

This entire grievous issue has been cleverly converted by the language of democracy — freedom, choice, equality, and rights — into a matter of broader civil rights: a case of the victim-mother freeing herself by right of choice from the slavery of biology so she can be equal to everyone else (especially to the male). This equation means that anyone who opposes abortion opposes the right to be free *and is therefore anti-democratic.*

A moment's reflection reveals that what pro-abortion types want is not really the freedom to choose. All lovers have that, and some botch it. What they demand (at taxpayers' expense) is *the freedom to undo their original choice and its natural biological consequences.* They want the power of God . . . and have gotten it. This outcome means there has been a dreadful modern merger between democratic ideology and personal appetite.

RADICAL PANSEXUALISM

The radical homosexual, incest, and pornography movements — all subdivisions of the pansexual movement in the West — seek to overthrow the *sexual order* of natural biological society. Inspired by such as Rousseau, Whitman, and de Sade — modern gnostics all — pansexualism argues that because the self is naturally good, all sexuality is naturally good. Modernity stands accused of being a "sex-negative" society based on repressive conditioning, a hangover from the Judeo-Christian or "Victorian" system. The objective of all authentic pansexualists, therefore, is "sexual freedom."

In contrast, the predominate sexual order is grounded in four traditional prohibitions based on Number, Gender, Age, and Incest: You can only marry one person at a time, only someone of the opposite sex, never someone beneath a certain age, and not a close blood relation. All four measures, grounded in morality and the law for millennia, protect a procreative society and rely on binding insider/outsider distinctions with all the important and binding rewards and stigma these generate.

Yet once again, leaning almost exclusively on the democratic language of freedom and rights found in our Charter, the privileges and protections normally reserved exclusively for those who commit themselves to this sexual order are now being given to all claimants regardless of qualification. "There shall be no insiders or outsiders!" is the democratic demand.

In essence the prototypical cry for freedom issued by sexual democrats is indistinguishable from the urge that underlies all freedom movements. As early as 1972, the U.S. National Gay Rights Platform published its demands for the abolition of all age of sexual consent laws; repeal of all laws against sodomy and child prostitution; the right of homosexuals to adopt children; and repeal of all laws restricting the sex or number of persons in a marriage unit.

An even clearer expression of this freedom cry came from the Task Force on Child-Adult Relations. This is the marketing arm of the North American Man-Boy Love Association, whose putative slogan is "Sex before eight, or else it's too late." TFCAR seeks "to establish the principle that the goals of all liberation groups are the same: the elimination of sexist, authoritarian regimentation of human lives; and that *the liberation of children is the sine qua non of all human liberation*" (italics mine).[25] In an even more breathless hyperbole, the leader of Toronto's "Lesbian, Gay, Bisexual, Transgendered, and Transsexual Pride Day Commmittee" lauded the prime-time lesbian confessions of Ellen Degeneres, saying without a hint of humour that *if human freedom is the value* her action may rival the destruction of the Berlin Wall in importance.[26] Alas, the German Mark didn't budge, and I'm sure the thousands who died in East German camps or while attempting to escape that evil empire would not have appreciated the comparison of their plight to sexual dalliance.

LEGAL RADICALISM

Last but not least, we have the legal radicals who populate every law school in North America, sit on many benches, and have been enormously successful in challenging the *legal and tax order* constitutive of a family-based society, again in the name of democratic rights. For example, since World War II, co-habitation (or marriage-avoidance) has had substantial legal and tax advantages over legal marriage; tax codes continue to penalize the traditional family that wishes to rear its own children; welfare rights financially reward single motherhood; and no-fault divorce now means no-responsibility marriage. In Canada and the U.S. it is presently impossible legally to bind yourself for a lifelong marriage. By all of these measures, freedom and equality rights enthusiasts have succeeded in undermining the entire contractual and sacramental basis for marital union.

The root concepts of the legal campaign against the family and family-based society may be found smouldering away in the dark junk-yard of Marxism. It is there we find the old gripes against private property, the biological sexual order, patriarchy, free enterprise, class warfare, and inequality. The utopian urge to rectify these "problems" through legal channels finds expression in modern concepts of "sub-stantive" in contrast to "formal" law. Legal radicals are fed up with formal law and the liberal-democratic framework of justice. These have always stood for freedom as "rules of just conduct, equal for all," a framework of law under which personal freedoms and differences (that is, natural inequalities) may be fully expressed.

Nuts, say the legal radicals. Power groups in society, especially the rich, use the cover of formal freedom to exert control and "hegemony." The result is widespread inequities in income, property, and influence. A true democrat must therefore despise this system and work hard to replace formal law with substantive law: law that is not satisfied merely to speak of "equality of opportunity" or "before the law" but that seeks to ensure it is provided in *substance*. From this springs the whole framework of affirmative action and the revolutionist idea of changing society not through liberal democratic means but through the courts, law journals, and interest-group politics. As Canada's Ian Hunter put it so well, "The religious vision of Heaven, a land beyond time and morality and very far off, has been replaced by a Utopian vision of an egalitarian society, to be obtained through Charters, Commissions, Affirmative Actions, and Legislated Codes of Behaviour."[27]

This means the appearance of what F. L. Morton (in this volume) calls the "Court Party," an interlocking system of legal scholarship, commissions, tribunals, and activists who are at heart radical democrats who have given up on the processes of liberal democracy. Liberal democracy does not produce utopia quickly enough because it relies on the opinion of masses of uninformed people who will not surrender the natural biological and sexual orders of human life to utopian schemes. So freedom, choice, equality, and rights? These can be enforced affirmatively to correct social imbalance by circumventing the people and their political process entirely. How? Mostly by spurning the "original intent" method of constitutional interpretation that insists we stick to the intentions of the founders in favour of a "living tree" approach that encourages "reading into" the abstract words of judicial codes and constitutions meanings that were never intended to be there or, more typically, that the authors of such codes, it is argued, would have put there if they had lived among us today.

Under regimes that accept such judicial revisionism, charters and constitutions become a broad form of licence for radical democrats to reshape and eliminate organic society by altering the meaning of the law, challenging the traditional common law, and *disciplining and correcting the assemblies of the people*. Thus does a concept of *higher democratic freedom* (gnostic-inspired and radically democratic) control and direct *lower democratic freedom* (one that reflects traditional morality and organic society and which is loosely grounded in true liberalism).

This is the new *modus operandi* of hyperdemocracy. Thus today do the people's legislators in the U.S. and Canada make law with great trepidation. Their first consideration is the conformity of proposed laws not to the original constitution but to the opinions of appointed radical judges on the bench or appointed bureaucrats on human rights tribunals. These latter bodies, not the people, are increasingly ordering legislators around.

At the international level, anti-family legal radicalism rooted in the language of radical democracy radiates mostly from United Nations "Conventions" on women and the child. During its recent "Year of the

Family," the United Nations announced to the world that the family is "the smallest democracy at the heart of society." Now this is pure bureaucratic hype and drivel, because the family has never been a democracy, nor should it be. Just try to imagine a family with three children voting against their parents on whether they should attend school or be allowed to burp at the table. But here was a bizarre trumpet call for the enforcement of "rights," "choice," and "freedom" of children against the authority of their own parents. Such bureaucrats are aware that children are too young to pursue rights. Thus what the U.N. hopes for, intoxicated with its Rousseauvian, gnostic faith in the spark of goodness in all children, is the enforcement of children's rights as interpreted by these officials against parents. The ordinary undemocratized natural family is regularly described in journals that uphold such conventions as "authoritarian" and, when attacked by homosexual advocates, as "privileged." Remember, this is not an international program to cure manifest evils such as smallpox, hunger, or war. No, it is a *call to become liberated* even from the healthiest of natural family-based societies *in the name of higher democratic equality*.

At the extreme, what such progressives dream of is the forcible top-down creation of the perfect society — the creation of Whitman's religious or "cosmic" democracy (the religion of nature, that is) — by intervening as early as possible via gnostic insight specifically to *prevent* the biological influence of the natural family and its awful gender-based consequences such as patriarchy, moral authoritarianism, oppression of sexuality, inequality, enslavement by the demands of "unwanted" children, and so on. That is the program.

A recent article, "Equality Rights and Sexual Orientation: Confronting Heterosexual Family Privilege," by a Canadian legal scholar[28] virtually obsessed with the language of democracy fulminates fanatically at the "discriminatory" injustice of having an "age of consent" law forbidding homosexual anal sex until age eighteen, but permitting "other sexual acts" — by which he means between heterosexuals — at the age of fourteen. He ignores that society wants to protect young children from adult homosexual predation, and sorrows at the injustice of society privileging any particular chosen mode of sexual relation. He wants a merely procedural sexual republic. In this pathetic and simple-minded view, humans are to be but life-support systems for genitalia.

Not least, the language of freedom radicals virtually infests the U.N. Convention on Women; its operating assumption is that to be free, women the world over *must* be provided universal daycare, must find work under affirmative action guidelines, above all *must* leave the family to work, work, work (read: be free from biology and pay taxes), and *must* be provided with sexual freedom through "family planning," by which is meant tax-funded contraception and abortion services. Nothing neutral here.

EDUCATIONAL RADICALISM

Lastly, we have all encountered the education radicals. Public-school teachers must of course act as trustees of children for someone, either for the parents and their community, or for the state. Ultimately, if the radical positions taken by North American teachers' unions are a guide — and they surely are — then in curricula, teaching philosophy, textbooks chosen, and especially in every aspect of modern sex education, abortion, homosexuality, multiculturalism, and so-called social and global engineering, teachers clearly tend to side with the state and its officially promulgated views against those of the private family, which they deride as "Victorian," "bigoted," "homophobic," or, most damning of all, "from the fifties." (Oh, the pain . . .)

WHAT IS TO BE DONE?

So to conclude, the course for those of us who wish to resist and conserve what is good, is clear. We must first understand that a certain amount of democracy may be a good thing, but that as the democratic logic proceeds it inevitably gets hijacked by radicals who purge it of an informed liberalism then use the language and the logic of democracy outside the political process to break down traditional community by taking special aim at the natural family as the chief source of inequity and moral authority.

The moral revolution required to reverse this process will mean we must reclaim and revivify democracy with true classical liberalism and a rule of formal law once again; defend the possibility of discerning right from wrong, and the social and moral hierarchy this produces as natural to, and a mark of, free and spontaneous societies; reject the sterile idea of a procedural republic and insist on open public discussion of the proper ends of a virtuous society; vigorously reject the modern liberal ruse of moral, legal, and judicial neutrality and the utter fable that contemporary liberal society is not adamantly pursuing ideological ends of its own; expose the indefensible, unworkable, and morally deflating goals of the modern liberal welfare state; and, not least, repudiate the radical notion of the imperial self as sovereign by democratic right over the people and their society.

Only then will we recognize what to conserve in a newly civilized, disciplined, and restrained democracy.

NOTES

1 For the most of the 1980s and '90s, approximately 76 percent of all Canadian families have been married mother-father-children families. If we include "common-law" families with children, then about 87 percent of all families still live in the traditional form. (For the sake of my argument, even common-law co-habitation is a form, if far less stable, that models true marriage and thus fits a kind of shadow definition of the natural family.) After the last major analysis, in 1991, Gordon Priest, social data expert of Statistics Canada, said: "The family is alive and well, with 86 percent of all children under age 15 living in two-parent families. The old values, of men and women forming couples they intend to last, having children, supporting them, are still there. Those who utter gloom and doom about the death of the family won't find it in our statistics" (*The Daily*, Statistics Canada Catalogue 11-00E, Tuesday, July 2, 1992). Lone parent families in Canada continue to hover around the 13 percent mark — about the same percentage shown for the 1930s and '40s. What has changed alarmingly in both the U.S. and Canada, however, in addition to the skyrocketing levels of illegitimacy and abortion, is the percentage of the total represented by common-law marriages. At the beginning of the decade these totalled about 9 percent in Canada, and by 1997, 14 percent. For a variety of reasons likely due to various legal changes, increased divorce liability and easy availability of sex, we are seeing increased marriage-avoidance and postponement.

2 A full treatment of this subject is found in William D. Gairdner, *The War Against the Family*

(Toronto: Stoddart, 1993).

3   A good essay collection on the role of society under Greek democracy is Josiah Ober and Charles Hedrick, eds., *Demokratia: A Conversation on Democracies, Ancient and Modern* (New Jersey: Princeton University Press, 1996). Also very useful are Mogens Herman Hansen, *The Athenian Democracy in the Age of Demosthenes* (Oxford: Blackwell, 1991), and of course, Numa Denis Fustel de Coulanges, *The Ancient City* (Baltimore: Johns Hopkins Press, 1980).

4   This view of the primacy of society (as distinct from the state) over the individual has been standard in all world history until recent times in the West, where alone it has suffered a reversal in the name of individual rights from the the Renaissance until today. The rise of modern "conservatism" in the past two centuries has been largely a reaction to this reversal. Conservative thinkers such as Joseph de Maistre and Louis Bonald in France underlined this primacy of natural society a century ago with great passion. The latter wrote: "Man exists only in and for society. Not only is it not true that the individual constitutes society, but it is society which constitutes the individual" (cited in Robert Nisbet, "Conservatism and Sociology," *American Journal of Sociology*, no. 58, September 1952, pp. 167-73).

5   Two thoroughly sobering analyses of this phenomenon for Sweden, a sort of model of the "middle way" for Canada under Prime Ministers Lester Pearson and Pierre Trudeau, are David Popenoe, *Disturbing the Nest: Family Change and Decline in Modern Societies* (New York: Aline de Gruyter, 1988) and Allan C. Carlson, *The Swedish Experiment in Family Politics* (New Brunswick, NJ: Transaction Publishers, 1990).

6   The best analysis of this process of social decomposition at the hands of the state, ancient and modern, is, again, Robert Nisbet, *The Quest for Community: A Study in the Ethics of Order and Freedom* (San Francisco: Institute for Contemporary Studies, 1990). His brief foreword to Joseph R. Peden and Fred R. Glahe, *The American Family and the State* (San Francisco: Pacific Research Institute for Public Policy, 1986), is a fine summary of his thinking on the family.

7   Robert Nisbet, "Rousseau and Totalitarianism," *The Journal of Politics*, 5:2, May 1943, pp. 93-114.

8   Michael Sandel, *Democracy's Discontent* (Cambridge, Massachusetts: Harvard University Press, 1996), p. 7. Sandel outlines in great detail the movement away from organic towards radical democracy, to what he calls the "procedural republic," in a progression of seminal court judgments over the past two centuries, each of which in the name of solely individual good gradually eliminates the notion of any corporate or collective or transcendent social good.

9   The importance of gnosticism for political life in the West was well recognized by late eighteenth- and nineteenth-century historians. Then, with the rise of statism, it was forgotten. It was roundly and incisively analysed in recent times by Eric Voegelin in his *The New Science of Politics* (Chicago: University of Chicago Press, 1952), and again in *Science, Politics and Gnosticism* (Washington: Regnery Gateway, 1968), originally published in German in 1959. Unfortunately, Voegelin did not have the benefit of the first masterful examination of gnosis by Hans Jonas, *The Gnostic Religion* (Boston: Beacon Press, 1958),

which itself was prior to the translation of 52 gnostic "secret gospels" discovered at Nag Hammadi in 1945 but kept from the world until the mid-1970s. The best treatment of the gnostic religion that includes the Nag Hammadi gospels is Kurt Rudolph, *Gnosis: The Nature and History of Gnosticism* (San Francisco: HarperCollins, 1987), first published in German in 1977. It is true that Plato and even many pre-Socratics believed that we are all born with full knowledge inside us and that our task is to discover it. Plato has often been described as a gnostic thinker for this reason. However, he promoted a discovery process based on reason and dialectic, not on a diffuse spiritual insight, and in contrast to the modern court pronouncements above, he certainly never believed that truth could be personally defined. For him, truth lies in absolute, unchanging eternal forms.

10 R. Haardt, in Rudolph, *op. cit.*, p. 327.

11 Insight into the life of the medieval Cathars, or Albigensians, centred in the south of France, may be found in Le Roy Ladurie, *Montaillou: The Promised Land of Error* (New York: George Braziller, 1978).

12 The Christian view is that all the faithful will be resurrected bodily as well as spiritually on Judgment Day. The gnostic view is that on death the spirit leaves the body behind and alone joins with God. Of note is that most practising Christians today when asked what they believe will happen to them upon death will give the gnostic interpretation rather than the Christian one. The Christian eschatology has somehow become gnosticized, and it's not as if Christians are protesting.

13 An especially good survey and analysis of this phenomenon is Paul C. Vitz, *Psychology as Religion: The Cult of Self Worship* (Grand Rapids, MI: Eerdmans, 1977).

14 See especially Claes G. Ryn, *The New Jacobinism: Can Democracy Survive?* (Washington: National Humanities Institute, 1991). This brief and insightful book puts in perspective the key moral, philosophical, and political aspects of original and modern Jacobinism. My own thesis flirts with Ryn's title, in that I increasingly believe that Western political mysticism runs far deeper than I could ever have believed (the public cant about Western reliance on reason and science has masked all this) and that in fact Jacobinism is an expression or fulfilment of pure democratic theory. Without the brake of religion and transcendent standards, democracy will always push itself towards Jacobinism, which, ironically, is itself a form of secular millenarianism.

15 For an insightful version of this argument for Canada, see Janet Ajzenstat, "Modern Mixed Government: A Liberal Defence of Inequality," *Canadian Journal of Political Science*, 18:1 (March, 1985). What many feared, she writes, "was the emergence of simple democracy, by which they meant a form of government in which the mass of the people are left without means to oppose or resist political leaders ruling in the name of the people."

16 It must be said here that this "progressivist" slant often attached to gnosticism, even by such distinguished scholars as Eric Voegelin, is not truly gnostic. The underlying distinctive feature of true gnosticism is repudiation of the material world, and retreat, not social revolution. This latter aim to repair the evil in this world, an ambition so influential throughout the history of the West, comes from Christian millenarianism, and this ever-present force is fascinatingly detailed in Norman Cohn, *The Pursuit of the Millennium*

(London: Random House, 1970).

17 James E. Miller, Jr., ed., *Walt Whitman: Complete Poetry and Selected Prose* (Boston: Houghton Mifflin, 1959), p. 490.

18 Stanton Evans, *The Theme Is Freedom: Religion, Politics, and the American Tradition* (Washington: Regnery Publishing, 1994).

19 The French political philospher Julien Freund maintained there were only three conflicts or distinctions central to all politics: command vs. obedience, the public vs. the private, and friend vs. enemy. See Gary Ulmen, "Reflections of a Partisan: Julien Freund (1921-1993)," in *Telos*, no.102, winter 1995, pp. 3-10.

20 Socialist-style or communalistic groups are the most rigidly defined by such boundary phenomena. The difference is that such communalities must be held together by force, walls, barbed wire, and/or persistent moral and social engineering. They are not natural and tend to define uncooperative sub-groups within the main insider group as outsiders, or "enemies of the people," or "internal enemies," whose fate too often is liquidation.

21 We should not miss the sloppiness and redundancy in the modern claim for "freedom of choice," in that all choices are by implication already free or else they could not be made. What moderns want is not freedom of choice but the power to control the consequences of their choices, and more than this, to command a menu of specific options.

22 Rudolph, *op. cit.*, p. 271.

23 Jerome Carcopino, "Marriage, Woman, and the Family," in *Daily Life in Ancient Rome* (London: Penguin, 1941), pp. 89-115.

24 *Saturday Review*, June 14, 1975, p. 12.

25 Rueda and Schwarz, in *The War Against the Family, op. cit.*, p. 373.

26 Letter to *The Globe and Mail*, Toronto, May 5, 1997.

27 *The Idler*, April-May 1975.

28 Bruce Ryder, "Equality Rights and Sexual Orientation: Confronting Heterosexual Family Privilege," *Canadian Journal of Family Law*, vol. 9, 1990, pp. 39-97.

THE FAMILY AND
THE WELFARE STATE

ALLAN CARLSON

At one level, the relationship of the family to the welfare state is obvious and direct. The welfare state component of Leviathan has grown only as the family has surrendered or abandoned functions that, for millennia, had belonged to it and to related small communities, including the central role of moral and practical education of the young and the dependency functions of care for the sick, the infirm, and of those at the very beginning and the very end of life.

Now some say that the family, in consequence, is changing, adapting, or evolving into new forms better suited to modern life. I reject that contention. My own experience, and my study, tell me that family structure is rooted in human nature, and is no more subject to rapid secular change than is the instinctual blink of the eye or the shiver down the back. The "changes" we can see are either deterioration from a *natural* order, or restoration towards that order. Holy Scripture affirms these truths. So do the modern sciences of sociobiology and paleoanthropology, which are rediscovering the powerful, biologically imprinted force of human nature on our behaviours.[1]

This means that in all corners of the globe, and in every historical age, the family can be understood as a man and a woman bound in a socially approved covenant called marriage, for mutual care and protection, for sexual intimacy, for the begetting and rearing of children, for the construction of a small home economy of production and consumption guided by altruism, and for ensuring continuity between the generations, those that came before and those coming after. The only important free cultural choice here is between monogamy and polygyny: that is, between a society composed of one husband and one wife or a society with one husband and multiple wives. Within the civilization known as Christendom, monogamy has been the rule.

Vocational specialization and the exchange of products through barter and sale are also in consonance with human nature, and universal to the species. Markets are where the altruistic economy of the family, based in sharing, meets the larger economy rooted in competition and the quest for profit. A challenge lying before every modern human society is protection of the boundary between these two economies from deep intrusion either way, so that "family altruism" is not forcibly extended to all of society (a system known as socialism) and "competitive individualism" is not injected into the family circle.

In our age, both the permanent revolution known as industrial capitalism and the exponential growth of state power have made extraordinarily difficult the protection of that boundary between the competitive and family economies. For example, large portions of the welfare state found initial justification as mechanisms to "save the family" from the depravations of competitive individualism. At the same time, it is clear that public bureaucracy, considered in the abstract, also holds an interest in family dissolution.

In this essay, I will examine four episodes in the development of the welfare state in the Western world. These episodes illustrate the deeply problematic place of the family in the modern age. I will also look for lessons that chart a better future.

THE FAMILY WAGE EXPERIMENT

The first episode was the attempt by workers and altruistic reformers to construct a "family wage." Few terms are better calculated to start a fight. As two feminist analysts explained a few years back: "Attacking the family wage is . . . like an atheist attacking God the Father: she wants to say that it does not exist, that the false belief that it does has evil consequences and that even if it did exist it would not be a good thing."

A fair conventional definition of the term comes from *The Trades Newspaper*, printed in England in 1825:

> The labouring men of this country . . . should return to the good old plan of subsisting their wives and children on the wages of their own labour and they should demand wages high enough for this purpose. . . . By doing this, the capitalist will be obligated to give the same wages to men alone, which they now give to men, women, and children. . . . [Labourers must] prevent their wives and children from competing with them in the market, and beating down the price of labour.

It is normal today to view language such as this both as sexist and as an artful attempt at restraint of trade, a cleverly veiled descendant of Christian "just price" theory. However, if phrased in terms of my earlier comments, a "family wage" system — if it truly existed — could be seen as a shelter for household units from full immersion into the industrial economy, by limiting to *one* the number of family members entering its employ. Competition *between* family members for the same outside work would be discouraged. At the same time, other forms of non-market social labour — meaning home production such as gardening, food preservation, education, simple carpentry, the production and repair of clothing, and child care — would remain *outside* the industrial economy (and, indeed, the taxable economy) with its value retained wholly by the family. In this way, families would hold to some degree of economic liberty and independence from the giant institutions of modern life, be they corporate or state.

Now it is true that a great deal of mischief has been done in the quest for a family wage. Labour unions in Great Britain and the United States placed the "family" or "living" wage at the centre of their agendas, demanding male wages that would support a "family of five" in reasonable comfort. Such efforts at officially defining the typical worker and injecting "social content" into wage rates quickly ran into the obvious difficulties. For example, since few households had exactly three dependent children at any given time, a family of five standard conjured up a vast horde of fictitious children needing support: 16 million in the England of 1930, and 48 million phantom children in the U.S. Meanwhile, families with four or more children faced continuing strains, while bachelors made out quite well.

The "family wage" also lay behind the Minimum Wage campaign, starting in Australia in 1896 and spreading elsewhere in the English-speaking world over the next few decades. State Wage Courts in Australia quickly succumbed to the temptation of defining a proper family budget, including precise sums for items ranging from "union fees and one newspaper" to "tobacco and drink." In the effort to sustain heads-of-households, the wage courts also fixed female wages at 54 percent of the male wage. This had the quite unintended effect of driving male workers out of certain professions, as employers hired from the legally cheaper female labour pool. The gender-based wage differential also overlooked the fact that a significant number of children depended on their mothers for financial support, due to the death, sickness, or desertion of the father.

A VOLUNTARY SYSTEM THAT WORKED

On the other hand, I think it possible to show that the American people, at least, did craft, without *state* coercion and under *modern* conditions, an informal family wage system that enjoyed popular support; this system worked as intended, delivering on average greater income to families with children and protecting the domain of the household economy. Allow me to elaborate.

During World War II, it was the U.S. federal government that forced private employers and states to eliminate direct wage discrimination against women. General Order Number 16 of the National War Labor Board, issued in November 1942, required government contractors to eliminate so-called "marriage bans" and to pay men and women equally "for comparable quality and quantity of work on the same or similar operations." Over the next three years, thousands of firms reported their compliance. Scientific job and wage classification, adopted by the U.S. government in 1923, was also forced on government contractors during the war years, with elimination of gender distinctions a central purpose. During the Cold War period, the Equal Pay Act won political support as a measure to improve defence mobilization in the war on communism, by expanding the labour pool with married women and improving industrial efficiency.

Despite these developments, though, the so-called wage gap between male and female workers actually *grew* during this quarter century. In 1939, median female earnings in the U.S. were 59 percent of men's. By 1966, the figure had fallen to 53.9 percent (curiously close to the Australian figure of 1920). Preferences for part time or seasonal work played only a slight role in this change. Although direct wage discrimination against women had vanished, another, more powerful, non-governmental force had more than compensated for this change: job segregation by gender, or the cultural recognition of "male" and "female" jobs.

The postwar period witnessed the accelerated crowding of women into only 21 of 250 distinct occupations (including file clerk, secretary, and nurse). Indeed, between 1940 and 1970, women actually lost substantial ground in occupational groups that were overwhelmingly male, including attornies, engineers, chemists, and heavy industrial workers. During these years, the pay rates rose most sharply for "men's" jobs, while the slowest growth was among "women's" jobs. The system encouraged specialization within the household, so enhancing the economic gains of family living and the scope of the household economy. And oddly enough, the system was popular, existing without complaint or meaningful dissent from any quarter of American life. Even the Lyndon Johnson administration, dedicated in many respects to egalitarian civil rights, in a 1964 report to the International Labour Organization cited this wage differential as a necessary aspect of "the basic [American] legal principle which places on the husband the primary responsibility for support of his wife and family with secondary liability devolving on the wife."

PROTECTING FAMILIES THROUGH THE MARKET

Through these culturally imposed preferences, the American people had found an accommodation between the needs of the family and the demands of the market economy. Whether biological or cultural in origin, assumed differences in the family roles of women and men served as a refracting lens through which market signals were bent to accommodate family autonomy, to protect family bonds from excessive intrusion of the "competitive principle." Not coincidentally, I believe, the 1945-65 period also witnessed an unexpected blossoming of family life in the U.S., with the marital birth rate rising 80 percent, with the divorce rate declining, and with the proportion of the adult population in married-couple house-holds reaching an historic high. Through the *cultural* construct of a normative barrier between the public and family economies, Americans had found a way to have economic growth *and* social stability.

It was the Jacobin principle of abstract *equality*, enforced by the state, that destroyed this successful American version of a *family wage* order. The venue was the addition of the word *sex* to Title VII of the Civil Rights Act of 1964. The story of how this occurred legislatively is peculiar enough. As originally proposed by the Johnson administration, this title would have prohibited U.S. employers from segregating or classifying employees, for any purpose, on the basis of race, colour, religion, or national origin. Yet, during debate on the floor of the U.S. House of Representatives, a "Dixiecrat" (Southern Segregationist), Howard Smith of Virginia, proposed an amendment to the bill, adding the word *sex* to the list of prohibited discriminations. His apparent purpose was either to scuttle the bill by adding frivolous amendments, or to swamp the intended protected class — Black males — with an equal legal focus on the much larger class of *white females*. Despite the fact that there was no organized support for this change, the measure won approval on a 168-133 vote, after brief and uncertain debate. The House amendment survived a conference with the Senate (which also never debated the issue or purpose of placing the word *sex* in Title VII), and this change became law.

For a few years, the impact of the measure was uncertain. In 1967, however, President Johnson issued Executive Order 11375, which prohibited federal contractors from discrimination in employment on the basis of sex, and mandated "affirmative," "result oriented" measures to eliminate job segregation by gender. Between 1968 and 1971, according to a sympathetic commentator, the Equal Employment Opportunities Commission (EEOC) "converted Title VII into a magna carta for female workers, grafting to it a set of rules and regulations that certainly could not have passed Congress in 1964, and perhaps not a decade later, either." The effect was large. One analyst suggests that in the absence of enforcement of Title VII, "the male/female earnings gap would not have remained constant, but would have increased, between 1967 and 1974." Instead, EEOC efforts *directly* narrowed the male-female earnings differential during these years by 7 percent. A measure I have developed of the family wage, called the Family Wage Ratio, shows surprising strength in the system as late as 1968, and its accelerating decay over the next 25 years. Again, it is not a coincidence that these same years have witnessed a mounting disruption of American families, marked by a low marriage rate, a very high rate of divorce, soaring illegitimacy, and a sharp decline in marital fertility.

The lesson here is fairly simple: a culture can create mechanisms that do protect the family; an ideologically driven state can destroy them.

THE CORRUPTION OF POLICY: HOUSING

A second episode casting light on the relationship of welfare state and family is housing policy in the U.S. Here we may see how good intent, and even initial success, can quickly turn socially destructive.

Viewed in the mid-1960s, the state-stimulated and -regulated housing industry in the U.S. appeared to be a dazzling triumph. The Federal Housing Administration, created in 1934, had devised the long-term, amortized mortgage, featuring a low downpayment, which made a sense of "home ownership" possible for persons with little capital. The Federal National Mortgage Association ("Fannie Mae"), organized in 1938, mobilized many billions of postwar dollars for housing investment. The GI Bill of 1944 provided millions of war veterans with insured mortgages and the waiver of downpayments. Reconfiguration of federal income taxes in the 1930s and 1940s gave preferred tax status to owner-occupied homes. The underwriting rules for government-backed loans also ensured that only traditional, child-oriented, married-couple families would qualify. The preamble to the Housing Act of 1949 proudly declared: "The general welfare and security of the nation . . . require . . . the realization as soon as feasible of the goal of a decent home and a suitable living environment for every American family."

Between 1945 and 1960, and under the stimulus of these state-inspired changes, the number of owner-occupied homes in the U.S. nearly doubled. U.S. suburbs grew exponentially, and the new housing tracts were filled by Baby Boom families. In a mere fifteen years, a nation of renters had become a nation of child-centred homeowners. To be sure, some dour economists complained about an over-investment in housing, or about housing tax breaks that had a tendency to redistribute income from the poor to the rich, or about housing subsidies that unfairly penalized renters. But in the exciting new America defined by Levittown and the shopping mall, these comments seemed to be sour grapes.

BUREAUCRACY AND MARKETS AGAINST YOUNG FAMILIES

Around 1970, however, the incentives within the housing market shifted (although the effects were not apparent for another ten years). Subtle changes in bureaucratic rulemaking on mortgage underwriting eliminated the implicit bias that was in favour of young, married-couple families. Why? "Fairness" and "equality" were the public explanations given. More important, though, was recognition that the housing market was slowing down. Most young married couples now had a home, and demand was weak. The industry needed more buyers, and the unmarried and the formerly married loomed large as "underserved" populations. Between 1970 and 1987, the number of one-person house holds in mortgaged units rose 216 percent, while the number of married-couple households in owner-occupied units barely changed. Reflecting this shift statistically, average household size plummeted.

The real process was more perverse, though. As economists George Sternlieb and James Hughes put it in their 1980 study of housing demand: "The very decline in the size of household, with its nominal generation of increased demand for housing, *may in turn be a consequence of the availability and costs of housing units generally*" (emphasis added). Non-marriage and divorce, they implied, were now being *encouraged* by the *availability* of federally subsidized mortgages, while the housing industry itself needed divorce to survive at the level to which it had grown accustomed.

Not only had federal housing policy ceased to *encourage* family life, it had now become an engine intentionally *destroying* families. The regulators and the regulated had conspired to keep the housing industry afloat by sabotaging the very social institution they had once sworn to serve. A recession could be avoided, industry advocates explained, only through the maintenance of residential construction at an artificially high level. The U.S. economy was hooked, with a superheated housing market as its drug-of-choice.

In retrospect, the lesson is that neither the massive state intervention into housing, nor the complete reconfiguration of the mortgage market by government institutions, nor even the family bias built into the early housing programs, were necessary or useful to the family. The "marriage economy" already contains within itself *natural* benefits relative to *shelter* and other consumption patterns; as the old adage had it, *two can live cheaper than one*. Compared to single adults, whether never-married or divorced, the married couple does not really need state subsidy to compete. In a truly free "lifestyle market," marriage will always win. It is divorce, illegitimacy, and cohabitation that require subsidy from the state to survive.

GENDER WARS

The third episode involves efforts by government to regulate gender roles.

The paleoanthropologists offer mounting evidence that human males and females have a "natural affinity" towards each other, a desire to be together that goes beyond the sexual act. They argue that monogamous pair-bonding, intensified parenting relationships, and specialized sexual-reproductive roles are behavioural traits *defining* the human species for over one million years.[2] This seems to be an evolutionist's way of understanding the biblical language of "two becoming one flesh."

The modern state, though, shall put asunder what nature and nature's God have joined together. This might be seen most concretely in modern employment patterns, which have a peculiar relationship to the welfare state.

Data from Denmark, to choose an example, show that the number of female homemakers in that country declined by 579,000, between 1960 and 1981. Over the same years, the number of employees in the Danish public sector climbed by 532,000, with most of the growth in just four areas: day care, elder care, hospitals, and schools. Roll these numbers together and the process emerges primarily as one of women moving from tasks of family-centred home production to the same tasks performed now for the government. But there are obvious differences. First, the women do these tasks less efficiently because the objects of their attention are non-family members in whom they have no stake. And, second, their labour has now been transferred from the private family to the state, and so must be paid for by taxation.

PUBLIC PATRIARCHY

Recently, feminist analysts in America have abandoned their once fashionable New Left pretensions and have become brutally blunt in their embrace of the welfare state as the *only* possible vehicle for their ideological success. Carole Patemen, for example, argues that women's *dependence on the state* is preferable to dependence on individual men, since women do not "live with the state" or sleep with the state as they must with the male creature.[3] Francis Fox Piven is equally frank in her stated preference for public *patriarchy* over *private patriarchy;* the former offers a better venue for the exercise of female power. She adds: "Women have also developed a large and important relationship to the welfare state as employees of these programs. . . . By 1980, fully 70 percent of the 17.3 million social service jobs on all levels of government were held by women, accounting . . . for the larger part of female job gains since 1960."[4] So, while it is true that women living under a system of *public patriarchy* do not have to sleep with the state, they *do* have to work for it.

The stark lesson here is the inevitability of patriarchy, resembling the title of Steven Goldberg's infamous book. Steely-eyed feminist analysis makes the only choice plain and clear: Will that patriarchy be private or public?

THE REAL "ME GENERATION"

The fourth, and final, episode involves the bonds between generations of a family.

Some of the best work being done on this phenomenon comes from Australia and New Zealand, where analysts David Thomson and Alan Tapper have described "the two welfare states."[5]

The first welfare state emerged after World War II and was designed to help young couples and their children. Tax rates for such families were low, while child allowances were generous. Young Australian families also had access to subsidized housing, at a level not unlike that found in the U.S. at the same time.

Yet, as Thomson and Tapper show, this "Youth State" of the 1945-70 era gave way to the second welfare state, or the "Elder State," of the post-1970s. The welfare system now became a vehicle for aiding the relatively old, inserting into society large and generously indexed state pensions unrelated to earlier and low social security "contributions"; fully subsidized health care; favoured tax treatment; and an array of other special programs for those over age 60.

The critical fact to know about the two welfare states is that *one* generation has been the principal beneficiary of both: persons born *in the 1920s.*
They gained dramatically from the benefit package available under
the Youth State, 1945-1970, and they have gained dramatically under the
Elder State of the last 25 years. The losers were the generation born circa
1910, who funded the Youth State, and the generation born in the late
1950s and 1960s, who are funding the Elder State. Thomson calculates
that to enjoy comparable real incomes, couples from the second, *losing* age
group will have to work at least fifteen more years than couples born in
the favoured 1920s. Converting this disparity between generations into
dollars per average household, the Greedy Geezers (or the true Me
Generation) born in the 1920s will enjoy a gain of $500,000 (Australian)
over their lifetimes from state transfers, while the poor souls born in the
1950s will suffer an average half-million-dollar loss per household.

On top of this, married-couple households with adults born in the 1950s
and 1960s will have to support, through taxes and welfare, single mothers and their children. Tapper estimates a *net gain* of $50,000 to $100,000
for couples with children who separate and take the state benefit.

With the old cosseted by the Elder State, and with the unmarried-
with-children cohabitating with the Provider State, only younger
married couples are left to pay the bills. In Tapper's calculations, the
annual average cost for the "Elder and Illegitimacy States" is between
$10,000 and $15,000 per intact household. To meet these costs, younger
couples are driven to deeper immersion in the industrial economy (that
is, towards the "two career family") and they are likely to forego additional, or any, children.

By way of contrast, under a truly free order, the economic incentives
bind the generations of a family tightly together. Each generation has a
vested interest in the success of those going before and those coming
after. This takes form in the communal nature of family wealth, in security centred on family relations, and in retention by the family of the
talents of progeny.

The modernist responds that such principles are no longer possible,
given the complexities and demands of the contemporary economy.

To which I always reply with my favourite counter-cultural example: the Old Order Amish in America.

Amish society violates every modern rule. Relative to the industrial economy, they use true horsepower rather than tractors in the fields. They rely on horse-and-buggy for transport, rather than auto and truck, make their own clothes, furniture, and candles. They avoid credit. They resist most uses of electricity and electronic devices. And they build and sell products using hand labour, dedicated to craftsmanship.

Relative to the state, the Amish are, at their request, exempt from Social Security and Medicare. They refuse welfare, relying instead on help from their neighbours and relatives in time of crisis. They keep their children out of state schools, operating their own schools through grade eight, after which children are to learn trades from their parents or neighbours. Indeed, the Amish shamelessly exploit child labour from age three on, and they maintain harshly segregated gender roles in all aspects of labour and life.

Living by such rules in twentieth-century America, the Amish should have disappeared long ago. Instead, the Amish population has grown from 5,000 in 1900, found only in Lancaster County, Pennsylvania, to 150,000 today, found in colonies in a dozen American states. To place this growth in context, it is important to remember that the overall U.S. farm population *fell* from 35 *million* to 2.5 *million* over these same years. Using even the modernist measure of mathematical success, I ask: Who succeeded here? And who failed?

Someone, though, will surely ask in shocked tones: Do you mean to imply that we should all become Amish?

I can imagine worse fates for the world, but that is not my message.

This is the lesson I draw from the Amish example: We *do not* have to live as we do, in a regime of mounting family and social disorder. The modern economy and the modern state *do not* make inevitable only one pattern of life. Human beings can use the power of culture to *build and maintain barriers* that protect their families (and their family or household economies) from functional ruin, and still participate with success in the larger economy. It has happened on a broad scale in the recent American past; it is happening now among communities such as the Amish; and it can happen in the future.

NOTES

1 An argument ably summarized in Thomas Fleming, *The Politics of Human Nature* (New Brunswick, NJ: Transaction Books, 1988), chaps. 4, 5.

2 See C. Owen Lovejoy, "The Origin of Man," *Science* 211 (January 23, 1981), p. 348.

3 Carol Pateman, "The Patriarchal Welfare State," in A. Gutman, ed., *Democracy in the Welfare State* (Princeton, NJ: Princeton University Press, 1988), pp. 231-60.

4 Francis Fox Piven, "Ideology and the State: Women, Power and the Welfare State," in L. Gordon, ed., *Woman, the State and Welfare* (Madison, WI: University of Wisconsin Press, 1990), pp. 251-64.

5 See Alan Tapper, *The Family in the Welfare State* (Sydney, Australia: Allen and Unwin, 1990); and David Thomson, *Selfish Generations? The Aging of New Zealand's Welfare State* (Wellington, NZ: Bridget Williams Books, 1991).

A CONSERVATIVE
EDUCATION

MARK HOLMES

TRADITION

*Yet human beings . . . do not fare well in a disordered world. They need
to live within the framework of a world in which they possess a chart.
They need categories and rules; they need criteria of judgment. They cannot construct these for themselves. This is one of the limits to the ideal of
total emancipation and total self-regulation. . . . Human beings need the
help of their ancestors.*

— EDWARD SHILS[1]

Aconservative education for children and young adults is based,
before all else, on tradition. Because *tradition* is a term of abuse in modern
educational circles (a privilege it shares with *authority, conservative, élite,*
and *discipline*), it is not surprising that the term is misunderstood. To its
critics, tradition means doing the things the way they have always been
done because they have always been done that way. To believe this, one

would have to believe that tradition springs, instantly formed, like a miraculous geyser.

Much of Shils's book, *Tradition,* is devoted to the ways in which traditions actually develop and change. It is precisely because traditions have been developed, tested, and changed over time that they are defensible. Conservatives do not believe that schools should return to some supposed golden age, but rather that schools should be founded on ideas that are believed to work, rather than chimera of change agents' imaginations. As philosopher Michael Oakeshott put it, it is not that we prefer traditions to other possible patterns, but rather that tradition is all the knowledge we have.

Contrast the idea that we should first educate our young by reliable methods, just as we prefer either traditional or tested medicines, with the contemporary mainstream liberal idea that change and improvement are essentially synonymous. Michael Fullan, a highly regarded and internationally respected liberal dean of education at the University of Toronto, puts it this way: "Today, the teacher who works for or allows the *status quo* is the traitor."[2]

TRUTH

Nothing worthy can be built on a neglect of higher meanings and on a relativistic view of concepts and culture as a whole. . . . behind these ubiquitous and seemingly innocent experiments of rejecting "antiquated" tradition there lies a deep-seated hostility toward any spirituality. There is no God, there is no truth, the universe is chaotic, all is relative.
— Aleksandr Solzhenitsyn[3]

If traditions grow and change, in education and elsewhere, there must be some means of determining whether a change is desirable or harmful. There is no rule-book to determine the good and the bad, whether subject specialization should begin in grade five or grade nine, whether history and geography should be compulsory in grade twelve. Indeed, any such set of arbiters would require a plan or mission statement, loved by managers but inconsistent with conservative growth by accretion. It is the slow and steady change of the conservative school that prevents whole systems from falling over the cliff, like so many lemmings, all determined to be first to try the new innovation. A few changes work, most do not. Conservative schools learn from others, from the tried and tested.

Nevertheless, there must be some overall objective standard if everything is not to be judged by whim or, in Alasdair MacIntyre's useful term, *emotivism*.[4] Although conservative schools in different parts of the world follow a host of traditions, in the context of this essay I refer to the Greco-Roman and Judeo-Christian traditions that undergird the societies and ideals of the English-speaking democracies. In that context, most traditional schools are Christian, a few Jewish. Their bedrock is God, who comprises the truth, the good, and, in the general sense of the word, beauty. Other traditional schools may base their beliefs on a classical tradition, such as neo-Platonism, but in all cases there must be recourse to an absolute, however imprecisely it may be discerned. Once there is acceptance of an ultimate truth, the virtues and values that are consistent with its traditional expression are more readily discovered and agreed on. It is possible to imagine a traditional school based on relativism, a Summerhill,[5] but difficult to see how it could be sustained over generations. Communities based on an absolute are themselves notautomatically sustained; while the vigour and longevity of the Western tradition form an important part of our society's distinctiveness, that tradition is under acute stress today.

Within the absolute, which is variously interpreted within the tradition, there is growth and change. Most conservatives today agree, for example, that girls and boys should have very much the same education and should have the same employment opportunities as they enter adulthood. At the same time, they would agree that sensitivity to the views of the community (i.e., the community or communities to which the school belongs, not the geographical area, municipal identity, or political constituency in which it happens to be situated) and to individual parents is crucial. Obviously, some conservative communities do not agree with the change in roles of men and women, and appeals to the absolute do not provide an unambiguous response. Nevertheless, the conservative consensus is acutely aware of the sensitivities involved, and the overarching importance of motherhood, principled child-rearing, and the maintenance of the family. Conservatives agree that lessons in sex education should emphasize morality rather than plumbing, that sexual relations should be postponed at least until adulthood, and, for most conservatives, until marriage. Those teachings are easily derived, both from traditional practice and religious belief and from an appeal to the good and its attendant virtues.

Virtue is an important component of truth; conservatives support the traditional virtues as components of the absolute: truth itself expressed by integrity, courage, justice, prudence, consideration of the other person, and humility.

ORDER AND CONTENT

[pride, ambition, avarice, revenge, lust, sedition, hypocrisy, ungoverned zeal] are the causes of . . . *storms ['that render life unsweet'].* Religion, morals, laws, prerogatives, privileges, rights of men, are the *pretexts . . . You would not cure the evil by resolving that there should be no more monarchs, not ministers of state, nor of the gospel; no interpreters of law; no general officers; no public councils. You might change the names. The things in some shape must remain.*

— EDMUND BURKE[6]

Authority is an essential, desirable, and visible element in a conservative school, just as it must be in any conservative society. Few aspects of the conservative school are more misunderstood by its critics than authority. They see authority, exemplified in the principal and the teaching staff, as being arbitrary and capricious. They see authority as being enforced by a lengthy set of rigid rules set within expanding bureaucracies. The truth is that they are observing either its abuse or its degeneration in modern hands. In contrast, they hypocritically pretend that the principal should be just a "member of a team" and that teachers and children should work together as equals, an equality attested to by the use of forenames to address one another.

Principals of traditional schools do not arbitrarily define right and wrong behaviour and then deliver punishment. They act within the tradition and only within that tradition. Principals, like all others, have their failings, and some may abuse their authority. Checks and balances are important. Teachers in a traditional school share the tradition. Their first loyalty, unlike their colleagues in unionized and bureaucratized schools, is to that tradition, not to their colleagues or to the leader (except to the extent they constitute the tradition). They accept reasonable interpretation of the tradition by the principal, who is appointed for that purpose. Similarly, parents, who typically delegate part of their parental authority to the school, have a duty to the tradition and to their children that transcends the school's managerial authority.

Punishment, as distinct from the distinct notions of revenge, consequence, and deterrent, lies at the heart of traditional order. In that sense, punishment is an essential and desirable part of school (and family) life. Without a recognition of evil there can be no human apprehension of good. Punishment expresses the community's abhorrence of behaviour that is morally wrong. Lying, physical and verbal abuse, and destruction of property are examples of wrong behaviour that must be, and must be seen to be, punished. The degree of harshness varies with the level of moral harm and the persistence of the misbehaviour; punishment, however, is not crucially defined by its harshness, but *by the moral imperfection it denotes*. Beyond punishment lies the hope of penitence, forgiveness, and redemption. Punishment is not primarily a deterrent, but rather a mitigation of harm to the community and the marker of wrongful behaviour. Many acts of misbehaviour are trivial and are quickly dealt with; but lying, cruelty, and theft, as examples, are never trivial.

A true traditional school in a true traditional community (of which few remain in the late twentieth century) has no need of lengthy written rules and lists of "consequences." Parents, teachers, and students all

know the difference between right and wrong, and those who misbe-
have expect to be punished. They can usually anticipate the level of
punishment. Even uniforms rarely have to be spelled out in lengthy dress
codes, because newcomers learn from those already there, or from
suppliers of the uniforms. Even in recently established schools, written
codes should wither.

Increasingly, lists of rules and consequences expand in the
modern, progressive school precisely because there can be no assumption of agreement on right and wrong, or even on their existence. A
modern school defines unacceptable behaviour as "inappropriate" rather
than wrong. Rules require definition, limitation, and new sub-sections,
proliferating together with school boards' policies, contractual agreements, and provincial regulations. A few ultra-progressive schools and
classrooms claim, falsely, to have no rules. To the extent the claim is
valid, the underlying rules just become more permissive. It is not
that there are no rules about dress, violence, and attendance, but that
the permissible limits are extreme (often capricious and therefore
contested). The student in a traditional school gains attention by deliberately dropping a candy wrapper on the hall floor; in the contemporary
cafeteria high school,[7] attention is gained by daubing the walls or lock-
ers with abuse of authority — the very authority that is cloaked,
averted, and denied.

The low level of bureaucracy in the traditional school is enhanced by
the professional authority of the teacher, who has responsibility for
teaching and order. Essential to an understanding of the authority and
order in the traditional school are the opposed concepts of the social
contract (related to mechanical solidarity) and the authentic gift (related
to organic solidarity). In the modern school, beyond the bureaucratic
structures lies an assumption of a social contract between individual and
state, between parent and school, and even, increasingly, between parent and children. This notion is both absurd and corrosive to the
conservative; absurd because a contract assumes voluntary agreement to
the terms of an agreement, corrosive because it reduces human action
to terms of individual advantage or, at best, enlightened self-interest.

Children do not choose their family or state, rarely their school; even parents are frequently, unfortunately, given little or no choice of school or classroom. Conservative parents delegate some of their authority to the school because it shares their belief in education as a good. If the school does not share their beliefs, even minimal delegation of authority is reluctant. Belief by educators in a contract when there is none (either because there is no choice involved or because there is deliberate refusal to share authority) leads to bitter misunderstandings.

The ideal family develops on organic (as distinct from mechanical) lines, with children learning: by example, from teaching, through emotion and intuition, with abstract reasoning, and by imagination. Parents give their children gifts (not contractual presents) because they love them, because they are family. Contractual presents, always material, come on birthdays and days of religious or secular celebration. Organic gifts, more often emotional than material, come at any time, as genuine and spontaneous gestures, without expectation of return. (Sociologists often claim there is no such thing as a genuine gift, just as there is no interest other than self-interest. And, increasingly, saying makes it so.) Organic gifts bind more firmly than contractual exchanges, which are always measured for value and comparability. That is why marriages built on true commitment without prior trial last longer than those built on prenuptial test drives followed by a written contract.

So in the classroom. A social contract, supported by written rules perhaps, even a signed document, may provide a minimum level of civil order, but an organic classroom where teacher and student are equally able to provide the other genuine gifts lays a foundation, always fragile, above and beyond civility — a climate of mutual trust, acceptance, even a kind of respectful affection (and I do not refer here to the very different adoration of the primary teacher, often as a substitute parent). Teachers in organic classrooms help children beyond their contractual responsibility, after school, as individuals or small groups. One measure of an organic classroom is the ability of the teacher to deal, simultaneously, with different groups in the classroom after hours, one being given the gift of extra help, another being punished, both understanding and

emotionally accepting of their different roles. Can this situation deteri-
orate into sets of teachers' pets and villains? Of course, as in all but the
most impersonal of classrooms. But the true organic classroom, like
the organic family, values all its members: the rebels are also loved. Part
of the tradition is the belief that all children are fundamentally equal,
not in the absurd modern sense that they all have (or should have) the
same mathematical probability of becoming neurosurgeons, but in
the primary sense that they are equally deserving of respect and dignity,
equally potential recipients of reward and punishment, equally capable
of good and evil.

The family analogy can be carried too far. Similar in some respects,
structure and function in an organization cannot be the same as in a
nuclear family. Although teachers in the classroom can and should attend
to the individuality of the students, they also respect, in the traditional
school, a considerably higher level of universalism than they would in
their homes. Students expect fairness and equal treatment above all (even
wise parents understand that there are limits to particularistic treatment
of their children, even when the children become adults). So, when it
comes to questions of habitual behaviour, treatment of work, and application of punishment, equality is the norm, with limited attention to
imperfectly understood motivation, which readily becomes manipulative
in the modern classroom where children soon learn to couch their behaviour in psychologically convincing terms for personal advantage. The
differential treatment of young people, favouring those who come from
bad homes because they do not know better, or those from good homes
because their parents will support them, making inevitably faulty, pseudo-
psychological diagnoses of motivation, is directly destructive of trust and
order, both of which are essential in a successful school. Ideally, students
in a traditional school recognize what they have done wrong and
correctly identify the appropriate punishment. The student is trusted to
understand the misbehaviour and to understand why the community
requires some penalty. In the modern school based on individual rights,
the assumption is that individuals will automatically deny guilt and
personal responsibility; in the traditional school, meanwhile, the

assumption is one of honesty and personal responsibility. Dishonesty and denial of responsibility cause more moral harm to the community than most acts of misbehaviour and defiance.

An important aspect of the order of the traditional classroom is the teacher's discretion. Discretion requires that teachers have genuine authority in the classroom. Teachers determine how to teach and much more: they are responsible for the moral climate. They are not subject to continual interruption, whether from public-address systems, administrators, consultants, parents, or disruptive students. They take responsibility because they have authority. Not left to the teacher are the goals and the desired results: high levels of academic achievement, students who learn and want to learn and who are morally aware, students whose deportment is civilized and demeanour open, and students who support both the classroom and the school as members of the community. There is minimal direct supervision of teachers, but there are concrete expectations of what young people will become under their direction.

Discretionary freedom is required if the epitome of education is to be achieved: the transcendental moment when the student's mind is reached by the teacher, and the mind is turned from the shadows in the cave to the true light of learning. Admittedly, conservatives have no proprietary right to this magic moment, a preserve of the few never reached by some teachers and many more students. It is, after all, equally a part of the nineteenth-century liberal tradition. It is, however, definitively excluded by the progressive, therapeutic classroom dominant in Canada today, and by its rival, the looming technocratic, computerized classroom.

COMMUNITY

[Dostoevsky's Grand Inquisitor] explains to the returned Jesus the absolute necessity of abandoning the freedom Jesus had brought to his followers: "For these pitiful creatures are concerned not only to find what one or other can worship, but find something that all will believe and worship; what is essential is that all may be together in it. This crav-

ing for community of worship is the chief misery of man individually and of all humanity from the beginning of time" . . .

The feeling of community lost and community needed is powerful. One indicator of the actual loss of community in America is the exploding rate of crime. It is not poverty but the breakdown of the social bond in family, neighborhood, parish and local community that leads directly to crime, as an escape from boredom with the void.

— ROBERT NISBET

Nisbet's two statements illustrate the paradox of community for conservatives. On the one hand, the power of community can sometimes hide or suppress truth. Jesus rejected the narrow confines of his Jewish community, insisting that God's grace is available to all. On the other hand, community is necessary to support and maintain truth and virtue, particularly in a time of overriding disbelief verging on nihilism. Traditional communities may lose their way, and modern communities, such as street gangs, may not have a tradition of truth and virtue in the first place. Conservatism, as with most of the major mythical narratives, has to deal with an uncomfortable dialectic between community and individualism.

It is increasingly clear that conservative education can only survive the modern (postmodern if the reader prefers) age within schools based on community. Those schools are rarely based on geographical community, for the simple reason that geographical, residential "communities" no longer possess community. Traditional schools are either, in James Coleman's words, *functional* communities or *values* communities.[9] The former are typically based on local religious communities, the latter are schools of choice, usually independent, where parents with similar wishes come together solely for the purpose of their children's education.

A community has a recognized membership with a system of shared beliefs. Those beliefs form *bounds*, in that they limit approved behaviour, and *bonds*, in that members are united against the world without, a world infelicitous for the community's tradition. Nowhere has the spirit of community in a school, for good and evil, been better captured, in fact and emotion, than in the brilliant film, *Au revoir, les enfants*. The film tells of Jewish boys hidden within a Catholic boarding school during World War II. The Jewish boys are gradually accepted as associate members of the community but are ultimately betrayed to the Nazis by an outsider, a young disabled servant at the school who is ridiculed and despised by the clever, upper class boys of the community. The task of the conservative school is to build a shared community on good terms with its rebels, its associate members, and its outsiders. If the bounds are too weak, the bonds loosen and the community decays. If they are too strong, rebellious outsiders proliferate and those delineated as beyond the community are vilified and despised.

The key to a harmonious resolution lies in the acceptance of family, community, and individuality. Some of the late nineteenth — and early twentieth — century boys' public (independent boarding) schools of England became travesties of traditional community, within which a muscular Christianity replaced humility with arrogance and the search for truth with one for superiority, and where the unavoidable organizational hierarchy was rigidified in legitimated abuse. It is no coincidence that the influence of parents was effectively removed from those communities and that there was little interaction with communities outside the schools' own boundaries. The boys' own individuality was denied, and the roles of family and the larger society restrained.

The nuclear family is, today, the bedrock of conservative society simply because it is the only surviving traditional institution other than a minority of churches (most having succumbed to trendy secular causes). Conservative and other sympathetic families coming together to choose a traditional school (a values community) are increasingly diverse in race, culture, and political values. That fact has the advantage of reducing the danger of overly strong community bounds, the disadvantage of increasing the probability of the school's corruption by the external secular culture, which appears to have been the fate of some traditional independent schools. One prominent independent school I visited showed confusion following a succession of modernizing principals. Another, affiliated with the Anglican denomination, had abandoned formal religious instruction in the junior school altogether and provided a program *about* rather than *in* religion at the senior level. They both served their changing markets. Authentic functional communities, typically schools catering to those of narrowly shared religious beliefs, are in greater danger of falling victim, like the Grand Inquisitor, to the abuse of authority.

Just as conservatives, well aware of the inevitability of hierarchy and social differentiation, must be constantly reminded of the fundamental equality of the human beings in their schools, so they must be constantly aware of young people's individuality. The purpose of order and universalism is not to produce identical human beings. It is to provide an environment in which effective education may take place and where individuals may search and choose truth in their own way in an atmosphere of faith (in the good) and reason, without fear of contempt and derision from teachers and peers.

THE PURPOSE OF EDUCATION

Education . . . is nothing and its costs in terms of deprivations of liberty unjustified unless it is a discipline enabling its initiates to distance themselves from their present concerns and perceptions. Through education we should enter into those human achievements that have endured and which have provided some distancing of the individual from his own greed and need and from the greed and need of others.

— ANTHONY O'HEAR[10]

Educational purpose is not an expression with which conservatives feel particularly comfortable. If a school is based in truth and virtue, its purpose is self-evident; specifying exactly what one is or is not about may lead to divisive argument about detail and priority and unhelpful restrictions on the excellent teacher. It is unsurprising, then, that O'Hear, perhaps England's foremost representative of conservative education, discusses purpose by differentiating it from current trends.

Aversion to narrowly conceived "relevance" (to the flavour of the month) is a key to understanding the direction of conservative education; the ultimate purpose of education is to transcend our daily circumstances, to see the light. The conception of truth discussed earlier is also a far cry from a blinkered, rationalistic, scientific view. Christopher Lasch described verification, "that much-vaunted principle of modern science," as a technique for "avoiding error, not for wresting truth from chaos."[11] At the same time, the purposes of studying a given subject are "immediate," in the sense that they are intrinsic to the subject itself. If study of subjects such as literature, history, biology, and music are seen only in material terms, then we have lost the greatest value of education. In Roger Scruton's words, "The aims of education are inseparable from the means by which we arrive at them."[12] We do not study literature because of some real or imagined material advantage, but because good literature is an expression of truth, beauty, and the good.

It follows that young people should be inducted into all the major traditions of knowledge and wisdom — all those subjects worthy of study for intrinsic reasons — so that they may be enabled to obtain better access to the various truths, explored through science, history, literature, music, art, mathematics, religion, and philosophy.

Conservatives are seen by outsiders as being dedicated to "the three R's," and so they are insofar as the basic skills are prerequisite to educational advancement (as well as to employment). It must also be recognized that schools, appropriately, are not only concerned with education. A conservative criticism of contemporary schooling is less that it is not confined to education than that true education is virtually excluded. The twin modern emphases on self and technocratic materialism inevitably oppose and exclude the conservative idea of education; not to be found in the current pedagogical vocabulary are God, transcendent truth, the good, virtue, beauty, community, punishment, and the intrinsic value of subjects.

Schools, reasonably enough, do or should concern themselves with training and socialization, with preparation for post-secondary schooling or work, and with skills necessary for survival in modern life (use of the computer, for example). However, it is very important that by the age of fourteen, at the latest, young people should have received strong instruction in all areas of intellectual, aesthetic, and physical endeavour, so that they may come to understand the intrinsic value of education and may ascertain their own strengths, weaknesses, interests, and abilities, whether they choose to build on their strengths or to overcome their weaknesses.

There is, then, considerable separation in the conservative school between education and training, between distinct subjects, between inquiry into transcendent truth and scientific investigation of empirical knowledge, as well as between levels of learning. This separation does not imply the total separation of subjects. Parts lead deductively to wholes, and wholes inductively to parts. Science should be seen in the context of religious belief, and history in the context of science.

There is one further aspect of conservative purpose requiring mention. It is part habit, part attitude, and part virtue — what Jacques Maritain elegantly called "an openness to life." This is not identical with an appetite for life, which may imply a hedonistic search to fill an existential vacuum. Nor is it to be confused with reckless self-indulgence. Put negatively, it means that young people are not permitted to close off their ideas on any topic, to dismiss a different idea out of hand, to reject a particular activity thoughtlessly. Such openness should not be confused with the psychological trait of extroversion. It is also unrelated to optimism; conservatives choose hope and realism rather than the morally and intellectually lazy habits of optimism or pessimism. Adults open to life are not necessarily particularly intelligent or well-schooled, but they are usually well-read. They do possess a lively interest in what goes on around them. While they have a firm worldview, and a grounded sense of virtue, they recognize their imperfect perspective of both the good and the physical world, and are open to further education, and to prudent risks. They are not brilliant — indeed, they may not be very good at anything and not jacks-of-all-trades, but they have persistent interests and are open to new pathways to understanding.

At this time in educational history, it is necessary for conservatives to put their purposes in writing, if only to dispel the false expectations that some parents may have. These false expectations include: that the school exists to allow students to express themselves freely and "creatively," to develop their self-concepts in the overall search for self-fulfilment and self-gratification; that the school will make all students equal and lead to social equality; that school activity will arise from the students' own expressed interests and motivation; that punishment will be banned, even if certain consequences may unfortunately result from failure to heed the school's minimal requests for order; and that students will only be expected to work at "their own rate."

A conservative education demands: that students accept their humble human status; that they recognize and respect, but not necessarily embrace, their traditions and the related ideas of virtue and the good; that they work hard, aspiring to independence, and participate fully in all aspects of school life; that they acknowledge their strengths and weaknesses without pride, self-pity, or envy, but with a sense of personal responsibility; that they understand reward and punishment, that they practise and accept forgiveness; that they look beyond immediate gratification or ambition to the transcendent rewards of education; that they develop their interests, skills and abilities in all areas of the school curriculum and develop a habit of mind that is open without being negatively sceptical.

LEADERSHIP

Managers themselves and most writers about management conceive of themselves as morally neutral characters whose skills enable them to devise the most efficient means of achieving whatever end is proposed. Whether a given manager is effective or not is on the dominant view a quite different question from that of the morality of the ends which his effectiveness serves or fails to serve.

— ALASDAIR MACINTYRE[13]

The principal of the conservative school is first a moral leader. This does not mean that administrators are or can be saintly exemplars of perfection, but that they should sincerely attempt to model and teach the school's ideals. Just as some students will graduate tone deaf, or physically inept or mathematically bewildered, so conservative principals are imperfect; failure is an important and valuable part of human experience, for teachers and taught.

Hypocrisy and manipulation, of which conservatives and conservative schools are sometimes accused, are antithetical to the central idea of conservatism: truth represented by integrity, openness, and authenticity. They do not usually derive from our inevitable human imperfections and regular failure to achieve our ideals; they stem from a deliberate betrayal of those conservative qualities.

That assertion may seem ironic, because hypocrisy is precisely the failing believers in absolute values are most frequently accused of. Hypocrisy is not the inevitable error of judgment, the inevitable mistake, the sin that is essential to our human nature. I mean by hypocrisy the deliberate continuation in a pattern of life that is inconsistent with one's teaching. This may be a pattern of sexual relationships outside marriage or it may be an insincere approach to consultation within the school. Liberals may maintain that they cannot be hypocritical because they do not claim to believe in absolute virtue in the first place; morality to them is essentially relativist. But they are no strangers to hypocrisy. They claim tolerance but are fierce in their condemnation of religion within education.

Manipulation is less open to ambiguous interpretation. Manipulation, as MacIntyre so incisively portrays, is the essence of contemporary leadership. Leadership, in the modern, secular school, is the art of getting others, principally teachers, to do things by "empowering" them to claim a "sense of ownership" of the latest innovation the leadership wants implemented. Parents are brought into the school not because they are the primary educators of their children, but so they can be co-opted into the school's worldview. Manipulative behaviour is definitively lacking in transparency, in integrity. Truth is the centre of the conservative school, and nothing is more corrosive of truth than manipulation, whether it be of teachers, students, or parents.

There is much discussion as to whether the management of schools should be directed by parents (in some form of school council representing parents, as a majority, and teachers) or by the principal. Such managerial issues are not central to the conservative ideal. What is essential is the recognition that parents are the first educators of the child, and that they may delegate authority, usually informally, to the school.

There are inherent managerial problems either way, with a closely involved school council, or with a more distant board of governors removed from day-to-day knowledge of the school's operation. The problems are mitigated when the principal and the majority of teachers and parents share a core sense of the purpose that education and the school are about. What makes today's large, cafeteria-style public school an impossible educational enterprise is precisely the unavoidable lack of sharing of an ideal as to what education and schooling are about, both within and between the differing participating groups.

THE PROSPECT FOR CONSERVATIVE EDUCATION

If there is one lesson we might have been expected to learn in the 150 years since Horace Mann took charge of the schools of Massachusetts, it is that the schools can't save society. Crime and poverty are still with us, and the gap between rich and poor continues to widen. Meanwhile, our children, even as young adults, don't know how to read and write. Maybe the time has come — if it hasn't already passed — to start all over again.
— CHRISTOPHER LASCH[14]

There are few Canadian schools that would claim to be conservative in the sense conveyed in this essay, and not many more in the other English-speaking countries. There is no possibility that the local public school will become substantially conservative.

The contemporary debate about educational policy is between the dominant Progressives, following the teaching of Rousseau and Dewey in a quest for self-fulfilment and a Utopian relativist secularism, and Technocrats, wanting more efficient schooling for competent workers in the global economy. There is also substantial public support, according to research I have carried out in Ontario among samples of educated Canadians, for the Cultural philosophy, the nineteenth-century liberal tradition based on science and "great books," some of which is shared by many conservatives.[15]

More numerous than the Egalitarian and Individualist minorities lie the Traditionalists represented in this essay, who form, I estimate, around 20 percent of the population. If there is some overlap with the Cultural worldview, there is strong, potential support for more schools based substantially on conservative thinking. This proposition is bolstered by the evidence that parents leaving the public system for independent schools do so principally because they are seeking higher academic standards, more firmly based values, and better discipline, all attributes of conservative education. Empirical research increasingly shows that the massive efforts to improve the public schools have little effect, but that the most effective schools, looked at in academic terms alone, are small and focused and are places where there is some consensus between parents and teachers. Egalitarians and Traditionalists, disagreeing on almost everything else, both demand consensual schools, but, while Egalitarians unreasonably demand that their minority beliefs be imposed on everyone within a common school for all, most conservatives would be content to have their own school of choice, accessible to all.

Lasch believed the United States should start over again with the public schools; there is little evidence that a monopolistic, public school system started afresh in Canada would look very different from the one we have, except that it would be more technocratic and less "child-centred." There is no instant mix that would create a conservative school, which, by definition, must grow over time. What is so infuriating, and engaging, about the conservative school is that there is no pattern.

The best prospect for conservative schools is increased support for minorities, with the result that those parents genuinely committed to a conservative education will be given access, but still make sacrifices to get it. A choice for conservatism based on a passing fad is no foundation for a traditional school.

It is a delusion to imagine, at the beginning of the 21st century, that public schools in a secular and freedom-worshiping society, where decisions are based on conflicting individual rights rather than on what is right, and on enthusiasms rather than on the good, will be turned back in search of our severed Western roots.

Conservatives are practical people. They do not like to categorize their beliefs as ideological, because ideology implies plans for a Utopian future. Believing in neither Utopia nor planning, they prefer the step-by-step cultivation and growth of conservatism in whatever unlikely corner it persists. While conservative education is most likely to be sustained in the new dark age in what I have called fortress monasteries,[16] it will be supported and defended in any school serving strong communities aware of their traditions.

NOTES

1 *Tradition* (Chicago: University of Chicago Press, 1981), p. 326.

2 *Change Forces* (The Falmer Press, 1993), p. 14.

3 "And How It Wrecked the Century," in *The New York Times Book Review*, February 7, 1993, p. 4.

4 Emotivism is the term MacIntyre uses to describe the modern habit of pulling together loosely defined, usually emotional, terms in lists of purported fundamental values. Popular examples in contemporary education are self-concept, collaboration, environmentalism, gender equality, and anti-racism.

5 Summerhill, an ultra-progressive private boarding school in England, has survived many decades. Its sister school, Dartington Hall, did not endure.

6 Quoted in Conor Cruise O'Brien, *The Great Melody* (Chicago: University of Chicago Press, 1992), pp. 603-4.

7 A "cafeteria high school" has a large enrolment and offers a wide range of courses and programs at different levels. It is typically characterized by lack of community, low standards, alienation, and a high level of individualism.

8   *Prejudices* (Cambridge, MA: Harvard University Press, 1982), p. 51.

9   *Public and Private High Schools: The Impact of Communities* (New York: Basic Books, 1987). Written with Thomas Hoffer.

10 "Education Beyond Present Desire," in Roger Scruton, ed., *Conservative Thoughts* (The Claridge Press, 1988), pp. 244-45.

11 *The True and Only Heaven* (New York: W. W. Norton, 1991), p. 289.

12 *The Meaning of Conservatism* (Penguin Books, 1980), p. 154.

13 *After Virtue* (South Bend, IN: University of Notre Dame Press, 1981), p. 71.

14 *The Revolt of the Elites and the Betrayal of Democracy* (New York: W. W. Norton, 1995), p. 160.

15 *Educational Policy for the Pluralist Democracy: The Common School, Choice and Diversity* (The Falmer Press, 1992), pp. 20-30.

16 "The Fortress Monastery: The Future of the Common Core," in Ian Westbury and Alan C. Purves, eds., *Cultural Literacy and the Idea of General Education* (Chicago: University of Chicago Press, 1988), pp. 231-58.

CONTACT
CONSERVATISM

PETER STOCKLAND

O n the first warm spring night of
the year when we could finally
leave the windows open a little at bed time, I asked my daughter what
smell she remembered best. Without hesitation she answered: "Grandma.
Her skin from the soap she uses."

After I had tucked her in and said goodnight, I went into my son's
room and asked him the same question. He, too, said without pause:
"Grandma. Her house when you first come in the door."

As I adjusted the blankets under his chin, I asked him what that smell
was like.

"I don't know," he said. "It makes me think of being a little kid."

Those responses illustrate for me the inherently conservative quality
of childhood, and the inherently childlike quality of conservatism.

By *childhood* I do not mean some idealized state of near-nirvana where
trouble never treads. Anyone who spends ten attentive minutes around
children knows that trouble of one sort or another is a constant in their
lives. Those troubles — getting a glass down from a shelf; fretting that
mom or dad or both will be angry about the broken glass — may seem

small to adult eyes. But that is a trick of perspective caused by the distance of the eyes, not an accurate measure of the troubles for those experiencing them. Stars are small, too, until we bend ourselves to a telescope and see them as big. Nor do I mean by *childlike* some Rousseau-like state of natural innocence uncomplicated by civilization and its discontents. As G. K. Chesterton reminded us in *The Everlasting Man*, the shape of the movement from yesterday to today is not a single line from primal purity to contemporary decay but rather a parallelogram of past and present: "Barbarianism and civilization were not successive states in the progress of the world. They were conditions that existed side by side, as they still exist side by side. There were civilizations then as there are civilizations now; there are savages now as there were savages then."[1]

It is this concrete connection with time that I mean in speaking of the natural conservatism of childhood and the childlike nature of conservatism. It is the connection to history as memory of place; to the past living and lived. As the timeless smells of grandmother's skin and house, remembered.

What better to illustrate this than the passage in Proust's *A la recherche du temps perdu* where the narrator recalls the childhood punishment of being sent upstairs to bed before dinner without having a chance to kiss his mother goodnight? "That hateful staircase, up which I always went so sadly, gave out a smell of varnish which had, as it were, absorbed and crystallized the special quality of sorrow that I felt each evening and made it perhaps even crueller to my sensibility because, when it assumed this olfactory guise, my intellect was powerless to resist it . . . my anguish at having to go up to my room invaded my consciousness in a manner infinitely more rapid, instantaneous almost, a manner at once insidious and brutal, through the inhalation — far more poisonous than moral penetration — of the smell of varnish peculiar to that staircase."[2]

The complex co-penetration of memory and the sensate world in this passage presents a dynamic process that contradicts the English translation of Proust's title as *Remembrance of Things Past*. It shows the novel as truly a *recherche*: a seeking out, an inquiry into, a searching for — a lost time. Not time lost in any nostalgic sense but in the objective sense we might speak of "keys lost" before tracking them down, locating them, recovering them in the knowledge they still exist, as do the locks they open.

In his book of literary essays, *The Critical Wager*, William D. Gairdner probes the way Proust uses language to effect a "formal arrestation of the *durée* or life-process, a distillation of past moments and the literal presentation of them, transported within a skin of sound, to contemplation. . . . "[3] Gairdner continues: "Proust's *Rememberance of Things Past* is a monumental celebration of this activity in which he attempts to demonstrate that the essence of life, as embodied in the words used to describe it, remains timeless."[4]

Curiously for a conservative (though perhaps not for a York University professor as he was when *The Critical Wager* was written), Gairdner claims it is only the nature of language itself that is ultimately realized in this demonstration. "It would be difficult to show that this timeless Proustian world was anything other than the words used to purvey this illusion because Proust's very thought is itself his words."[5]

Such a conclusion confounds the passage from Proust above, which makes clear the essence of life in time is realized by the absorption, the inhalation, of a spiritual air — a pneuma — that precedes emotion, morals, intellect, and therefore language itself. It is timelessness not as words, but as realized reality. It is the telling of history only as a subset of untellable memory. It is knowing the smell of grandma's house as part of the universal mystery of what it means to be human: that is, to be a child.

~

It is this timelessness that conservatism seeks to conserve — or did before it became confounded as a catch-all term for a series of preferred policy options for issues of the day. Rather than general attitude to, say, taxation rates or free market economics or crime and punishment, it is a particular relationship to time, history, and memory. As Russell Kirk wrote in *The Conservative Mind*, its best expression should be found more frequently among a nation's poets than its politicians.

Its antithesis is the creed of the modern liberal as espoused by the late Robert F. Kennedy when he said: "Some people look at things as they are and ask why? I look at things as they could be and ask why not?" Conservatives undertake the far more complex and childlike task of looking at things that are because they were and asking why they should not always be. It is true that this does risk confusing conservatism and antiquarianism. Proust satirizes this attitude by having one of his elderly relatives give as gifts objects so old and weak they crumble at the slightest touch. But it is not true that even a fetish for the antique condemns conservatives to the political pathology of nostalgia.

Nostalgia, after all, is the affliction not of memory but of forgetting. As such, it is a liberal disorder because liberalism, by definition, promises progress as freedom from the living and present past. To presume freedom from the past is a good thing, or that we can get by in a pinch with the ersatz historical re-creations that are a product of nostalgia, can only constitute a corruption of the natural order. At its extreme, it requires nothing less than denial of the interconnections between life, death, and history. The dead leave us bodily, but in so doing they leave behind the whole body of our traditions. In political terms, those traditions comprise what Chesterton famously called "the democracy of the dead . . . democracy extended through time (by) giving votes to the most obscure class of all, our ancestors."[6]

Alas, even by the time Chesterton had made that appeal for tradition at the dawn of this century, Tocqueville had already demonstrated that giving the past a political place in the present is virtually unthinkable in a liberal democracy. A fact as basic as the system of land tenure outlawed it. "In virtue of the law of partible inheritance, the death of every proprietor brings about a kind of revolution in the property," Tocqueville wrote in *Democracy in America*. "The law of equal division exercises itself not merely upon the property itself, but it affects the minds of the heirs, and brings their passions into play. . . . Where family pride ceases to act, individual selfishness comes into play. When the idea of family becomes vague . . . a man thinks of his present convenience; he provides for the establishment of his next succeeding generation and no more."[7]

Those who can think only a generation forward are hardly likely to extend democracy even that much behind. Indeed, the fleeting nature of TV-image, virtual politics makes it literally unthinkable for many North Americans to conceive of any need for such constancy.

A contemporary French thinker, Pierre Manent, contends in his *Intellectual History of Liberalism* that the very deformation of being human in a liberal democracy produces this revolutionary impulse. Manent says this political ontology was established by Hobbes at the beginning of the modern liberal project "to escape decisively from the power of the singular religious institution of the Church [by] renounc[ing] thinking about human life in terms of its good or end, which would always be vulnerable to the Church's 'trump.' Since, therefore, power in the body politic can no longer be considered the power of the good that orders what it gives (the Augustinian definition of grace), man can understand himself only by creating himself."8 This line of thought surely finds its apogee in Nietzsche's attempt to fulfil humanity's destiny beyond good and evil by liberating it through perpetual values-creation, an activity that is now the hallmark of Western liberal democracies. As biographer Walter Kaufmann reminds us, forgetting was as important a part of history as remembering for Nietzsche: "A people with absolutely no memory of their past would be unable to govern themselves successfully, to abide by a proven way of life, and to keep the law. . . . On the other hand, a people or culture without the ability to forget would be unable to make decisions, to act, to be creative."9

I am not for a moment suggesting Nietzsche himself was a liberal in the remotest sense. But as Allan Bloom showed so brilliantly in *The Closing of the American Mind*, what has passed as progressive thought for three-quarters of this century has really been the appropriation and distortion of Nietzschean ideas to fill the void created when left-liberal intellectuals could themselves no longer believe their own dogma. In Bloom's pithy phrase: "The continuing effort of the mutant breed of Marxists has been to derationalize Marx and turn Nietzsche into a leftist.

Today, virtually every Nietzschean, as well as Heideggerian, is a leftist."[10]

Given this stunning demonstration of its capacity to conveniently forget itself, it is little wonder that the political amalgam known as modern liberality predicates its promised freedom on transformation of the past from the enduring, sensual, and concrete into the utilitarian, invented, and abstract. That is the unmistakable symptom of nostalgia: the creative ordering of the past to present purpose. It is what makes nostalgia pathological, particularly in political form, because its very nature is to lie about history itself. Such a nature is the negation of the very soul of conservatism which is the constant awareness, in T. S. Eliot's phrase, "not only of the pastness of the past, but of its presence."

In Eliot's words we find the justification for Russell Kirk's emphasis on the importance of poets in the preservation of nations. It is why Kirk regards Eliot as the principal conservative thinker of this century whose "whole endeavor was to point a way out of the Waste Land toward order in the soul and in society."[11] Eliot, Kirk stresses, saw early the dangers of considering conservatism as simply the conservation of what is now because that too often leads to the petrification of evils within a society, as happened in the former Soviet Union when Marxist-Leninists came to be called conservatives for their efforts to ossify the privileges their revolution brought them.

As Kirk puts it: "Eliot's real function . . . was one of conserving and restoring: melancholy topographer of the Waste Land, but guide to recovered personal hope and public integrity. Having exposed the Hollow Men, diseased by life without principle, Eliot — like Vergil in a comparable age — showed the way back to the permanent things."[12] The real conservative's function, Kirk adds, is to ensure "the struggle to uphold the permanent things has no surcease."[13] It is to guarantee, repeating Gairdner's word, the literal presentation of the past.

But if conservatism really is about time and history more than about politics and policy, can conservative minds possibly give concrete meaning to an age so adulterated by liberal democracy that forgetting has become the natural state of being for most people? Can the conservative impulse survive when generation after generation happily lets the grass grow high and tangled over the tombstones of its ancestors?

American essayist Guy Davenport, in *The Symbol of the Archaic*, raises serious doubts about the prospect given what he considers the last-gasp failure of artists earlier in this century to make the permanent things endure. Davenport argues that in their quest to make present lost time Proust, Joyce, Rilke, Eliot, and Pound succeeded only in showing how utterly unrecoverable that past is to us: "Our search for the archaic may have contributed to our being even more lost. Persephone and Orpheus have reverted to footnotes in anthologies. The classic sense of the city perished rather than revived in the Renaissance of 1910, which had spent its initial energies by 1914 and was exhausted by 1939, the year of the publication of *Finnegans Wake* and of the beginning of the second destruction of the world in 25 years. The world that drove Ruskin and Pound mad has worsened in precisely the way they said it would. Eliot's wasteland has extended its borders; Rilke's freakshow outside which the barker invites us to come in and see that the genitals of money . . . is a feature of every street."[14]

This *carnival de morte* now clearly includes more than capital and acts of sex. It features the thinking life itself, at least as it falls under the ominous shadow of the modern multiversity. Our academies are now the grounds for the realization of Lawrence Ferlinghetti's "Coney Island of the Mind" with professorial theorists of class, gender, race, queerness who are "constantly risking absurdity above the heads of [the] audience" and actually achieving it in their publications, their media pronouncements and, bleakest of all, in their classrooms.

The damage unleashed by such lunacies is too well known to require repetition here. It is enough to point out the fallacy of rejecting the past merely on the grounds that it is the product of the neologism Eurocentric thinking — as if Socrates taught at the Sorbonne; as if Jesus drove the members out of their parliamentary seats in Brussels.

The measure of our disconnectedness is that we even take seriously a body of thought based on rejection of an idea that did not even exist at the time it produced the works being rejected. Granted, the union of Athens and Jerusalem produced the Western tradition. But to dismiss the Western tradition because of its places of origin, when those places had no thought of originating anything Western let alone traditional, is a nonsensical anachronism. It is not to find the past in the present, but to force the present into the past. To dismiss that past on the basis of prejudices towards that present is the kind of logical inversion that would allow finding fault with the balls for dropping the juggler. It is nostalgia in its final, most pathological phase.

Carleton University's Peter Emberley explains succinctly in *Zero Tolerance: Hot Button Politics in Canada's Universities*, that much academic prejudice and animosity arise either from deliberate political distortion or a pitifully narrow view of how the broad and fertile Western tradition came to be.

Emberley insists the mere historical distance of the lives of Socrates and Christ from the routines of those who occupy university classrooms in no way diminishes their power as primary symbols for intellectual and spiritual searching. "It would be reducing severely the richness and suggestive quality of these symbols to believe they are narrowly 'Western' or 'Christian Platonic.' One might say, instead, that these two primals contain a vast range of meaning and that vital threads present at the origins of the 'West' are always available to be unearthed and used for their restorative possibilities. If we see 'Socrates' and 'Christ' in this way, it would not be inappropriate to suggest that these two symbols form a significant key to understanding our culture. To speak of 'our' culture is to see identities within world culture, convergences of need and expectation, or a universality of adventures and predicaments."[15]

The failure to locate life in that universality, especially by those charged with safeguarding the Western university, is the fulfilment of liberalism's fateful reliance on Nietzschean forgetting, or its eagerness to deny democracy to the dead. It is the triumph of the disembodied present over the substantial past.

The resulting danger is hardly limited to the horrors academic fashion can inflict. It extends to the very way we have come to think about knowing. For centuries now, the Western liberal doctrine of progress has been based on the dogma that knowledge is power. For ancients such as Plato, the purpose of knowledge was to permit the perfection of life through philosophy. For moderns, knowledge became merely the fuel driving everything forward into an ever-unfolding future and permitting the past to be left behind cold and dead. As modernity itself recedes into that cold, dead past, knowledge itself has become indistinguishable from information. The simple delivery and receipt of data has become confused with doing something experiential.

In his essays popularizing the thinking of Martin Heidegger, George Grant lamented the co-penetration of thought and technique underlying the age of technology, and making it impossible for us to think non-instrumentally about the world.

Yet less than a decade since Grant's death, we have stood his concern on its head so that we now permit the reception of largely undifferentiated and disembodied thinking (or at least information) about the world to replace instrumental engagement with the world.

Grant's essay "Thinking About Technology," for example, reiterates what I believe was essentially Heidegger's argument about the effects on Being of our cultural imperative of regarding knowledge as the exclusive domain of the modern scientific method: that we will not Let It Be. Grant wrote: "What is given in the modern use of the word 'science' is the project of reason to gain 'objective' knowledge. And 'reason' is the summoning of anything before a subject and putting it to the question, so that it gives us reasons for being the way it is as an object. . . . this paradigm of knowledge stamps the institutions of (the educational) system, their curricula, in their very heart, in what the young are required to know and to be able to do if they are to be called 'qualified'. . . . [It] is central to our civilization destiny and has made possible the existence of computers."[16]

He expands the point in the essay "Faith and the Multiversity" by defining the word *objective* not only as active knowing, but as a radical and aggressive supplanting of the contemplative tradition; that is, of disallowing it even as an alternative mode of thought: "Objective means literally some thing that we have thrown over against ourselves. 'Jacio,' I throw, 'ob' over against; therefore 'the thrown against.' The German word for object is Gegenstand — that which stands against. Reason as project (that is, reason as thrown forth) is the summonsing something before us and the putting of questions to it so that it is forced to give its reasons for being the way it is as an object. Our paradigm is that we have knowledge when we represent anything to ourselves as object, question it, so that it will give us its reasons."[17]

Grant's argument in both essays is designed to show that the tools produced by the techniques of modern science require a particular way of thinking about the world that makes bringing those tools into being possible, and therefore determines how those doing the thinking will use them. His purpose is to explode the fallacy that such a cognitive model is morally neutral by demonstrating how it makes a life of faith aberrant, if not impossible, in modern institutions and thus society at large.

I mean no slight to the worthiness of his argument or purpose when I say the very tool Grant saw as emblematic of the knowledge model he lamented — the computer — has so rapidly changed our way of knowing that the active and the contemplative have themselves been virtually obliterated by their synthesis into the purely informational. Not, it must be stressed, informational even in Grant's sense of calling forth to question and demand answers for passing on to future generations or salvaging links to the past. Not, in any sense, information about actual objects that we disturb and objectify by holding them in our hands to study them with our eyes. Rather, reams and streams and torrents of pure facts and factionalisms, statistics and statements, whose very value is their volume and whose very significance is their suitability for the storehouse of forgetting.

The Catholic theologian Romano Guardini foresaw this in the 1920s when he warned in his *Letters from Lake Comeau* that the impulse of industrialization was not only to turn raw nature into finished consumables but, much more importantly, to turn the concrete world into mere concepts: "We are now no longer in the first living relation to corporeal things and people; the relation has been attenuated. We are in an abstract and artificial world, a substitute world, an improper world of significant signs."[18]

That impulse has become overpowering in the post-industrial age when the significant signs are further reduced to the binary codes of ceaseless computerized information exchange, and the concrete world has become as foreign to us as the votes and voices of our ancestors.

This is perhaps most readily apparent in the illusion relied upon by the mass communications media to persuade us that their din and uproar of random particulars on foreign wars and fashions, natural disasters and professional sports are necessary for us to be complete and participatory citizens.

The June 1997 report of the U.S.-based Rockford Institute Center on Religion and Society cites a study showing the reality of the media-driven information invasion. It notes 51 percent of American viewers can't remember a single report half an hour after the news is over. "But even those who do remember find themselves well-informed only about the last 24 hours, but hardly at all about the last 60 years."[19] Or, the report adds, about the basics of Western civilization.

The report recounts the case of a Lutheran bishop in Germany who was called by a television reporter asking about the existence of some kind of "commandments" in the Church. The Bishop asked if the reporter meant the Ten Commandments, to which the reply came: "What do they say? Could you fax me a copy of them?"[20]

It's insufficient to shrug this off as an example of pitiful ignorance. Much more, it is an outcome of knowing the world as information rather than using information to know the world. Its more serious form is found in that pillar of the modern economy, the stock market, which largely operates without tangible stock in an imaginary marketplace where adults spend their lives using computer screens to trade nothing but data about the psychological dispositions of others.

The acme of the stock market's information-as-world pattern was reached during the fiasco over the non-existent Bre-X gold mine in Indonesia. There did not actually need to be real gold in the mine for many people to hit the motherlode. The only thing required was the capacity to traffick in substanceless information about the mythical mine. In one afternoon, nearly half-a-billion dollars changed hands purely on the strength of a rumour spread through the Internet that reports of the mine being bogus were themselves untrue. Fortunes were reaped, and lost, dealing in the high-tech equivalent of medieval phlogiston.

There is something more than magnitude that distinguishes the Bre-X saga from other great tricks and traps, frauds and forgeries, baits and switches in history. It is that the preponderance of those buying and selling, wagering and paying off Bre-X shares were dealing purely in information as information and accepted it as pure information regardless of the real world effect.

We may consider Eve's temptation of Adam a myth, but even as such we demand she offer him real — not computer-digitized — fruit. We would not accept Judas e-mailing Christ a betraying kiss. When Julius Rosenberg sold secrets to the Soviets, they were secrets about actual plans of atomic bombs that really could destroy the world.

The larger phenomenon at work came home to me as I was sitting on an Air Canada flight at Toronto's Pearson airport. Our departure was delayed because the computer that gives the reading to the flight crew for the fuel levels disagreed with the computer the ground crew used to measure the amount in the tanks. After 40 minutes of waiting, a computer-generated video flashed on the movie screen showing two players for the Toronto Raptors slam dunking basketballs through a hoop attached to the tail fin of a plane. Their feats were followed by a message from the airline promising us that whenever we were ready to soar like that, we should choose Air Canada.

Now, the image being presented to us was a flat contradiction to — if not an actual lie about — what we were physically experiencing at that moment. We were not soaring. Whatever a computer said we could be doing, the reality was that we were stuck on the ground in a hot, stuffy, crowded airplane because of a computer malfunction. Yet no one stood up and openly challenged the digitally generated misinformation. No one even scoffed at the juxtaposition of the message to the reality, as they certainly would have had the captain come through the cabin announcing: "We're really soaring folks."

In part that may have been because Canadians are too polite or practical to protest openly in such circumstances. But I also think it had a great deal to do with the transitions in our relationship to data effected by 40 years of television and the computer revolution. Through five decades, disembodied voices and images have shilled from our TV screens. Cartoons have sold us food. Actors have sold us miracles. But even they have rarely done it in situations that allowed us to directly compare the claims being made with the concurrent reality. Our scepticism towards the products hawked, or our disappointment after purchase, testify to the division between the information and expectation. The computer, however, changes that by changing the information into the reality.

We have begun to accept information as information to the extent that we no longer expect its connection to the objective world even when it is demonstrably at variance with our traditional means of knowing that world — through our physical senses and our reason. We accept the neologism of a "multimedia experience" as though the experience is indistinguishable from the media through which it is transmitted; as though we are sharing the experience with the transmitting media; as though the mere reception of digitized impulses is, in fact, an experience of the real world.

In other words, we have already gone far beyond Grant's concern about using the computer in accordance with the nature of knowing that allowed it to be created. We have increasingly internalized its working principles as our own. The heart of any computer is its BIOS — Basic Input Output System. The BIOS is the cachement area for the computer's input-output system (I/O Sys), which takes the information we put in and transforms it into a series of 1s and 0s that the computer "reads" as yes-no binary propositions or digital "gates" and reproduces as output.

The words input and output are already so natural a part of the vernacular that people speak of "putting in input" to a meeting, project, or political party. What even that infiltration of computer language to our thought processes fails to fully reveal is the extent to which we have become part of the computer BIOS. It is not just that the computer requires us to make it work. It is that too many of our expectations of the world — its possibilities and requirements — now conform to the computer's capabilities and needs.

The symbol I/O Sys is now as subliminally a part of our engagement with the world as the Latin letters INR were to Christendom. It is not that the computer is merely atop the hierarchy of powerful tools humanity has created. It is that it alters the very nature of human knowledge by transforming it from sensory action upon the world to abstracted, virtual information about the world.

It is reasonable to protest that such a transformation is far from complete. Yet there are those such as Derrick de Kerckhove, director of the University of Toronto's McLuhan Program in Culture and Technology, who confidently predict the information revolution is proceeding so fast and inexorably that it is only a matter of years before we are so habituated to our niche in the I/O Sys ecology that our habit of distinguishing between "virtual" and "real" worldly engagements will simply stop.

The improvement and expansion of virtual reality to all phases of our lives, de Kerckhove wrote in his 1995 book *The Skin of Culture: Investigating the New Electronic Reality*, will provide the "pliancy" to demolish the barriers between our own bodies and the "world" created by the computers generating the VR experience. Quoting Jaron Lanier, de Kerckhove agrees that the body will become the part of us that can move as fast as we think. Through what is called proprioception, our bodies are extended by the electronic devices at our disposal. The telegraph and telephone allowed us to listen and speak over vast distances. The computer goes infinitely beyond that by allowing us to re-shape reality provided we are prepared to think like a computer about the world.

As de Kerckhove put it: "[The] effect is to expand the self from its private mental space into on-line shared mental space. . . . Logging in and out of the Internet amounts to spreading oneself in cyberspace and out of time. . . . The 'on-line self' is supported by neither time, space nor body and yet is unmistakably present."[21]

This may sound like what might be called traditional futurist fantasy. Yet it's important to stress that de Kerckhove is not making predictive but descriptive claims about an epistemological environment that he shows exists right now. More importantly, he shows that this environment is the culmination of two historic factors: money and the alphabetization of language. By the reduction of language to alphabetic symbols, de Kerckhove argues, "human intelligence was released from the burden of remembering to be applied to innovating,"[22] and the result was the "privatizing" of that intelligence through reading and writing: "What alphabetic literacy achieved to an unprecedented level was to feed back a very strong degree of self-consciousness. . . . What the alphabet accomplished in the Greek, then Roman, then all western empires was to endow each and every reading citizen with a personal handle on reality and intelligence."[23]

Minted money as a representation of value was a cognate of the alphabet as a representation of language. Instead of driving a cow before one with a stick to the [stock] market, one took information — abstraction — in one's purse or pocket. Value, too, became privatized. "This allowed money to become one of the main tools of human intelligence . . . the universal system of most goods and services . . . [the] way of parsing time, space and individual human effort. Money played in society the role of the timing clock in the central processing unit of the computer — synchronizing all the calculations. . . . "[24] De Kerckhove labels this cultural process "fragmentation" and "de-contextualization" and argues effectively that its outcome has been a "recombination" producing the innovation of computer digitization that supersedes both the alphabet and money as "the new universal translator of all heterogenous substances. . . . Together, fragmentation and de-contextualization form the basis of recombination, which is the source of the typically western drive for innovation, the well that, in *Finnegans Wake*, James Joyce called the 'Cartesian spring.'"[25]

We might do well at this point to recall Guy Davenport's point that *Finnegans Wake* was published on the cusp of the world's second attempt to destroy itself this century. We might also do well to look at Simone Weil's brilliant critique of the Cartesian spring in her essay "Science and Perception in Descartes." This is not the space for detailed examination of the difficult essay that was Weil's dissertation for the diplome d'études supérieures at the Ecole Normale. But even a summary must be framed by noting her thought reveals the same metaphysical perspicacity towards Descartes that Weil showed politically towards Hitler when she wrote in 1932 that the situation in Germany was "literally a life-and-death question for a great many German workers. . . . Despite electoral defeats, as long as the crisis continues, the Hitlerite storm troops . . . constitute a permanent threat of extermination for the . . . working class."[26]

The comparison is not accidental, for in both cases Weil perceived — and argued eloquently against — the menace of substituting abstractions for active work in the world. During her time in Germany, she recorded the power of lost work not only to spread physical poverty and hunger but to demoralize and almost literally disembody individual human beings. It was a power she had penetrated a few years earlier in the more benign depths of Cartesian thought.

Weil admired Descartes as a genuis who had effected the "double revolution [whereby] physics became an application of mathematics and geometry became algebra." But she replaced the famous dictum arising from Cartesian doubt, "I think therefore I am," with her formulation, "je puis, donc je suis" — I can (or I can act; or I have power) therefore I am: "As for knowing my own being, what I am is defined by what I can do. So there is one thing I can know: myself. And I cannot know anything else. To know is to know what I can do; and I know to the degree that I substitute 'to act' and 'to be acted upon' for 'to enjoy,' 'to suffer,' 'to feel,' and 'to imagine.' In this way, I transform illusion into certainty and chance into necessity. . . .

"In the end, the only wisdom consists in knowing there is a world, that is, matter that work alone can change, and that, with the exception of the mind, there is nothing else. To take one step is to make the universe appear. Between one step and another, I touch the world directly. Between the numbers one and two, I have only a presentiment of the world; for that matter, to count is merely to understand that one can walk. . . . "27

This is the essence of what all children know and what the history of growing old — individually, collectively, culturally — requires us to forget. Weil's steps are Proust's staircase where perceiving and knowing have what Eliot memorably called objective correlatives in the order of memory and time. It is not, as Gairdner would have had it when he was a York University professor writing on Proust, merely the abstraction of language, let alone the further abstraction of alphabet. It is what the conservative impulse truly seeks to conserve.

⌒

Though I cannot say whether she succeeded, or even possibly could succeed, Weil's purpose in "Science and Perception in Descartes" is ultimately to show that the intent of the "double revolution [whereby] physics became an application of mathematics and geometry became algebra" was not the virtual binary culture that surrounds us today, but rather a re-symbolization of universal order, and a reunion of humanity with that order: "In short, we understand that . . . when the mind applies itself to the world, it may take geometrical figures, algebraic signs, or even sensations as intermediaries, but it is always the same mind, the same world, and the same knowledge; and it is this that Descartes, in all his writings, makes very clear."28

Sadly, perhaps not clear enough. For the nature of the innovation springing from the Cartesian well has been precisely the opposite. It has been the reduction of the world to the option of 1 or 0 by which digitization works. Those numbers no longer offer only "a presentiment of the world" — as Weil put it — but form the irreducible core of the I/O Sys that provides the world of information with the power to reconstitute reality as it chooses.

My sense is such a change represents a metaphysical shift with political consequences that give the phrase "computer terminal" an ominous meaning. Admittedly it would seem the binary proposition of 1 or 0 is little different from similar formulations ever-present to Chesterton's everlasting man. Are not positive and negative, right and wrong, good and evil, God and man, the same kind of polar opposites?

No. Counter-intuitive though it may seem, they are not. They are not, precisely because they are opposites while 1 or 0 is an option. We can choose the symbol for affirmation or the symbol for negation, but both produce results. And not even results as definitive as whether we go in or out the gate. Results only as a choice. More, only as an instrumental choice, not a moral choice. Results so far beyond good and evil that there no longer is need of that hypothesis. How could it be otherwise when, as de Kerckhove says, we exist "in cyberspace and out of time" where "'the on-line self' is supported by neither time, space nor body"?

Morality may not require God, but it does demand memory. Memory is a function of time in a space where between one step and the next we touch the world directly. But the 1-0 choice that eradicates our bodies must necessarily eradicate bodily contact with the world. The loss of that contact is the loss of the memory that makes it possible for us to understand that "when the mind applies itself to the world . . . it is always the same mind, the same world, and the same knowledge."

In the world of information-as-world, body and mind are both as private and as universally interchangeable as money and alphabetized language. Like those fragmented and de-contextualized parsings of culture, body and mind are superseded as symbols by the binary formulation working through the I/O Sys. We are free to be 1 or free to be 0 or free to be whatever form their infinite recombinations can provide. We are more than free to look at what we could be and ask why not. We are free to become it — and un-become it — as we choose not through work upon matter, nor even through imagination, but because we will the distinction between information and reality away.

A world without distinction between data and doing is a world that has done away with childhood. For childhood, above all, is the concrete discovery of that which is not us. It is the looking at, the finding of, things that are because they were and always shall be. It is a time of startling freedom, but a freedom very different from the now-infamous definition provided by Judge Stephen Rheinhardt of the U.S. Ninth Circuit Court who said in the 1992 ruling *Casey* v. *Planned Parenthood* that "at the heart of liberty is the right to define one's own concept of existence, of meaning, of the universe, and of the mystery of life."[29] Or, by extension, to change eternal truths, ancient codes of conduct, the moral principles of our ancestors, according to the binary mood of the moment.

Social conservatives do not fail to point out that this definition of liberty was presented as support for the providers of abortion, nor that its understanding of existence was cited repeatedly in later court briefs submitted by six leading U.S. philosophers arguing for legalization of physician-assisted suicide. What has piqued my conservative sensibility about that statement since I came across it, however, is its curious use of the word *mystery*. There is, of course, the non sequitur of a mystery being something definable. More compelling is the assumption that a mystery can be an individual matter. When I went to school, a strictly individual mystery — something everyone else knew but you did not — was called ignorance or, worse, stupidity. I have since heard the term *obscurantism* — a style in art or literature characterized by deliberate vagueness or obliqueness.

Yet as Flannery O'Connor wrote in *The Nature and Aim of Fiction*, art should be concretely directed at the kind of mind that "is at all times the kind of mind willing to have its sense of mystery deepened by contact with reality, and its sense of reality deepened by contact with mystery." This seems exactly the opposite of Judge Rheinhardt's definition, for it demands that reality and mystery both stand outside the mind contemplating them, and are neither creations nor ephemeral definitions of that mind. They cannot be known. But they can be contacted. They can be used for the deepening of the understanding that there are parts of the world, of existence, whose unity is our universal inability to turn them into information. It's instructive that in this same essay, Flannery O'Connor locates in childhood this process of the mystery of art. "The fact is, anybody who has survived his childhood has enough information about life to last him the rest of his days. If you can't make something out of a little experience, you won't be able to make it out of a lot."[30]

In her familiar, plain-spoken words lies the hope for the survival, indeed the flourishing, of the conservative heart, mind, and soul. Certainly conservatives concerned about overcoming the obstacles of this age would do better to ponder them than to simply pick sides in a debate over, say, minimum wage laws or the right to work. For crucial to those words is the understanding that information and experience are separate phenomena, and that the former proceeds from the latter through the history of a life. This is something our ancestors knew implicitly. It is something we deny explicitly with our emphasis on knowledge as disembodied data about the present. We deny it by forgetting that the universal mystery of life can only be approached through the past; that is by the childlike and inherently conservative task of retracing our steps through the active memory of the smell of grandmother's skin and house.

This is something I know on the basis of a memory of a place. My family had a houseboat on a lake in the Interior of British Columbia. A ritual of autumn was to drive up, pull it onto shore, and make it ready for winter. The lake was part of the cycle of salmon spawning, and as a result every four years when the run was at its peak the beaches and rocks would be littered with red and green rotting fish.

I remember as if it were yesterday at the age of nine working around helping my dad while the smell of dead salmon ripened the warm fall air. Taking a break, I watched a female nosing in the gravel, swishing her tail, making ready to lay her eggs. As I stood there, my dad came over and watched, too. He explained what I already knew about the salmon coming back to the rivers and lakes where they were born, and then he asked me: "Do you know why?" I thought up some fairly inventive answers, but he shook his head at each one. Finally, he said: "No one knows." Then he went back to work. I stood there for a little while longer, watching the female who would lay her eggs and then join the other battered and decomposing bodies on shore. She would join them right there, where I stood, not somewhere else. She would join them there because it had to be there and could not be anywhere else in space or time. No one knew why. No one knew why.

One of my childhood habits was to make shapeless songs out of things people said, and as I went back to work beside my father I sang in my head: "No one knows why; no one knows why; no one knows why." It was a song about the timeless contact of mystery and reality; about the glorious impossibility of turning some precious things into mere information. At the end of the afternoon, as I walked behind my father up the bank through the green reeds towards the car, I sang my song out loud. I remember because that made him smile, though I don't know exactly why. I was probably still singing it as he pushed the fedora he always wore back on his head a bit, and the motion of his arm rising made the scent of his perspiration fill the car. Perhaps I rolled down the window and sang it to the wind all the way home. I must have because, in many ways, I have never stopped.

Against all obstacles, the answers my own children gave to my questions about memory give me hope that they have just begun to sing. And will continue without surcease.

NOTES

1   G. K. Chesterton, *The Everlasting Man* (San Francisco: Ignatius Press, 1993), p. 62.
2   Marcel Proust, *Remembrance of Things Past* (London: Penguin Books, 1989), pp. 29-30.
3   William D. Gairdner, *The Critical Wager* (Downsview, ON: ECW Press, 1982), p. 23.
4   *Ibid.*, p. 24.

5 *Ibid.*

6 G. K. Chesterton, *Orthodoxy* (New York: Dodd, Mead and Co., 1954), p. 84.

7 Alexis de Tocqueville, *Democracy in America* (New York: Mentor Books, 1956), pp. 50-52.

8 Pierre Manent, *An Intellectual History of Liberalism* (Princeton: Princeton University Press, 1994), p. 114.

9 Walter Kaufmann, *Nietzsche: Philosopher, Psychologist, Antichrist* (Princeton: Princeton University Press, 1974), p. 145.

10 Allan Bloom, *The Closing of the American Mind* (New York: Simon and Schuster, 1987), p. 217.

11 Russell Kirk, *The Conservative Mind: From Burke to Eliot* (Chicago: Regnery Books, 1986), p. 493.

12 *Ibid.*, p. 495.

13 *Ibid.*

14 Guy Davenport, *The Symbol of the Archaic in the Geography of the Imagination* (San Francisco: North Point Press, 1981), p. 28.

15 Peter Emberley, *Zero Tolerance: Hot Button Politics in Canada's Universities* (Toronto: Penguin Books, 1996), p. 32.

16 George Grant, "Thinking About Technology" in *Technology and Justice* (Toronto: Anansi, 1986), p. 21.

17 George Grant, "Faith and the Multiversity" in *Technology and Justice* (Toronto: Anansi, 1986), p. 36.

18 Romano Guardini, *Letters from Lake Comeau* (Grand Rapids, MI: Eerdmans, 1994), p. 22.

19 *The Religion and Society Report* (Rockford Center Institute for Religion and Society, Rockford, IL, 4:6, June 1997), p. 4.

20 *Ibid.*

21 Derrick de Kerckhove, *The Skin of Culture: Investigating the New Electronic Reality* (Toronto: Somerville House, 1995), p. 204.

22 *Ibid.*, p. 196.

23 *Ibid.*

24 *Ibid.*, p. 199.

25 *Ibid.*, p. 201.

26 Simone Weil, "The Situation in Germany" in *Formative Writings 1929-1941* (University of Massachusetts Press, 1988), p. 100.

27 Simone Weil, "Science and Perception in Descartes" in *Formative Writings 1929-1941* (University of Massachusetts Press, 1988), pp. 59, 85.

28 *Ibid.*, p. 87.

29 Flannery O'Connor, *The Nature and Aim of Fiction* in *Mystery and Manners* (New York: Farrar, Strauss, Giroux, 1989), p. 79.

30 *Ibid.*, p. 84.

WHAT'S RIGHT, WHO'S LEFT, AND WHAT'S LEFTOVER

MICHAEL A. WALKER

The National Media Archive, a division of the Fraser Institute, has for many years been documenting the extent to which television commentators use labels in their descriptions of certain groups.[1] The purpose of this essay is to explore the use of labelling by the media and others in connection with the work of the Fraser Institute, Canada's largest independent economic policy research organization. It is written as an exploratory essay and concludes with a simple test with which the reader can locate his or her own beliefs within a political spectrum.

THE INTELLECTUAL WING OF THE KU KLUX KLAN

My first encounter with the issue of "right" versus "left" came within months of the founding of the institute, in 1974. We had given an interview to a person from the business section of *The Vancouver Sun* about what it was that the institute would try to accomplish. Our published statement of purpose was (and is): "The Fraser Institute is an independent Canadian economic and social research and educational organization. It has as its objective the redirection of public attention to the role of competitive markets in providing for the well-being of Canadians. Where markets work, the institute's interest lies in trying to discover prospects for improvement. Where markets do not work, its interest lies in finding the reasons. Where competitive markets have been replaced by government control, the interest lies in documenting objectively the nature of the improvement or deterioration resulting from government intervention." The interpretation of this by George Froehlich, a business journalist working with *The Vancouver Sun*, was that "the Fraser Institute will be an intellectual wing of the Ku Klux Klan."

NO CONSERVATIVES NEED APPLY

Such was the general posture of the journalism community in 1975 when an interview that had been conducted with Friedrich Hayek at the Fraser Institute was withdrawn by the CBC. The interviewer, Wendy O'Flaherty, had been so taken aback by this Nobel laureate's unabashed and candid conservative policy prescriptions that she refused to allow her employer to air the segment. Apparently her contract with the CBC permitted her to have this control — itself a remarkable fact.

Now lest you think that Hayek — regarded as having been generally correct in the areas where John Maynard Keynes was generally incorrect, in the assessment of the causes and consequences of economic developments — was on some rant, let me assure you that he was not. Hayek was merely talking about the business cycle and the requirement for monetary restraint because of the coming inflationary process. The fact that Hayek had been really the only notable economist of his time to predict the Great Depression had no standing with this CBC reporter. During the interview, Hayek exactly foretold, four years before it would happen, the necessity of the coming assault on worldwide inflation which was to be led by Paul Volker, then chairman of the Federal Reserve Board of the United States. I have often wondered whether Ms. O'Flaherty or the CBC remember the event and ponder their own lack of insight and the extent of their own ideological displacement. But that would require a degree of self-reflection that might have prevented the unfortunate development in the first place.

The episode didn't end there. The institute had taken the precaution of keeping a copy of the interview — on video and audio — and showed it to a few select people at private gatherings. One way or another, word of this got back to the CBC, and soon we received a phone call from Ottawa indicating that we were engaged in an illegal act. If we did not return all copies of the interview in any form to the CBC by the following day, RCMP officers would be around to collect them! Not the last time the institute would get threatening phone calls from media lawyers. Nor was it the last time that the CBC would tape and then fail to air comments by a visitor to the institute — a few years later they did the same thing to Milton Friedman, also a Nobel laureate and also a "conservative" economist.

THE SPIRIT OF THE TIMES

It is evident to me now that the *Sun* commentary and the CBC's refusal to show an interview with one of the greatest economists of all time together were a capsule comment on the spirit of the times.

Canada was generally taken up with the economics of redistribution. The government of the day, led by Pierre Trudeau, was in the process of pointing out to Canadians that "the market has failed and must be replaced by government-organized economic development." It is important to remember that while the economic paradigm guiding this government was typified by Trudeau's embracing the ideology and the aspirations of Fidel Castro and his Mexican counterpart Lopez Portillo, Trudeau and his government were among the most popular in Canadian history. Westerners in particular are inclined to regard Trudeau and, certainly for most of the period of the '70s, the rest of his cabinet, as a species of plague because of the National Energy Program. Nevertheless, at the time there was a deep and abiding satisfaction across the country, which included deep pockets of support in the west.

The Fraser Institute raised its impertinent head against this wave of popular leftist sentiment and with three employees began a process of reconsidering some of the presumptions that guided national economic policy and coloured its politics. By 1978 the institute was producing six or seven books a year, articles at a ferocious clip, and was beginning to publicly challenge the conventional wisdom. While in the country as a whole the output of the institute was regarded with amused scepticism, the institute was regarded as an evil threat in British Columbia, at that time the most polarized political environment in the country. The strength of this feeling can be gauged by the fact that in 1978 an unknown party placed what the police department referred to as "an incendiary device" in the elevator and sent it to the second floor offices of the institute. When the elevator doors opened, this device blew out into the lobby area of the institute, causing $10,000 (1979 dollars) worth of damage to the institute's premises, but fortunately no harm to any of the institute's staff.

While the vitriol behind the initial description of the Fraser Institute by *The Vancouver Sun* should have prepared us for the depth of feeling that was attached to people's disagreement with our views, I think it is fair to say that we were not prepared for the fire bombing incident. Nor was this to be the last incident we would have with those who chose a violent response. Far from in any way staunching the flow of ideas from the institute, the bombing incident served to emphasize in our own minds the importance of the work we were undertaking and, if anything, encouraged us in our activities. And so our output increased and the knowledge of what we were doing became ever more widespread in the community. One of the consequences was the pursuit of the institute by policy makers, both elected officials and their top deputies.

ROBESPIERRE OF THE RIGHT

By 1983 the institute was asked by the government of British Columbia to appear before its cabinet to outline a program of economic restructuring to deal with the incipient gap between revenues and expenditures that was emerging in government accounts. While the institute is non-partisan and does not engage in lobbying efforts, it is always willing to meet with political actors, whether in government or outside it, for the purpose of sharing the institute's views on the course of economic policy. We therefore sprang to the task of mapping out the desired economic policy course correction for the government.

Within months the government had enacted 26 bills which in broad outline resembled the policy advice the institute had, at the government's request, provided. Milton and Rose Friedman, in their book *The Tyranny of the Status Quo*,[2] refer to the B.C. program as one of the most comprehensive ever attempted and related it to the Thatcher program in Britain. It was not long before the journalistic classes seeking a villain to associate with the 1983 restraint program began to "accuse" the institute of being the source of these ideas. In the general hysteria of those times, and in the context of a general strike organized by the trade union movement in the province, it did not take long before physical abuse, or the threat of it, began to emerge. Attempts to occupy the offices of the institute were followed by bomb scares requiring the evacuation of the institute's premises periodically and a spate of death threats against me, finally producing 24-hour surveillance of my home at the request of the police department.

Of course, the foregoing was precipitated by an outpouring of media accounts, many of them completely fanciful, that sought to find the evil eminence behind the government's policies. So the premier was depicted as a ventriloquist's dummy on the institute's knee, and I was referred to as the Robespierre of the Right. Robespierre, of course, was the leader of the Jacobins in the French revolutionary period, was a chief ideologue of the revolution, and, most importantly, was the initiator of the Reign of Terror by which he eliminated most of his ideological foes within the revolution by way of liberal use of the guillotine.

GREATER THAN THE MARCH OF ARMIES

Whatever one might think of the unacceptable means they chose to use, the people who in the early days resorted to violence, or the threat of it, against the institute had a deeper understanding than many in the population of an essential truth, that ideas are important. As John Maynard Keynes so aptly put it in the last pages of his revolution-causing *General Theory of Employment, Interest and Money*: ". . . the ideas of economists and political philosophers both when they are right and when they are wrong, are more powerful than is commonly understood. Indeed the world is ruled by little else. Practical men, who believe themselves to be quite exempt from any intellectual influences, are usually the slaves of some defunct economist. Madmen in authority, who hear voices in the air, are distilling their frenzy from some academic scribbler of a few years back. I am sure the power of vested interests is vastly exaggerated compared with the gradual encroachment of ideas. Not, indeed, immediately, but after a certain interval; for in the field of economic and political philosophy there are not many who are influenced by new theories after they are twenty-five or thirty years of age, so that the ideas which civil servants and politicians and even agitators apply to current events are not likely to be the newest. But soon or late, it is ideas and not vested interests which are dangerous for good or evil."[3]

In other words, the issue of whether you are on the left or on the right — to use, for the moment at least, this now outdated taxonomy — is a matter of absolutely essential importance.

BE CAREFUL OF WHAT YOU THINK — YOU MIGHT BE RIGHT WING

What are the ideas that led media and ideological opponents to be so fearful and to label the institute "right wing"? It's useful to review some of them to see the pattern that emerges. I feel compelled to warn readers that some of you may find the following sections uncomfortable since you may discover that you, too, are "right wing."

Rent Control is a policy that has been pervasively adopted throughout the world. Controls are popular in the first instance because they involve imposing a tax on landlords and giving the proceeds to tenants. Since tenants vastly outnumber landlords, the political chemistry is perfect. The institute opposes them on the grounds that the historic evidence indicates quite clearly that the net result of rent control is a destruction of the housing stock gradually over a long period of time, the benefitting of sitting tenants at the expense of landlords and new entrants to the rental housing market, and finally the acceptance of a discriminatory tax that penalizes people simply on the basis of the fact that they have offered rental housing to the population.

As we soon discovered, for many people rent control is not simply an economic policy that might be good or bad for its intended recipients. It is, rather, a crucial battle in the class warfare between "the capitalist class and the worker class." When the NDP government moved to adopt rent controls in its first term of government in British Columbia, 1972-1975, it encountered problems and hired an expert from the United States, Emily Paradise Achtenberg, to assess the effect that rent controls were having and to advise them on the design of a more appropriate rent control regime. Ms. Achtenberg's immediately preceding qualifications included her having been the author of a book, *Less Rent, More Control*,[4] which was self-described as a handbook on how tenants can get a rent control regime installed, and keep it. I know it will come as a great surprise that Ms. Achtenberg concluded that rent control would be a good idea. But she was opposed to those right-wing ideas of the Fraser Institute, and *she* had the best interest of tenants at heart.

From a technical point of view, rent control is simply a form of price control that tends to expand the demand and reduce the supply of the controlled item. It is a policy about which economists, left and right, are universally agreed; it is a policy which, if you find yourself disagreeing with it, will lead you to being labelled "right wing."

A close relative of rent control in the policy toolbag is wage and price controls of a more general sort. These were adopted in Canada in 1975 as part of the federal government's commitment to the idea that the market was dead and needed to be more tightly controlled. Of course the practical impetus for them was the fact that wages and prices in Canada were escalating because the supply of money was being expanded too rapidly. Wage and price controls are an attempt to permit the government to enjoy the benefits of inflationary finance on the one hand, and not have to live with the inflationary consequences and the political backlash, on the other.

Needless to say, the institute opposed wage and price controls, expounding on the policy's some 4,200-year history and its dismal inability to control inflation, along with its untoward effects on economic development.

Since one of the principal losers in the imposition of wage and price controls is workers, wage and price controls were also opposed by the Canadian Labour Congress of the day, and *The Illusion of Wage and Price Controls*, published by the institute, occasioned a congratulatory letter from the president of the Canadian Labour Congress, then Mr. Joe Morris. Curiously enough, the institute was not referred to as right wing by the members of the journalism guild when the wage and price control study was being reviewed.

HOW ABOUT A LEFT-WING LABEL FOR A CHANGE?

One of the early targets of our program of research on bad market interventions was agricultural marketing boards. Properly construed, marketing boards are a government-sponsored cartel that empowers the producers of agricultural products to prevent their competitors from selling the controlled product. Correspondingly, the price in the market for agricultural products is higher than it would otherwise be, causing a transfer from consumers to producers. The central concern about this policy from the point of view of a transfer program is that it, in a more or less systematic way, transfers income from low-income families to higher-income families and is in that sense a very poorly conceived transfer program. From the point of view of economic efficiency, the cartelized production is typically produced in units of too small a size, ensuring that the overall costs of production in the industry are higher than they need to be to produce the corresponding agricultural output.

The institute's concerns about government-created monopoly were not exclusively focused on marketing boards. Over the years, studies on the medical monopoly conferred on physicians by virtue of the requirement for licensing, the way in which the legal fraternity is able to control the supply of legal services, and the quasi-monopoly power of trade unions were all subject to critical scrutiny. Curiously enough, our work on producer cartels has sometimes earned us the label "left wing," since the producers in these cartels usually fancy themselves to be, well, right wing.

Owing to this positional promiscuity of businesses who benefit from government preference, the label "right wing" hasn't always been applied to institute studies. The label "pro-business" or "conservative" has, however, been consistently used. This labelling has in no way been affected by the fact that we have over the years done a number of studies critical of the government's provision of subsidies to business. Perhaps the most celebrated of these is our long-standing opposition to subsidies to research and development or high technology. A series of books on this topic, pointing out the dismal history of research and development subsidization and the untoward likely consequence of pursuing it, did very little to cause the media or special interest critics to revise their estimation of the institute's work. Of course this is not surprising given the reason for the use of the labelling in the first place.

A FUTURES MARKET IN STOLEN PROPERTY

Two strands of the institute's research program have been particularly productive of labels: our work in the area of fiscal studies relating to the tax and expenditure policies of government, and our work on privatization. Upon consideration, this is not in the least surprising.

My friend Tom Borcherding of Claremont Graduate School is fond of quoting H. L. Mencken's description of politics, and more particularly elections, as a kind of futures market in stolen property. By this Mencken meant that governments curry the favour of the electorate by taking resources from one segment of the electorate and giving them to another. For such a policy to work successfully in the winning of votes it must take, in what are perceived to be small amounts, from one group and give, in concentrated, significant amounts, to another group. As Mencken also pointed out, if you are going to take from Peter to pay Paul, you can rely on the unabashed support of Paul.

The activities of government in this way systematically create fan clubs for the various programs they adopt. These fan clubs then become the defenders of the programs in the event that there is an attempt to get rid of them or fundamentally change them. It is not surprising that groups like the Fraser Institute incur the opposition of these fan clubs when they question the desirability of the clubs' programs. And what better way to defend yourself from a demonstration that you are on the take from the public purse than to claim that your critic is nothing more than a right-wing bigot?

It is important to note that for the most part the people who are the recipients of these programs are not primarily ideological in their outlook. They are in many cases not even particularly liberal in their politics and may even be, as we noted above, "right wing." The problem is that they are beneficiaries of the programs and are simply defending their interest.

The beneficiaries of the programs are joined in their defensive tactics by the public servants who administer the programs and the politicians who form the third arm on what Milton and Rose Friedman have called the iron triangle of interests that make policy change very difficult. Of course, we know from Buckminster Fuller that a triangle is the strongest two dimensional structure. A collection of triangles goes together to make a geodesic dome, an igloo-like structure which is an excellent symbol for the structure of interests that make up the Canadian polity.

AN IDEOLOGICAL FAN CLUB

Privatization is another policy the institute has advocated in Canada and elsewhere around the globe. It is a policy the public sector trade unions have fought with every resource available to them. While this has been in part simply a case of special interests protecting themselves, for the most part I think we can see here a true ideological struggle.

The reality is that most of the privatized firms around the world have also been unionized firms. Of course the union in many cases has been different than the public sector union that originally represented the workers, but privatization, by and large, has not been an anti-union movement.

It has, of course, very much been a movement of reducing the reach of the state and, as the 1969 manifesto of the "waffle wing" of the New Democratic Party pointed out, an important function of government is to "control the commanding heights of the economy." (The manifesto was signed by such leading lights of the party as David Barrett, Gerry Caplan, Ed Finn, Steven Langdon, David Lewis, Laurier LaPierre, Gordon Laxer, Jim Laxer, James Lorimer and Mel Watkins.) State ownership is an integral part of market socialism. And so if you oppose state ownership or produce studies showing that it is inefficient and ineffective and that privatization would be a better option, you can depend on the label of "right wing," "pro-business" or "anti-social." The operative strategy of those who want more state ownership is, "If you can't question the research of an organization, question its motives."

The institute has produced nearly 200 books, thousands of articles, and tens of thousands of commentaries on economic policy development. In almost every case these products have been labelled "conservative," "right wing," "pro-business." This labelling has not limited the effectiveness of the institute's program. It is nevertheless interesting to observe the extent of the attempt to dismiss the work by labelling and the virtual absence of labelling put on those who have come forward to criticize our work. It is a rule of political discourse that those who oppose special interests will be labelled; the special interests themselves will not be.

There has been an interesting consequence of this practice of asymmetric labelling. Many who take the trouble to examine the work of the institute have found its conclusions and recommendations sensible and usable. The result is an increasing tendency for people to regard themselves as "right wing." This broad use of our ideas in many jurisdictions around the world has given us international exposure. One of the impressions that emerges from this exposure is the extent of the difference between Canadian and foreign attitudes towards the policies that the institute has advocated and the sort of labelling that people have thought appropriate to apply. In this regard it is interesting to consider the experience of New Zealand and the United Kingdom.

IN BRITAIN, THE "RIGHT-WING" CONSERVATIVES

In 1979 in Britain, and in 1984 in New Zealand, two remarkable groups of politicians were elected. In Britain it was of course the government of Margaret Thatcher, a person of impeccable conservative credentials and an absolutely unshakable confidence in policy direction based on a clear understanding of the issues and a sound grounding in market economics. While Mrs. Thatcher reflected the radical competitive market policies of the Institute of Economic Affairs in London, she also, in her courage, outlook, and aspirations, reflected the best instincts of traditional conservatives. She brought in a program of deregulation, privatization, marketization and denationalization of a kind that had never been seen on the face of the globe. For the first time since 1946 she brought to economic activity in Britain a predictable posture of government, an attitude designed to encourage development of the private sector, and to foreign policy a firm conservative outlook of honour, duty and the Thatcher doctrine — that it would be no longer acceptable for countries' boundaries to be changed by the use of force.

Quite predictably Lady Thatcher was labelled a "right-wing maniac," "the Iron Lady," "ultraconservative," "neoconservative," and "monetarist." For her policies of restraint she was reviled to such an extent by the left that the academic senate of Oxford University voted against a proposal that she be given an honorary doctorate. Like the labelling activities we have been discussing, this failure to honour one of the very greatest of British prime ministers is a comment more on the thin quality of the academic senate of Oxford than on Lady Thatcher.

IN NEW ZEALAND, THE "RIGHT-WING" SOCIALISTS

On the other side of the world a few years later, a lifelong socialist and cabinet minister in Labour governments and then a member of parliament in New Zealand's loyal opposition found himself writing a small book, *There's Got to be a Better Way*.[5] Roger Douglas, observing New Zealand's economic situation deteriorating day by day, week by week, and month by month, was moved to comment that the unmitigated program of nationalism and socialism being pursued by the then allegedly conservative government of Robert Muldoon could not possibly be the best way in which to organize government policy in New Zealand.

Douglas began to sketch out what was the only course left open to an opposition party faced by a conservative government following virtually every interventionist, statist policy imaginable. He turned to a pro-market, denationalization, privatization program designed to completely restructure the pattern of economic incentives in New Zealand. Announcing their purpose as a struggle against state preference, Douglas and his colleagues Richard Prebble, Geof Palmer, and David Longe successfully persuaded the people of New Zealand that indeed there had to be a better way and it must lie along the line of a pro-market policy program.

As many have observed, the policies Douglas espoused were very similar to policies that had been advocated in New Zealand by the Centre for Independent Studies, a New Zealand offshoot of an Australian organization formed in 1977 on the model of the Fraser Institute.

It was quite natural that Douglas should have been elected finance minister by his cabinet colleagues because among those in the new government he seemed to have the clearest vision of where New Zealand should go. He was fortunate to find in the New Zealand treasury, Graham Scott, the top treasury official. During the years when Robert

Muldoon was both prime minister and finance minister, Scott had very little to do in the way of strategic planning, so, he spent his time designing blue-sky schemes for what should be done to correct the country's economic difficulties. Scott's thinking and that of Roger Douglas coincided almost exactly and Scott simply produced his ready-made blue print for what became a pro-market revolution.

In 1986 Roger Douglas came to Canada at the invitation of the institute and gave a number of lectures in Canada regarding his government's reform program. The lectures were nothing short of remarkable. Their title, "How to Achieve Socialist Ends with Capitalist Means," is indicative of what Douglas and company attempted to accomplish. In his lectures and the paper associated with them, Douglas was careful to point out that he was a lifelong socialist. He had lost none of his socialist aspirations, but he simply had come to the conclusion after nineteen years in the New Zealand government that there were some things that worked and some things that did not. The things that did not were those policies that generally are referred to as socialist, left wing or, as we prefer to call them at the institute, interventionist.

From Douglas's point of view they did not work in the sense that they did not deliver employment to those who wanted it, they did not deliver prosperity, they did not yield to the government the kind of resources that would enable New Zealand to pursue the diminishment of poverty and need by those least capable of functioning for themselves. Therefore these policies for socialists were not effective.

Douglas went on to point out that he saw nothing particularly socialist about a program of state preferences that effectively took from one group in society and gave to others who were perfectly capable of getting for themselves. This was, as he pointed out, nothing more than a system of political preferences reflecting the political pressures mounted by the recipient groups rather than any socialist vision designed to help those most in need. And so Douglas abolished preference, from rent control, to agricultural marketing boards, to import subsidies, to export subsidies, to industrial assistance, to interest-rate controls and special finance arrangements for farmers, industrialists, and others.

Douglas could not bear to think of it as being quintessentially social-ist to tolerate over-manning, feather-bedding, and incompetence in nationalized industries, nor could he see it as particularly appropriate that a Labour government should maintain a labour code that gave one group of workers predatory opportunities over others. He could see nothing intelligent or attractive in a tax system that so heavily penalized income it led to widespread evasion and diminishing amounts of rev-enues available to the government. In short, Douglas was looking for policies that would work to help him achieve a society in New Zealand where government would have sufficient resources to help those who were unable to help themselves and to achieve other worthwhile inten-tions badly missed by the policies then in place.

THE CANADIAN LEFT IS MUGGED BY REALITY

An interesting incident during Douglas's first visit to Canada happened at a dinner in Toronto between Sir Roger and then leader of the NDP opposition in Ontario, Bob Rae. During the lengthy dinner meeting, Douglas explained in splendid detail his program of market reform and winding back the role of the state. It is fair to say that Bob Rae was flabbergasted by this socialist finance minister and his rendition of New Zealand's new approach to economic policy. But he listened patiently and asked intelligent questions about the transformation of New Zealand.

At the end of it all, Rae said to Douglas, "Well then, how, Roger, would you compare your policies to those of Mrs. Thatcher?" After a moment's thought, Douglas replied, "Well, on the whole I would have to say that Mrs. Thatcher's policies were somewhat less comprehensive in their scope than the program which we have followed in New Zealand."

So here we had a traditional left-wing government, the New Zealand Labour party, and a traditionally right-wing government, the British Conservatives, pursuing policies that were broadly consistent one with another but in which the New Zealand socialists were claiming to be somewhat more comprehensive in the denationalization and restructuring of their country's economic system.

These developments in different corners of the world, in conjunction with the remarkable developments in the former Soviet Union and the People's Republic of China, should by any sensible standard have brought an end to the traditional linear thinking that gave rise to the right-left distinction between people of different ideological persuasions. It should also have done away with the historical predilection to differentiate people according to their intentions.

As Douglas is at pains to point out, well-intentioned people in New Zealand, pursuing what had been traditional socialist policies, produced a reduction in New Zealand's standard of living from third to 23rd in the world over a period of several decades. Good intentions don't make good policies. Good analysis may, and it was the unrelenting implication of the onslaught of the evidence that interventionist, statist policies traditionally associated with the left, while undertaken for good intentions, were not in fact capable of delivering the intended outcomes.

On the other hand, according to Douglas and many others following in his footsteps, it is possible to achieve the good intentions of socialism by using the mechanisms of the marketplace. That is, by recognizing that incentives matter, that the state should not provide privileges, and that altruism is not a very reliable principle of human action. At base, the revolution in thinking that has occurred in Labour governments like those led by Douglas is that the model of the world to which old line socialists subscribed simply was not an accurate description of human nature and how it is expressed in economic undertakings and didn't provide good predictions of policy outcome.

ALL RIGHT WINGERS NOW — EXCEPT IN CANADA

Regrettably this revolution in thinking about the role of government has not yet penetrated the left in Canada. Rae's reaction to Douglas was to seek to arrange a private meeting so that he could dissuade Roger from his errant ways. Somewhat later the CBC's response to the New Zealand economic miracle was to air a screed of patent nonsense, authored by

Canadian labour-union publicist Murray Dobbin, which totally misrepresented the record of the facts about what had happened in New Zealand. Dobbin's rendition of New Zealand developments was so badly distorted that it caused the New Zealand High Commissioner to take the unprecedented act of issuing a press release decrying the lack of factual content in Dobbin's piece.

In countries ranging from Chile in South America, to New Zealand, to Shanghai in China and Tony Blair's Britain, the issue of right versus left in economic policy terms has been rendered almost meaningless as socialist governments increasingly pursue their good intentions using the techniques of free market incentives.

Of course, Canada is a deeply conservative place. I mean conservative in the sense that we are slow to change our ways. There are many attractive features about such an approach to life. But one of the consequences is that we, as a people, are subject to ideo-lag. Our ideas are slow to adjust to the mainstream of world thought. And so, notwithstanding the above, when we return soberly to *The Vancouver Sun* of July 2, 1997, we find buried in a story about the Pacific salmon and its plight, the comment, "Salmon, like the disciples of the Fraser Institute, instinctively turn right." Not much has changed at the *Sun*!

WHAT'S LEFTOVER?

While the labels "right" and "left" are no longer relevant, there obviously is a distinction between people and the values and views they hold. It is fascinating to discover where your views lie in the constellation of possible views. As a quick guide to thinking about these issues, the Fraser Institute in 1995 published a Canadianized version of a test that had been devised by the group Advocates for Self-Government, Inc. To find where you stand relative to this index, all you have to do is answer the questions, score your values, and then add the values to get a total score that will give you a position within the matrix. Of course you can add your own set of questions and try it out on your friends, provided you have a lot of them; otherwise perhaps you'd better limit the test to your acquaintances for you never know what political beliefs lurk beneath the apparently placid surface of your neighbourhood.

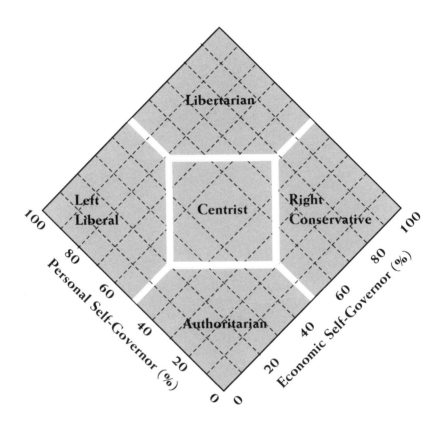

THE WORLD'S SMALLEST POLITICAL QUIZ

Take the *World's Smallest Political Quiz*. Then use the Self-Government Compass to find your political identity.
Circle **Y** when you agree with a statement,
M for Maybe, Sometimes, or Need-More-Information, or
N for No.

Are you a self-governor on PERSONAL issues? 20 10 0

Government should not control radio, TV
or the press (including books) . . . . Y M N
Drug laws do more harm than good and should
be repealed . . . . Y M N

There should be no laws or regulations concerning
sex between consenting adults . . . . Y M N
Private clubs and organizations should be free to
admit or refuse any member. . . . . Y M N
Government should not interfere in arrangements
between doctors and patients . . . . Y M N

Are you a self-governor on ECONOMIC issues? 20 10 0

Business and farms should operate without
government subsidiest . . . . Y M N
People are better off with free trade than with tariffs . . . . Y M N
Minimum wages cause unemployment and should
be repealed . . . . Y M N
Government should not dictate hiring or
employment practices . . . . Y M N
Union membership should be voluntary, not
compulsory . . . . Y M N

NOTES

1 "Name Calling in Parliament and in the Media," *On Balance*, 7:5; "Who's Right, Who's Left? A Catalogue of Television's Naming Conventions," *On Balance*, 7:7; "Media Labelling and the Legitimacy of Organizations," *On Balance*, 7:8; "Comparing Mandates: Ontario and Alberta," *On Balance*, 8:2; "Who's to Blame for the Oklahoma City Bombing?" *On Balance*, 8:5; "The Ontario Election: How did the Media Report the Harris Victory Compared to Rae's Five Years Ago?" *On Balance* 8:6.

2 New York: Harcourt Brace Jovanovich, pp. 6-7.

3 London: Macmillan, 1964, pp. 383-84.

4 Cambridge, MA: Urban Planning Aid, 1973.

5 Fourth Estate Books, 1980.

CONSERVATIVE POLITICS IN CANADA: PAST, PRESENT, AND FUTURE

TOM FLANAGAN AND STEPHEN HARPER

"The best of times, the worst of times" — that hoary Dickensian cliché could apply to the present state of the conservative movement in Canada. Intellectually and organizationally it is better off than ever, with conservatives in control of key provincial governments, but it is so divided politically that winning the federal government seems hopelessly out of reach.

In this essay, we examine the conservative political disarray. In particular, we look at three current debates in conservative politics — economic versus social conservatism, populism versus traditionalism, and the "One Canada" versus "Two Nations" views of the country. Our conclusion is that, because of the differences revealed by these debates, a working alliance of separate regional parties, rather than a unitary national party, is the most desirable and attainable goal. Some modest steps towards cooperation may be possible at the present time, but a full-scale coalition would require not only new leadership but also some institutional changes, most notably to the electoral system. There is unlikely to be any genuine resolution of conservative political divisions until conclusion of the debate over Quebec sovereignty. For the time being, conservatives will make more progress towards their goals by working to influence public opinion and a pliable Liberal party than by expecting to take direct control of the federal government.

THE CONSERVATIVE MOVEMENT

The conservative movement in Canada has grown remarkably in the 1990s, and the momentum continues to increase. An organizational network able to develop and communicate a sophisticated conservative message now exists everywhere in English Canada. We hesitate even to offer a list for fear of leaving out valuable contributors, but here are some major nodes in the network:

- *Research Institutes.* The Fraser Institute and the C. D. Howe Institute are the most cited Canadian authorities on economic policy, and new research institutes, such as the Atlantic Institute for Market Studies, continue to be founded. In the social sphere, there are now institutes such as the Centre for Renewal in Public Policy and the National Foundation for Family Research and Education.
- *Advocacy Organizations.* The National Citizens' Coalition and the Canadian Taxpayers Federation each have memberships in the tens of thousands. They are complemented by numerous smaller organizations, such as REAL Women and Citizens' Impact, that specialize in certain clusters of issues.
- *Publications.* For years, *Alberta Report* (and its sister magazines *B.C. Report* and *Western Report*) stood almost alone in conservative publishing. Now they have been joined by the interesting new quarterlies *Gravitas* and *The Next City.* And as a result of Conrad Black's purchase, the Southam newspapers are becoming genuinely pluralistic, rather than monolithically liberal and feminist as they were under previous ownership. Newspaper readers in metropolitan areas now get reasonable access to conservative national and local columnists.
- *Financial Support.* Unlike the labour-union, feminist, gay-liberation, and

environmental movements, conservatives do not seek, and would not get, government support. Conservative organizations have to combine corporate and foundation support with direct-mail fundraising in varying proportions. Recently the Donner Canadian Foundation has provided seed money for many new ventures, helping to knit the network together.

In addition, the conservative network is now starting to knit itself more closely together through the umbrella discussion group known as Civitas. Although Civitas takes no positions and does not engage in political advocacy, it provides a forum for writers and activists to get to know each other better; in that sense it will enhance the influence of the conservative movement over the long run.

The impact the conservative movement has already had is shown in the growing conservatism of public opinion and public policy. Canada is not the same country it was ten years ago. Sound money, balanced budgets, tax reduction, free trade, deregulation, privatization of public enterprise, and targeting of social welfare programs now constitute a broad consensus within the Reform party, the Progressive Conservatives, and the business Liberals, who currently dominate that party.

THE CONTEMPORARY DISARRAY OF CANADIAN POLITICS

The expansion and networking of the conservative movement stands in sharp contrast to its widening partisan divisions.

As recently as 1995, it was considered novel when Stephen Harper wrote that Canada might enter a "one-party-plus" phase, with the Liberals as "the only broadly based coalition capable of governing" and the other parties acting as representatives of more narrowly based regional, ethnic, or ideological constituencies: "The New Democrats might become the party of labour leaders and left-wing activists; the Reformers, the party of western populists and single-issue rightwingers; the Progressive Conservatives, the party of eastern traditionalists and the country clubs; and the Bloquistes, the party of Quebec tribalism."[1]

Today, after the highly regionalized and fragmented result of the 1997 federal election, that view is echoed by all commentators.

This configuration is, of course, partly an artifice of the first-past-the-post electoral system inherited from Britain. The requirement for a simple plurality in a single-member district produces a large number of "wasted" votes that do not translate into seats. First-past-the-post has an inherent bias towards a two-party system. An important exception, however, is regional concentration, which allows comparatively small support to elect members. A two-party system, if it begins fragmenting regionally, becomes a two-party-plus system, and in the extreme, a one-party-plus system.

Table 1 shows how genuinely dominant the Liberal party is. The real significance of Liberal victories in the last two election campaigns is neither the party's legislative majority nor its relatively strong popular vote, but its general superior competitiveness. The Liberal party is an electoral threat in most parts of the country, whereas the other parties are threats only in definable sets of constituencies. The Liberal party placed either first or second in roughly 90 percent of electoral districts, whereas no other party placed either first or second in even half the ridings.

Table 1

First and Second Place Finishes by Party

(Preliminary Figures for 1997)

	1993		1997	
PARTY	First	First + Second	First	First + Second
Liberals	177	269	155	260
Reform	52	131	60	117
BQ	54	75	44	67
NDP	9	32	21	61
PC	2	80	20	95
Ind.	1	3	1	2
	295	590	301	602

In this configuration, the Liberal party should be understood not as a centre-left party, like the American Democrats or British Labour, alternating in office with a centre-right alternative. Rather, it is a true centre party, comparable with the Christian Democrats in Italy, the Liberal Democrats in Japan, and Congress in India, standing for nothing very definite, but prevailing against a splintered opposition. It avoids definite ideological commitments and brings together people mainly interested in exercising power and dispensing patronage. The left-leaning period under the leadership of Pierre Trudeau was an historical aberration, which the current Liberal government has actively rolled back by, for example, making unemployment insurance less generous and reducing transfer payments to the provinces for welfare and medicare.

The 1997 election accentuated the "sectarian" opposition trends of which Harper first wrote. The PCs, whose vote was spread the thinnest in 1993, made a mild recovery in the eastern regions of the country but fell back even further in the west. Reform, already western-based, strengthened its presence there while slipping back somewhat in the east. The NDP made significant inroads in various regions — unprecedentedly so in Atlantic Canada — but almost always in inner-city and remote areas. Its historic position as a broadly based protest party in western Canada continued to slip away. The Bloc Québécois lost strength overall while remaining completely concentrated in francophone Quebec.

The danger for the Liberals is not defeat by an alternative government, for the opposition is too divided for that to occur. However, if the other parties continue to "segment" rather than "divide" the opposition vote, the Liberals will eventually lose their majority. A centre party can be driven from office if it suffers internal splits or if the other parties gang up on it. If the latter occurs, governing for any length of time would be a major challenge, usually culminating in a period of further partisan disarray.

THE HISTORICAL FRAGMENTATION OF CANADIAN POLITICS

Not very long ago, it seemed that the age of political conservatism had dawned in Canada. In 1984 the Progressive Conservative party, led by

Brian Mulroney, won a smashing victory — 50 percent of the popular vote and 75 percent of the seats in the House of Commons. Mulroney also won a reduced, but still solid, majority in 1988.

Students of history realize, however, that Progressive Conservative majority governments have been exceptional. For the past century Canada has usually been governed by the Liberal party, and during much of that time the opposition has been weak and divided. The lack of an alternative government today is merely a replay of the past. As we explained recently in *The Next City*, Canada's party system contains five major forces that have been present since 1935.[2]

- The Liberal party, with a national coalition capable of governing. There were times from 1972 through 1988 when the Liberals were virtually shut out of the west as they are today in francophone Quebec, but they have usually maintained appreciable strength in all parts of the country.
- The Conservative party (Progressive Conservative after 1942), commanding a nominally national base of support but in fact coming to power only in exceptional circumstances and then governing only for short periods of time.
- The Co-operative Commonwealth Federation, a socialist party claiming to be national but with real strength only in a patchwork of ridings. Emerging from the wreckage of the Progressives in the mid-1920s, it inherited some of their western protest base when it was formally established in 1932. In 1961 it recycled itself as the New Democratic Party, the official political arm of the Canadian Labour Congress.
- The Social Credit League, a right-wing populist party firmly rooted in western Canada. Federally, it elected western members as recently as 1965. The Reform party inherits this conservative populist tradition. Its first and so far only leader is Preston Manning, himself a federal Socred candidate in 1965 and the son of Ernest Manning, the long-serving Social Credit premier of Alberta.
- The Union Nationale, a francophone nationalist coalition in Quebec, founded in 1935 by Quebec conservatives and Liberal nationalists. In

the 1970s the Union Nationale was permanently displaced by a new coalition of separatists, the Parti Québécois. The Bloc Québécois is the most recent of such nationalist movements at the federal level, spanning almost the entire ideological spectrum, from socialist left to monetary-reform right.

The only times in the last 50 years that the Progressive Conservatives won majority governments were John Diefenbaker's victory in 1958 and Brian Mulroney's victories in 1984 and 1988. Diefenbaker's triumph depended on displacing Social Credit in the west while getting one-time support from the Union Nationale in Quebec. His majority slipped away when his chaotic, populist management style could not hold this diverse coalition together.

Brian Mulroney won his great victory in 1984 partly because he made a strategic alliance with the separatists in Quebec. He recruited numerous well-known nationalists to his cause, and he received the support of many workers from the Parti Québécois machine. Across a wide range of issues, however, Mulroney failed to govern on conservative principles, to the disappointment of conservatively minded voters. In the west, the Reform party, founded in 1987, attracted the allegiance of these voters, once the most loyal of PC supporters. In Quebec, Mulroney's erstwhile friend and cabinet colleague, Lucien Bouchard, founded the Bloc Québécois in 1990. The Mulroney coalition was saved when it stumbled, almost accidentally, into the 1988 free trade election, but its downfall came when it lost support both in Quebec and in the west. The Progressive Conservative party was like a barrel tapped at both ends. In 1993, previous PC voters flooded out in the west to Reform and in Quebec to the BQ.

Essentially, the formula has been the same ever since 1917. *The Progressive Conservative party has come to power only when the public has been desperate to remove the Liberals and a PC leader has managed to attract support from western populists and Quebec nationalists in addition to Tory core support in Ontario and the Maritime provinces.* Such a "throw them out" coalition can win an election but faces substantial difficulties in governing. The aspirations of these elements are not necessarily complementary and, in building the coalition, their differences have inevitably been ignored rather than brokered.

It might be possible to keep such an act together in the more loosely structured American system, where the requirement for party unity is not so great. But Canada's parliamentary constitution requires the existence of disciplined parties able to vote as a bloc in the House of Commons. Party discipline could be loosened, but it will always have to be quite high as long as the constitutional framework endures. Heterogeneous coalitions face grave strain, because one element usually sets the party line, making the others feel excluded from power. In the Progressive Conservative party, the predominant element has been centrist and eastern, anglophone and traditionalist, leaving both western populists and Quebec nationalists feeling that the party does not represent their views or interests.

With this review of the historical causes of conservative disarray behind us, let us examine the various divides that would have to be crossed in order to assemble an effective conservative coalition today.

ECONOMIC VS. SOCIAL CONSERVATISM

Ted Byfield, the publisher of *Alberta Report* and the dean of conservative writers in Canada, holds that the biggest threat to the conservative movement in Canada is the split between economic and social conservatives, or, as Byfield prefers to call them, "neo-cons" and "theo-cons." In his words: "Conservatism in Canada consists these days of two radically separate groups that are held together not by what they favour, but by what they oppose. Neither likes big government. But one lot dislike it for what it costs, while the other lot dislike it for what it does."[3]

Byfield's statement contains an obvious element of truth. There are, in fact, two rather different political philosophies commonly labelled conservative. One, sometimes called "economic conservatism," is derived from classical or Enlightenment liberalism. Its primary value is individual freedom, and to that end it stresses competitive markets, religious toleration, limited government, and the rule of law. In the United States, some authors, perhaps with a degree of distortion, are now calling it "libertarianism."[4] The other philosophy is Burkean conservatism. Its primary value is social order, and to that end it stresses respect for custom and traditions (religious traditions above all), voluntary association, and personal self-restraint reinforced by moral and legal sanctions on behaviour.[5]

Because these are two different lines of thought, parties based on them can, and in the minds of many must, oppose each other; and nineteenth-century politics in most countries, including Canada, had that configuration. On one side was a liberal party in the classical sense — rationalist, anti-clerical (but not anti-religious), free-trading, often republican. On the other side was a conservative party — traditionalist, explicitly or implicitly denominational, economically protectionist, usually monarchist.

The rise of the radical, socialist left at the beginning of this century demonstrated to classical liberals and Burkean conservatives how much they had in common and made possible a conservative movement in the modern sense. When confronting the left, neo-cons and theo-cons realized that they both opposed public ownership, government interventionism, egalitarian redistribution, and state sponsorship of secular humanist value systems, and that they both favoured private property, small government, and reliance on civil society rather than the state to resolve social dilemmas. Meanwhile, historical trends made some of their other differences, such as republicanism versus monarchy, decline dramatically as sources of political conflict.

If there were no egalitarian, statist left wing in our politics, classical liberalism and traditional conservatism might once again enter the field against each other as distinct parties and ideologies. Is this happening today? Certainly the socialist left has been in significant decline in recent years, particularly since the end of the Cold War. And both the libertarian and religious strains of conservatism have experienced a revival and renewed assertiveness over the same period. We believe, however, that a return to the old realignment is unlikely, and implausible in any realistic time frame. The legacy of the radical left is extremely powerful, whatever its current political weakness. There are far too many organizations and groups with vested interests in big government and redistributive politics, and dedicated to propagating and legitimizing collectivist values.

As well, there is no general evidence to suggest that the two kinds of conservatives are incapable of sustaining workable coalitions in modern politics. It has happened in Britain under the leadership of Margaret Thatcher and John Major, in the United States under Ronald Reagan and George Bush, and in many places in North America regionally. At the present moment, Progressive Conservative provincial parties, based on precisely this type of coalition, are governing Alberta, Manitoba, and Ontario and doing yeoman's service in trimming back the excesses of the welfare state. We see no reason why the same could not happen federally.

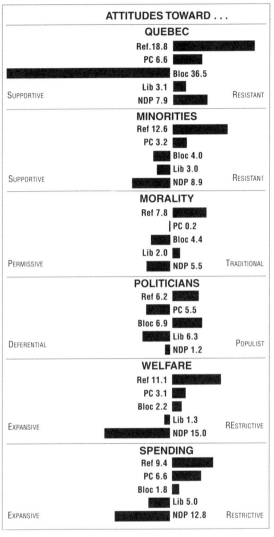

ATTITUDES TOWARD . . .

QUEBEC
Ref.18.8
PC 6.6
Bloc 36.5
Lib 3.1
NDP 7.9
SUPPORTIVE — RESISTANT

MINORITIES
Ref 12.6
PC 3.2
Bloc 4.0
Lib 3.0
NDP 8.9
SUPPORTIVE — RESISTANT

MORALITY
Ref 7.8
PC 0.2
Bloc 4.4
Lib 2.0
NDP 5.5
PERMISSIVE — TRADITIONAL

POLITICIANS
Ref 6.2
PC 5.5
Bloc 6.9
Lib 6.3
NDP 1.2
DEFERENTIAL — POPULIST

WELFARE
Ref 11.1
PC 3.1
Bloc 2.2
Lib 1.3
NDP 15.0
EXPANSIVE — RESTRICTIVE

SPENDING
Ref 9.4
PC 6.6
Bloc 1.8
Lib 5.0
NDP 12.8
EXPANSIVE — RESTRICTIVE

Let us examine more closely the fracturing of the PC coalition in 1993. The differences between Canada's main political groupings are easily visible in the figure in the sidebar, based on survey data collected by the Canadian Election Study team in 1993.

Reform supporters appeared to be the most conservative on both economic and social matters. Bloc supporters were all over the map on social and economic issues. PC voters were closer to the Liberals on social and cultural issues than they were to Reform supporters; in fact, they were to the left of the Liberals on several points. However, they were closer to Reformers on economic and fiscal issues. Socially, the Liberals actually located themselves to the right of the PCs — a phenomenon explained by the historic attachment of many Roman Catholics to the Liberal party.

Although survey data from the 1997 election are not yet available, there is no reason to think these patterns have changed much, except in one respect: Although the PC platform espoused conservative fiscal and economic positions, the leader, Jean Charest, actually ran a centre-left campaign in Quebec and Atlantic Canada, attacking the Liberals for having reduced federal spending. Because the new PC caucus was elected in this way and represents only dependent regions of Canada, one may expect a further leftward drift in fiscal and economic policy.[6]

The difference between economic and social conservatism certainly does not explain the rise of the Bloc, and the separation of Reform from the PCs is related to a split between conservatives and centrists generally within the old Mulroney coalition, not to a split between that coalition's economic and social conservative elements. In fact, both brands of conservative thought share a common ethos — free will, personal responsibility, family values — as well as a common electorate. Tensions between economic and social conservatives may run high in the United States, but in Canada they are the least of the problems confronting those seeking to build an effective conservative political force.

POPULISM VS. TRADITIONALISM

Despite the conventional "conservative" and "right-wing" labels assigned by the media to the Reform party, Preston Manning tenaciously insists on describing himself and the party as "populist" rather than

conservative.[7] In fact, he has consciously designed the Reform party c..
the model of earlier populist parties that were such a powerful force in
western Canadian political culture. Populism in the west cuts across
conventional political divisions and animates any political party that
emerges from or puts down roots in the region.

Populist parties originated in the late nineteenth century following
the settling of the western half of North America. A deep cleavage
developed between the mass of the population, mainly agricultural
producers with homogenous concerns, and a small number of powerful
actors (banks, trust companies, railways, grain dealers) who, despite the
apparently democratic nature of representative government, came to
control the local state apparatus.

A period of political turmoil gradually corrected this imbalance.
Through vigorous programs of political reform, many political movements sought to democratize the system. Although these populist
movements were short-lived, they have had enormous historical impact
on mainstream partisan politics in both Canada and the United States.

Populism is not as comprehensive and intellectually elaborated as
other ideologies, but populist movements do possess a common philosophical framework. This includes a rejection of the ideological discourse
of both the "conservative" establishment and its conventional "radical"
opponents (i.e., of both the "right" and the "left"), demands for political
reform and direct democracy, and leadership reflective of middle-class
priorities and mores but coming from outside the establishment.

Populist leaders insist that they go beyond conventional political
cleavages to articulate the true "will of the people," or in Manning's
words "the common sense of the common people."[8] They reject existing
ideological divisions, such as that between left and right, as irrelevant
and self-serving. For this reason, populist leaders are often accused of
simply pursuing popularity like other non-ideological politicians. There
is, however, a significant difference between the populist reformer and
the conventional centrist or pragmatic opportunist.

The centrist consciously brokers divergent interests and ideologies
and is acutely aware of the ideological pluralism in which he operates.

The populist rejects such ideological pluralism fundamentally; indeed, the populist framework is defined most accurately as "democratic monism."[9] The populist leader seeks the will of the people outside of the disputes between existing political forces. He elicits the common will, an idea which makes no sense in brokerage politics.[10]

Populism also differs from conservatism. Modern conservatives, beginning with Edmund Burke, have been leery of radical political change and have put emphasis on incrementalism and on traditional institutions as safeguards of order and freedom. Conservatism in this sense, sometimes called Toryism, has been marked by a cautious temperament, bereft of the zealous tinge that has been attached to populism of all political stripes. Burke himself advocated the trustee version of representative government, as evidenced in his famous speech to the electors of Bristol.[11] Ever since, conservatives have usually been sceptical of direct democracy. Conservatives have been especially leery of the direct, unfiltered will of the people and the local factionalism direct democracy tends to encourage.

Today, however, many active, self-described "conservatives" are proponents of direct democracy. This is especially true in the United States, but not only there; a leading Canadian example is Patrick Boyer.[12] This conservative advocacy of direct democracy is a reaction to the legislative log-rolling, judicial activism, and special-interest politics of the modern liberal welfare state. As governments have become bastions of liberal economic and social values, conservatives have recognized that the preservation of traditional norms often means the criticism of establishment institutions. Thus in an age where populism often appears right-wing, conservatism has simultaneously adopted some ideas about the political process originally associated with populism.

The 1993 Canadian Election Survey indicates that populism is a significant characteristic in contemporary partisan division. For example, Reform supporters, unlike the PCs, had a populist mistrust of government. Polls have also repeatedly shown the appeal of Reform to independent middle-class voters, while the economic and social elite among traditional PCs have rejected the new party. This is a strong characteristic of right-of-centre populist movements and has parallels in the older left-wing populist formations.

Also interesting is the distrust of government that Reformers share with supporters of the Bloc. Many, including Manning himself, have noted social parallels between Reform and Bloc support. Yet the BQ is a francophone separatist party dedicated to the division of the country through a unilateral declaration of independence by way of a referendum, regardless of constitutionality. The distrust of government shared by Reform and the Bloc underscores some of the perils of populism as a political philosophy.

The monistic nature of populism, on the surface identical with opportunistic centrism, explains its occasional association with political extremism. Populism, by assuming an essentially monolithic population, can lead to the elevation of a class, ethnic, or religious perspective to the level of "common will," beyond the claims made by mere ideology. Driven by this monistic outlook, social conservatism can degenerate into corporatism (state sponsorship of specific social groups) and nationalism into ethnic chauvinism.

Democratic monism even more commonly degenerates into personalized leadership and bonapartism (defined below), as opposed to constitutionalism. Since a populist party exists to express the popular will, not the voices of political factions and special interests, there is no reason to replicate these in the party's structure. In fact, there is good reason not to. Since the leader's only role, indeed his duty, is to discover and articulate what "the people" want, there is no reason why he should be inhibited in this task by rival authorities.

In the Reform party, almost none of the organizational diversity of other political parties exists, despite a large and active membership. There are virtually no organizations for demographic or occupational groups, no ideological or interest-group foundations, no contributors' clubs, and no provincial parties or regional wings within the federal party itself. The party has no elected president; its chairman is in effect appointed by the leader.[13] Its caucus, like its extraparliamentary wing, is organized exclusively for functional and operational purposes. Bodies embracing regional, ideological, or demographic perspectives have been officially (but not always successfully) discouraged or forbidden. In short, nowhere in this large political organization is there any other body, arm, or faction with an existence sufficient to have its own leadership in even the loosest sense of the term.

Likewise, Reform has no real intermediate levels of authority, but rather an organizational structure that could be called "balcony and street." At its worst, this recalls the practices of Louis Napoleon Bonaparte, who used plebiscites to create a virtual dictatorship in France. Preston Manning has sometimes used *ad hoc* popular consultations to ignore or replace procedures in Reform's constitution and policy book. At other times, he has declined such popular reference at all, merely asserting that, as a populist leader, he is able to ascertain the common opinion of his constituents without the encumbrance of such mechanisms.

Needless to say, such concepts of organization and leadership are fraught with potential for abuse. Thus far, Reform policy usually has reflected what its grass-roots members actually think, indeed more so than in other parties. But Reform's ideological and personality disputes have always been resolved by suspension, expulsion, or departure, rather than by the compromises over policy or position that make traditional parties work.

ONE CANADA VS. TWO NATIONS

Although the differences between populists and traditionalists, and between committed conservatives and conventional centrists, shed some light on the PC-Reform divide, they explain almost nothing about the rise of the Bloc Québécois.

The Bloc Québécois was founded in 1990 by Lucien Bouchard, a well-known Quebec nationalist recruited by Brian Mulroney to the PC cause. Bouchard was instrumental in Mulroney's decision to reopen the constitutional file in a campaign address delivered in Sept Iles in August 1984.[14] Within three years, Mulroney had secured all-province agreement-in-principle for the Meech Lake Accord, a series of constitutional amendments designed to address five major demands made by Quebec in exchange for formally signing the Constitution Act of 1982.

During the three-year ratification period following the agreement, a series of political events raised public concerns about its provisions and led to a precipitous decline in its public support, especially outside of Quebec. It ultimately failed to be ratified in a soap opera of high drama, rising public tension, and increasing support for Quebec separatism. The most, though by no means the only, contentious element was the clause declaring Quebec a "distinct society within Canada."

This clause raised fundamental questions about the nature of Canadian federalism. While these have existed since 1867, and have been the source of periodic crises, they have been more acutely dangerous since the rise of the Quebec sovereignty movement during the Quiet Revolution of the 1960s.

A very large proportion of Quebec's francophone population regards Canada as a partnership of "Two Nations," English and French, whereas a very large segment of English Canadian opinion regards Canada as a federal union of equal provinces. Different conceptions of the nature and ideal of this union have ranged from Trudeau's concept of a centralized, multicultural, bilingual state to Manning's concept of a highly devolved federation of provincial cultural entities. But they can all be summarized by Diefenbaker's slogan of "One Canada," his rallying cry against the formal adoption of the "Two Nations" slogan by the PCs in 1967. While Diefenbaker lost his argument within his own party, his position was ironically adopted in a more radical form by his Liberal foe, the Quebecer Trudeau, who used it to thrash the Tories the following year.

Shortly before the final defeat of Meech, Bouchard led a small contingent of Quebec PCs and Liberals out of their parties to form the Bloc Québécois as a federal separatist option. Bouchard's move radicalized Quebec opinion regarding "distinct society" across the political spectrum. Under this political pressure, Canada's three major federal political parties, and indeed the entire federalist political establishment of the country, arrived at an even more comprehensive constitutional deal, the Charlottetown Accord, in 1992. Again including a "distinct society" clause, it was defeated both inside and outside Quebec in a national referendum. Significantly, its organized political opposition consisted of little more than the Bloc Québécois and the Reform party, although Trudeau, emerging briefly from retirement, played a major role in swaying public opinion.

The Charlottetown referendum was the effective end of the Mulroney coalition. Although the Reform party was founded during the signing of the Meech Lake Accord in 1987, the agreement played almost no role in the party's early phases, including its emergence in Alberta as a political factor in the 1988 federal election. But the party's real growth occurred after 1989, after Manning delivered his "House Divided" speech to a Reform assembly in Edmonton,[15] and Deborah Grey became the first federal MP to launch strong public attacks on the Meech Lake Accord. The Meech crisis was again a major factor when Reform launched its expansion into eastern Canada, principally Ontario, in 1991. No other federalist political party opposed the Meech-Charlottetown agenda.

Again looking at the 1993 Canadian Election Survey, it is evident that the three fragments of the Mulroney coalition are most dramatically divided on their opinions about Quebec and on related issues such as bilingualism, distinct society, and constitutional change.

The entry of the Bloc and Reform into federal politics has radically overturned a key consensus of the previous players. For the last 30 years, the established parties have taken turns playing what the journalist Peter Brimelow called the "patriot game."[16] That is, they have used the fear of separatism to control national politics. A succession of prime ministers from Quebec — Trudeau, Mulroney, and Chrétien, with Jean Charest waiting in the wings — have built their careers on "saving Canada." Responding to the threat of a separatist referendum coming from Quebec provincial politics, they have made "keeping Quebec in Canada" a rationale and a test for virtually all important federal policies.

The advent of Mulroney led to an important shift in federalist strategy. Whereas Trudeau had sought to make federalism appeal to Quebecers through his bilingual reforms of national institutions, Mulroney took the unprecedented step of attempting to reconcile Quebec sovereigntists and nationalists directly. When his "distinct society" strategy failed, the separatists stepped into the federal Parliament itself. This could not help but expose the deep animosity to the "patriot game" long festering just below the surface in English Canada. This was especially true in the west and rural Ontario, the core of PC support ever since the Diefenbaker era.

Reform, with its slogan of equality of provinces and citizens, espouses the long-standing One Canada view of these English Canadians. The Liberals, and even more so the Progressive Conservatives, have embraced "distinct society" as a covert way of defining Canada as two nations. And the Bloc Québécois, taking matters to their logical conclusion, wants two sovereign nations. These differences are stark and visceral; they became the major defining issue in the 1997 federal election.

PROSPECTS FOR POLITICAL CONSERVATISM IN CANADA

Regardless of the growing conservative movement in Canada, the political reality is Liberal party government and a fragmented opposition. This fragmentation is not new, and is not based on contemporary debates within conservatism. Instead, it is founded on deep fault lines within Canadian political culture that the growing crisis over Quebec sovereignty has again exposed. The conventional political spectrum of left to right is now crosscut by a dimension of conflict over national identity, which was highlighted in the election campaign.

MERGER?

There are a number of possible resolutions to these divisions within the conservative camp. Most talked about is a merger of the Reform and federal PC parties. This has repeatedly been the subject of political punditry and urged by prominent outsiders. A national conference, entitled "Winds of Change," was even dedicated to the question.[17] However, merger seems to us to be simply out of the question. Too many careers would be at stake, which is why political parties almost never merge in the true sense of the term. In any case, these parties don't even cooperate on a limited basis, let alone a comprehensive one. Moreover, during the 1997 campaign, Reform questioned the ability of "Quebec-based" politicians to deal with separatism, and Charest responded by calling Manning a bigot.[18] The gap between Reform and the PCs has become a yawning gulf over the national unity question.

Another possibility is that either Reform or the PCs will win the war of attrition that both Manning and Charest seem dedicated to fighting. Both parties now have territorial bases that the first-past-the-post voting system rewards. Both have distinctive elements of the electorate and sources of members and funds.

While both parties could go on for a long time, Reform seems to be favoured in any conventional "fight for the right." It has clearly captured the most conservative constituencies, both regionally and ideologically, and as Canada's official opposition has the upper hand in terms of representation in the House of Commons.

Even more importantly, Reform is playing a significant role as an influence on the Liberal government, pulling it to the right on economic policy and towards a harder line against Quebec separatists. This "NDP of the right" role is similar to what that party did in the 1960s and 1970s when it set an agenda for the Liberals to enact. As long as the Liberals remain unchallenged as the dominant centre party, such an influence is critical for the long-term survival of any conservative faction.

The PCs, on the other hand, have an uncertain base and an uncertain political mission. Now a party exclusively for middle-ground pragmatists both inside and outside Quebec, it must offer a plausible prospect of forming a government in order to hold their loyalty. Yet, other than the popular appeal of Charest, there is nothing to indicate that government is within grasp.

Reform's limitations, however, are severe. These are rooted in its commitment to populism. As a populist, Manning has directed Reform away from a clear strategy of consolidating the conventional right. Ironically, the vagueness of his populism has also had the perverse effect of allowing the most right-wing elements in the party to define its image in the public eye. Reform's monolithic nature makes a big breakthrough into the east, especially Ontario, difficult. If Reform knew how to break into Ontario, it would have done so by now. In normal times, its efforts would appear to be hopelessly stymied. Populism simply seems to be outside of the cultural framework of most Ontario voters.

CONSOLIDATION

Another possibility is that one of the parties will make a major shift to consolidate the right. Such shifts usually involve seminal changes in policy or leadership, especially in the regional origin of the leader. It is, however, unclear what Tory policy shift could attract Reformers, since the differences between the parties are as much matters of political culture and style as policy. Reformers themselves have to be cautious lest opportunistic shifts expose their hard-won base to encroachment by the Liberals, who have demonstrated themselves to be seasoned and effective opportunists. Finally, voluntary leadership changes of any kind appear unlikely. Both Charest and Manning possess historically unparalleled control of their parties, and neither seems anxious for another career.

Even if such policy or leadership moves could re-create a national conservative party, we believe the resulting entity would be temporary and unstable, as has been the rule throughout the twentieth century. From an institutional perspective, the fragmentation of Canadian conservatism results from imposing the Westminster model of a parliamentary system and first-past-the-post voting on a society with deep ethnolinguistic and regional cleavages. Differences of political culture between Quebec and the rest of Canada, and between the west and the east, have repeatedly shattered the regimented coalitions necessary for political combat in the House of Commons.

Since experience suggests that a monolithic conservative party is unworkable, what might make more sense is the gradual construction of an explicit alliance of opposition elements, or "sister parties." An alliance would face many difficulties, to be sure, but it would also have two great advantages. It would reflect the regional and cultural character of Canadian society, and it would give that character an institutional expression without necessitating constitutional change. Also, it would allow leaders of regional parties to defend necessary compromises as precisely that — necessary compromises. Within the framework of a single national party, compromises have to be defended as hegemonic party policy, which tends to drive dissenters out of the fold.

CHANGING THE ELECTORAL SYSTEM

Outside the United States and United Kingdom, sister parties are actually the norm in the democratic world, particularly on the conservative side of the spectrum. Three examples are the Christian Democratic Union and the Christian Social Union in Germany, the Liberal/National coalition in Australia, and the various alliances of the centre-right in France.

But merely to make this enumeration raises the question of the electoral system. Each of these countries uses something other than first-past-the-post voting. Australia has a preferential ballot for the House of Representatives, making it possible for Liberal and National candidates to run in the same constituency without hopelessly dividing the right-wing vote. Conservatively minded voters can mark one as their first choice and the other as their second choice, thus facilitating the victory of one of the two. Germany has a mixed-member-proportional voting system that delivers a highly proportional result. The CSU operates only in Bavaria, while the CDU does not go into that province; but even if the two parties were to compete head-to-head, the electoral system would protect the existence of both. France has a two-stage run-off system that allows the Gaullists and the traditional centre-right parties to test their strength on the first ballot and make alliances for the second.

Plurality voting, on the other hand, encourages parties to wage a war of attrition. Smaller parties have so much trouble converting votes into seats that larger parties are always tempted to open up even a small margin over their rivals in the hope of consigning them to oblivion. But territorial concentration and the one-party-plus system create regional exceptions to the Darwinian logic of plurality voting. Thus Reform, the PCs, and the Bloc could go on for decades without ever becoming truly national parties, while through their survival as regional parties they could continue to prevent the emergence of a national conservative party.

If supporters of Reform and the PCs who want merger were to begin by pushing for changes to the electoral system, they could encourage cooperation in a way that should not threaten their leaders. For example, a simple preferential ballot would eliminate any possibility of a "split" vote among conservative parties, even if no formal cooperation occurred. The preferential ballot has Canadian roots; it has been used in the past in the western provinces, and it is essentially the voting system that all Canadian political parties use in the selection of their own candidates and leaders. A Reform party task force has now reported favourably upon electoral reform, but the party has not (yet?) made it a high priority.[19]

If even this small advance cannot be made, then it is perhaps time for more radical action. This would have to occur in Ontario, where the division of the conservative vote is most acute and the demands for merger most vocal. The "Blue Tories" that elected Mike Harris seem to be fundamentally uncomfortable with the western populism of Reform, despite a largely shared policy agenda. At the same time, they share little with the emerging Charest coalition, a combination of left-of-centre Red Tories and narrowly focused Quebec nationalists. Of the three traditional elements of Canadian conservatism, it is actually the strongest, the Toryism of Ontario, that is increasingly unrepresented by any political party.

Maybe it is time for Ontario conservatives to form their own consciously regional movement. Since there are virtually no Ontario leaders in either Reform or the federal PCs to combat such a formation, it could be organized from the ground up. If Reform activists were involved, that party would probably be forced not to oppose the new Ontario Tories if the latter were prepared to cooperate with Reform at the national level. Resistance by the rump PC party in Harris Ontario would be even more futile. In other words, a new Ontario conservative party could begin to encourage cooperation between western populists and Quebec autonomists.

o regional party seems like a novel idea, but it would fit into ɪgly regional character of Canadian politics. Witness the ɂ 1997 election, when the Liberals took 101 of 103 seats in Ontario but did not win a majority of seats in any other region of the country. The federal Liberals are not an Ontario regional party, but they do seem to be moving in that direction.

Whether or not any of these efforts occur, there is no doubt that the fragments of the Mulroney coalition will remain in play for the immediate future. The pending showdowns between Quebec separatists and Canadian federalists on the one hand, and between One Canada patriots and distinct society compromisers on the other, guarantee this. Bouchard's Bloc is awaiting its rendezvous with destiny. And both Manning's Reformers and Charest's PCs believe they are the only real guardians of their supporters' and their country's interests. In such a scenario, both see the potential of a sudden and massive breakthrough in Ontario, and so neither one will abandon the dream of forming a dominant national party.

There is a prominent mountain along the Trans-Canada Highway from Calgary to Banff called The Three Sisters. Legend has it that an Indian chief placed each of his three daughters on separate peaks to keep them away from unworthy suitors. The strategy was so successful that the three daughters died up there. Is Canadian conservatism also a family of three sisters fated to perish in isolation unless they forge an alliance?

If Canadian conservatism is ever to work, its three sisters must recognize that each represents an authentic aspect of a larger conservative philosophy. Reformers will have to realize that there is something genuinely conservative in the Tory penchant for compromise and incrementalism. Tories will have to admit that compromise, to be honourable, has to be guided by underlying principles and that Reformers are not extremists because they openly advocate smaller government, free markets, traditional values, and equality before the law. Both will have to recognize that Quebec nationalism, while not in itself a conservative movement, often appeals to the kinds of voters who in other provinces support conservative parties — voters who care about their local identity and culture and who see a centralized state as a threat to their way of life. And conservative Quebec nationalists will ultimately have to make a clear commitment to Canada, renouncing unconditionally the ethnocentrism that underlies the sovereignty movement. If Canada is to regain political stability, ordinary issues of governance and constitutional change must be decoupled from each other and from the separatist threat.

The prospect for reuniting the three sisters is bleak at the moment. The Bloc Québécois, though it commands the allegiance of some conservatively minded voters, is a separatist movement, not a conservative party. The Reform party seems content to confine itself to the populist tradition. And the conservatism of the Progressive Conservatives has become sadly attenuated as Ontario Tories dream of re-creating a monolithic party which they forget has failed time and time again.

Conservatives, however, should not despair. The purpose of the conservative movement is to change public opinion and public policy, not solely to elect to office a party with a particular name. Much has already been achieved and can be advanced further by working on public opinion and pressuring the governing Liberal party. Not a perfect solution, perhaps, but then conservatives are not *supposed* to chase after perfect solutions.

NOTES

1 Stephen Harper, "Where Does the Reform Party Go from Here?" *The Globe and Mail*, March 21, 1995.

2 Stephen Harper and Tom Flanagan, "Our Benign Dictatorship" in *The Next City* (Winter 1996/97), pp. 35-40, 54-57.

3 Ted Byfield, "The Harper-Flanagan Essay Was a Start; So Now Let Them Tackle This Issue" in *Alberta Report*, February 10, 1997, p. 44.

4 Charles Murray, *What It Means to Be a Libertarian* (New York: Broadway Books, 1996), p. xii; David Boaz, *Libertarianism: A Primer* (New York: Free Press, 1997), p. 25.

5 Russell Kirk, *The Conservative Mind: From Burke to Eliot* (Chicago: Henry Regnery, 1953).

6 Anne McIlroy, "Tories Tilt Platform to Left, Toward East," *The Globe and Mail*, June 20, 1997.

7　Tom Flanagan, *Waiting for the Wave: The Reform Party and Preston Manning* (Toronto: Stoddart, 1995), p. 22.

8　E. Preston Manning, "Building a New Canada: Leader's Foreword," *Reform Party of Canada, Principles and Policies: The Blue Book 1991*, p. v.

9　Thomas Flanagan, "The Politics of the Millennium" in *Terrorism and Political Violence* 7 (1995), pp. 166-71.

10　The definitive critique of populism is William Riker, *Liberalism Against Populism: A Confrontation Between the Theory of Democracy and the Theory of Social Choice* (Prospect Heights, IL: Waveland Press, 1988/1982).

11　*Burke's Speeches and Letters on American Affairs*, Hugh Law, ed. (London: J. M. Dent, 1908), pp. 72-74.

12　Patrick Boyer, *The People's Mandate: Referendums and a More Democratic Canada* (Toronto: Dundurn, 1992).

13　Flanagan, *Waiting for the Wave*, p. 28. According to the party's constitution, the chairman is elected by the other members of the Executive Council, but Manning has always orchestrated the choice.

14　Graham Fraser, *Playing for Keeps: The Making of a Prime Minister 1988* (Toronto: McClelland and Stewart, 1989), p. 48.

15　The speech is reprinted in Ted Byfield, ed., *Act of Faith* (Vancouver: British Columbia Report Books, 1991), pp. 76-78.

16　Peter Brimelow, *The Patriot Game: National Dreams and Political Realities* (Toronto: Key Porter, 1986).

17　Susan Delacourt, "Ontario Has 'Right' Stuff," *The Globe and Mail*, May 27, 1996.

18　Jack Aubry, "PC Chief Calls Manning a Bigot," *The Globe and Mail*, May 30, 1997.

19　Reform Party of Canada, Report of Electoral Reform Task Force, preliminary report, first draft, submitted February 1, 1997. The chairman of the task force subsequently published a book favouring the single-transferable-vote form of proportional representation. Nick Loenen, *Citizenship and Democracy: A Case for Proportional Representation* (Toronto: Dundurn, 1997).

THE QUEBEC QUESTION:
DEBT DIVISION AND
THE RULE OF LAW

SCOTT REID

The single theme that most clearly unites civilized democracies is their belief that a justly constituted society must be based on the rule of law, rather than upon the arbitrary actions of those who hold political power. Canada's policy makers must recognize the importance of this theme as they develop contingency plans to deal with the possibility that Quebec may attempt to secede.

It is obvious that Canada would be better off if Quebec did not separate at all. But it is no longer valid to claim, as some opponents of contingency planning have done, that the act of developing plans reduces the cost of separation, thereby making separation more likely. The near success of the separatists in obtaining a majority "Yes" vote in the 1995 referendum suggests that if the intention of the federal government in refusing to prepare contingency plans is to frighten Quebecers into voting against separation, it isn't working.

The secession of a member state from a federation means, among other things, that the constitution of the federation is temporarily incapable of providing a framework within which politics can be conducted according to the rule of law. Once the seceding state has established its own constitution and made clear the boundaries between its authority and the authority of the parent federation, a framework of legal order is once again established. However, there is an unavoidable transition period during which there is no generally accepted set of rules under which disputes between the seceding unit and the parent country, or between the seceding state and its residents, can be settled. In the absence of such rules, the result is that such disputes are typically settled by means of the party that has more power imposing its will on the party or parties that have less.

While the use of raw power is never the best way to resolve disputes, it need not always lead to disaster. For example, in the case of the secession of Quebec from Canada, the decision as to whether Quebec residents would be permitted to keep their Canadian passports would be decided entirely by the Canadian rump state, and the government of Quebec would have no say in the matter. The decision as to whether Quebecers would continue to use the Canadian dollar would be made entirely by the Quebec government, because there is no way in which Ottawa could prevent them from doing so without causing its own citizens more grief than the matter is worth. And so on.

But there are some matters where the absence of an enforceable law-based dispute-resolution mechanism could lead to enormous economic loss, or even to violence. In particular, one such danger zone is especially ominous. This is the question of dividing the federal government's accumulated debt. For this problem, Canadian political leaders must act in advance of a secession crisis to create a law-based, rather than power-based, dispute-resolution mechanism.

As a practical matter, it is clearly impossible to develop such a mechanism with the Constitution of Canada as its ultimate source of authority, since the entire point of the Quebec separatist movement is to reject the power of the Canadian constitution. It would therefore be possible to resolve the debt question only if Canadians recognized that the process of secession would leave all of us — Quebecers and non-Quebecers alike — temporarily incapable of acting as fully sovereign states. We must recognize that we would have to rely on non-Canadian authorities and institutions to ensure that Canada continues to enjoy peace, order, and good government throughout the transition period between a "Yes" vote in a referendum and the date at which Quebec's full sovereignty was granted.

I believe both the government of Quebec and the government of Canada will grudgingly consent to an invited non-Canadian presence in regard to the division of the debt if the alternative to such intervention is a negative-sum game in which both Quebec and the rest of Canada are likely to come out as net losers. Based on this premise, I will lay out a proposal for an international body to adjudicate and enforce a division of the federal debt.

THE PROBLEM

Use of the debt as a pawn in discussions of breakup could foreclose effective options for bargaining. . . . Moreover, both parties might use the debt after breakup to distort the policy options in other areas. In these less than ideal circumstances, the combined costs to ROC [the rest of Canada] and Quebec could leave a debt "burden" that substantially exceeded the value of the debt being divided.

— JOHN CHANT[1]

In the event of secession, the division of the federal government's $590-billion debt would represent a special category of dispute that, unlike disagreements over trade links or the use of a common currency, would not be easily resolved by means of bilateral negotiations. Why? Because in most negotiations on any subject, each side's ultimate negotiating tool is the option of withdrawing from negotiations and refusing to participate further. In negotiations over the percentage of the federal debt that should be assigned to each party, however, withdrawal necessarily involves the refusal of one side or the other to make interest payments to Canada's creditors, either in full or in part. But by refusing to pay — or even by *threatening* to refuse to pay, the negotiators will have the effect of scaring away new creditors, thus driving up the total cost of financing the debt.

To date, the possibility of using this negotiating tactic has been broached only by the separatists. Shortly before the 1995 referendum on separation, Lucien Bouchard linked federal support for Quebec's admission to the North American Free Trade Agreement (NAFTA) and its repayment of the debt. He warned: "One of the first steps of English Canada would be to run after Mr. Parizeau to ask him, to beg him, to sit down and discuss what would be the share [of the debt to be paid by] Quebec. . . . So there'll be negotiations and Quebec will be clever enough to bind things. . . . everything will be linked. . . . Don't forget that the debtor, the one that creditors will call first, will be the federal government."[2]

Former Bloc Québécois leader Michel Gauthier has suggested another strategic use for debt negotiations. He stated that a failure on Ottawa's part to join promptly in separatist-initiated negotiations following a referendum victory for the separatists could be answered by Quebec's refusal to pay its share of debt-financing costs: "Yesterday the minister of finance closed the doors to all negotiations with a sovereign Quebec and remained strangely silent as to the share of the debt. The tremendous debt would oblige the federal government in its own interests to instigate negotiations the very next day after the referendum."[3]

Similarly, while he was the premier of Quebec, Jacques Parizeau made rumblings about using debt repayment as a way of forcing Ottawa to negotiate on Quebec's terms. In 1995, he told a Rimouski audience: "If Canada says we will not be at the table, and there are some Canadians who get excited sometimes, and they say we won't be at the table even to negotiate the sharing of the interest payments on the federal debt, we'll say, under those conditions you'll just wait for your cheques."[4]

Quebec Finance Minister Jean Campeau has also suggested that Quebec might renege on its share of the debt.[5]

The dangers of this strategy are enormous. Any such talk, following a majority vote in favour of sovereignty in a future referendum, would have an immediate impact on creditor confidence. At the very least, new lenders would demand a very high risk premium for their money, thereby sending interest rates soaring. This could drive up the costs of refinancing the federal debt to unsustainable levels. Ultimately, lenders might refuse altogether to put their money in the hands of either the Canadian or the Quebec government, with the result that it would be impossible to finance the repayment of maturing securities. In this situation, Canada would be forced to start defaulting on payments as they come due. As one currency analyst put it on referendum day in 1995, "Who would want to buy Canadian government paper in the wake of a Yes vote, until such time as fundamental political, tax and revenue agreements between Quebec and the rest of Canada have been concluded? If your answer is 'Not me, not anyone I know, why . . . no one would,' well, Canada has a king-size crisis on its hands."[6]

Remember, all that would be required to trigger a default of Canada's debt obligations would be for creditors worldwide to conclude, for several months in a row, that it is wiser to invest their money in the debt instruments of any other country in the world rather than in new Canadian securities. In 1995, 43 percent of Ottawa's marketable debt took the form of treasury bills with an average term to maturity of 113 days. In a single four-month period shortly before the referendum, it was necessary to roll over one-quarter of the entire federal debt.[7]

Worse yet, a decision on the part of Quebec's leadership to withhold payments might cause the government of Canada to deliberately initiate a complete default on the debt, regardless of the economic costs. A logical — if unlikely — scenario of doing so would be as follows: Once it becomes clear that Quebec's secession from Confederation has served as a successful method of allowing the province to escape from paying an equitable share of the federal debt, other provinces would have a rational incentive to escape from paying their own shares of the debt by also unilaterally seceding from Canada. Given that the per-capita cost in the rest of Canada of refinancing the federal debt would have been greatly increased by Quebec's departure, unilateral action would seem even more attractive to these provinces. In order to pre-empt further secessions, Ottawa would have no choice but to initiate a complete default on the debt. This would force all provinces to share equally in the cost of debt default, thereby eliminating the possibility that further unilateral secessions could be used as a means of escaping these costs. At this point, international authorities would step in and impose a debt division settlement on Canada and Quebec, but the cost to the Canadian economy would be enormous.[8]

The costs of this worst-case scenario are so obvious that politicians on all sides may be dissuaded from using non-payment as a tool for negotiating such points as an independent Quebec's admission to NAFTA. However, even if a temporary *modus vivendi* were established between Quebec and the rest of Canada regarding the repayment of the debt, problems would still exist. As long as the debt is jointly held by the two states, the Quebec government might use its ability to suspend future payments as a tool of longer-term diplomacy. As Alan Freeman and Patrick Grady note in their 1995 book, *Dividing the House,* "[One] disadvantage of keeping all federal debt in Canada's name indefinitely is that it would give Quebec a lever over Canada that could be used in subsequent negotiations over unrelated issues. Quebec could always threaten to withhold the interest payments until it got its way on any issue."[9] Creditors would recognize this risk and demand a permanent risk premium on all new securities issued in order to refinance this debt.

Even if both governments acknowledge the enormous costs of protracted debt negotiations, they could find themselves forced into a worst-case scenario by circumstances beyond their immediate control. On one occasion, Parizeau casually suggested that "there are really two criteria to use [in determining how to divide the debt]: population and Gross Domestic Product. We will, I suppose, haggle for a few weeks before we come to something like a quarter."[10] (Quebec's share of Canada's population is just under 25 percent and its share of Canada's gross domestic product is around 23 percent.) However, Quebec's semi-official position, adopted by the secretariat of the provincial government's Bélanger-Campeau Commission in 1991, is that Quebec should assume only 18.5 percent of the federal debt.[11] In the midst of a secession crisis, it might prove politically impossible for the premier of the seceding province to unilaterally abandon the Bélanger-Campeau formula in favour of a population-based or GDP-based formula, when his supporters are demanding that a hard line be taken on the debt in order to force Ottawa to back Quebec's anti-partition efforts, or to prevent Canada from revoking the passports of Quebec residents.

This is an enormous problem, considering that Quebec's Cree and Inuit populations in turn would probably attempt to secede from Quebec, that some English-majority regions would also try to detach themselves from the province, and that the premier of Newfoundland would be under pressure from his own population to turn off the turbines at Churchill Falls unless Quebec agrees to renegotiate the lucrative hydro contract under which Hydro-Québec has the right to purchase all but 300 megawatts of the 5,225 megawatts produced by the facility until the year 2034.[12]

The problems faced by Canadian and Québécois negotiators would be worsened by the virtual absence of useful international precedents for the division of a marketable debt worth half a trillion dollars. Outside the colonial context, there are only a few cases of countries splitting apart. In most of these cases, the predecessor state was already in default of its debt obligations (for example, the German Empire and the Otto-man Empire at the end of World War I). Other well-known secessions, such as the separation of Norway from Sweden in 1905 or the Malaysia-Singapore split in 1965, have been the result of the breakup of very loose confederal relations in which there was no common debt and very few common assets to split.[13]

International law is similarly unhelpful. The best description of the international legal situation is provided by Patrick Grady in his book, *The Economic Consequences of Quebec Sovereignty*: "There is no one legally sanctioned method of dividing assets and liabilities under international law. Everything would be up for grabs at the negotiating table."[14]

The closest thing to a governing document for the division of assets and debts is the *Vienna Convention on the Succession of States in Respect of State Property, Archives, and Debt*. There are, however, a number of compelling reasons why the convention is not definitive. For one thing, it is intended to apply to colonies breaking away from their former imperial masters, rather than to territories seceding from integrated federations like Canada. Second, the convention has been ratified by only a handful of nations, but not by any major industrialized countries, including either Canada or any of Canada's major creditors.[15] Therefore it has no legal weight.

Third, the Vienna Convention is hopelessly vague on the question of debt division. It says only that debt "[shall be divided] in an equitable proportion, taking into account, in particular, the property, rights and interests [transferred to the successor state]." But what is meant by "an equitable proportion"? The secretariat of the Bélanger-Campeau Commission chose to interpret this phrase as implying that since 18.5 percent of Canada's federally owned assets are located on Quebec territory, it would be equitable for the province to assume only 18.5 percent of the federal debt.[16] But Quebec's percentage of Canada's population or GDP could easily be regarded as a more "equitable proportion." Furthermore, the secretariat arrived at the 18.5 percent figure through the use of some questionable valuation techniques.[17]

Fourth, the relevant section of the convention refers only to government-to-government debt; it makes no mention whatever of debts owed to private creditors. This has led Quebec lawyers Daniel Desjardins and Claude Gendron to argue convincingly that while the provisions of the Vienna Convention relating to assets are authoritative, the provisions relating to debts are of no weight.[18] Desjardins and Gendron gloomily conclude that "it is . . . difficult to assert conclusively that one theory or rule regarding the liability of the successor state to creditors of the debt of the predecessor state can be uniformly applied in all the diverse cases of state succession."[19]

In short, then, under current institutional arrangements, Quebec's leadership has powerful incentives to attempt to use the debt as a negotiating tool, and the leadership of the Canadian rump state has an incentive to react intemperately. International law provides no clear rules that could be applied to prevent this, and international precedents are few and mostly inapplicable anyway.

THE SOLUTION

We need a Solomon, and you, sir, by virtue of your position can play that role. What I beg you do is this: On coming to Canada, please announce the proportions of the debt which in the judgment of the United States ought to be borne by each party and then inform us — Quebec and English Canada — that either party refusing to accept its full share will be looked upon by the United States as willfully repudiating its financial obligations to the international community and will be treated by the United States like any other country that repudiates its debts.
— Dan Usher, open letter to President Clinton[20]

The best means by which to settle the question of the percentage owed by each party to the federal government's creditors and to determine the manner in which payments should be made would be to use an independently appointed, impartial court or tribunal, the authority of which is constituted so it is in the best interests of both Canada and Quebec to accept and adhere to its decision, even if the content of that decision seems unpalatable. As long ago as 1991, Simon Fraser University economist John Chant observed that the predictable federal response to the Bélanger-Campeau Commission's 18.5 percent/81.5 percent debt division proposal would be to produce an equally one-sided proposal of its own, so as to establish a strong negotiating position. Instead, he proposed, the rest of Canada "should avoid the predictable step of presenting its preferred criterion for debt division, however credible. Instead, it should declare that it seeks Quebec's agreement to refer the issue to an independent arbiter when and if separation becomes a fact. The arbiter would be commissioned to review the two parties' competing positions and use them to determine the division of the debt."[21]

Arbitration is normally used when two disputing governments find that "[their] own efforts to reach a negotiated settlement have been unavailing and are at an impasse, and where neither prefers such a failure to reach agreement to the alternative possibility of continuing to seek settlement through assistance by, or delegation to third parties.

In this case, both parties may choose to ask third parties for help in their attempts to reach an agreement or, at the extreme, they may simply ask or allow a third party to determine the settlement or outcome."[22] In the case of the division of the federal debt, Quebec and the rest of Canada would be at this sort of impasse before negotiations had even started. For this reason, it is pointless even to attempt to engage in bilateral negotiations over the debt. Logically, both parties should agree at the very outset of the secession process to refer the entire question to binding arbitration.

It might prove difficult, however, to ensure that a tribunal's decision would be recognized by both Canada and Quebec as authoritative and final. It would be even more difficult to ensure that the willingness of both parties to be bound by the decision is obvious to all creditors, so as to reduce to the lowest possible level the risk premium that creditors will demand during the period during which arbitration is taking place. A further consideration would be to reduce to a minimum the length of time needed for the tribunal to render its decision, since every delay lengthens the period of uncertainty and increases its associated costs.

There are precedents in Canadian history for the use of arbitration for the purpose of dividing a common debt or resource. Two such examples are outlined below. The appropriate structure for a debt-division panel will become apparent by studying the flaws of the first model (the panel established under Section 142 of the British North America Act for the purpose of dividing the debt of the united province of Canada between the new provinces of Ontario and Quebec) and the merits of the second (the court of arbitration established to determine the maritime boundary between Canada and the French possessions of St. Pierre and Miquelon).

In the course of the 1864 debates and negotiations between the representatives of Britain's North American colonies, preceding the creation of the Dominion of Canada, delegates from Nova Scotia and New Brunswick expressed their unwillingness to allow the government of the new federation to assume responsibility for the debt of the Province of Canada, since this would force taxpayers in the Maritime provinces to participate in paying for debts that had been accumulated exclusively for the benefit of residents of another colony.

That is why it was necessary to divide the debt of the old Province of Canada between the new provinces of Quebec and Ontario. To solve this problem, the Legislative Assembly of the Province of Canada voted on July 27, 1865, "that it is expedient that any Act of the Imperial Parliament which may be passed for the Union of the Colonies of British North America, should contain a provision that the division and adjustment of the debts, credits, liabilities, properties and assets of the Provinces of Upper and Lower Canada, should be referred to the arbitrament of three arbitrators, one to be chosen by the Local Government of Upper Canada, the other by the Local Government of Lower Canada, and the third by the General Government; it being further provided that the selection of the arbitrators shall not take place until after the General Parliament for British North America and Local Legislatures for Upper and Lower Canada have been elected — and that the third arbitrator shall not be a resident in either Upper or Lower Canada."[23]

Section 142 of the British North America Act used essentially the same language to establish a panel that would, following the enactment of the new constitution, allocate the debt. The three members of the panel were to be individually appointed by the governments of Quebec, Ontario, and the Dominion. The decision of any two members would be binding.

Unfortunately, the panel never functioned as intended. The panel's initial meeting took place on August 31, 1869. On July 9, 1870, the Quebec representative, Charles Dewey Day, resigned in protest, claiming that the Dominion and Ontario representatives were conspiring to produce an unfair formula, which would then be used to divide the debt in a manner highly disadvantageous to Quebec. On July 20, the government of Quebec revoked Day's appointment by letters patent and refused to appoint a new member. In the absence of any Quebec representation, the remaining two members reached a decision in September and presented it to Parliament.

There followed an appeal by Quebec to the Judicial Committee of Britain's Privy Council, which was the Empire's highest court of appeal.

The committee ruled that Day had had no right to resign, that the government of Quebec had had no right to revoke his appointment, and that the final 1870 decision was binding. Nonetheless, the government of Quebec refused to accept the legitimacy of the panel's decision; as a result it was politically impossible to enforce the panel's ruling, even though the ruling was technically binding on all parties.

It was not until 1890 that it was possible to gain all-party agreement to establish a second panel, and it was not until 1904 — 37 years after the date of Confederation — that the second panel's decision was ratified by all parties and the dispute was resolved. Even then, it proved necessary for the Dominion government to assume $62,500,000 of the debt of the former Province of Canada in order to gain the signatures of both provincial governments on the final debt division agreement.

Several reasons can be offered for the failure of the panel to bring the debt division issue to a quick resolution. The fact that only the debtors were involved in the discussions, while creditors were excluded, certainly reduced the sense of urgency. This was a luxury that could be tolerated in the 1867-1904 period, when Canadian government debt was minuscule by today's standards. Second, the small size of the panel meant that any member could use the threat of withdrawing from the negotiations as a tactic to gain concessions at the table. This worked because the withdrawal of any member would have the effect of rendering the entire process politically illegitimate in the eyes of the population of the province that had appointed the dissenting member. This is exactly what happened in 1870. Debt division negotiations ground to a halt, while somebody other than the abstaining province (in this case, the federal government) picked up the burden.

In contrast to the disastrous Quebec-Ontario panel, a particularly successful arbitration mechanism was employed by Canada and France in 1989-1992 to resolve the dispute regarding the maritime frontier between Newfoundland and the French *département* of St. Pierre and Miquelon. This five-member panel is an ideal role model for a tribunal to resolve the Quebec-Canada debt-division issue.

Disputes over maritime boundaries are in some respects similar to disputes over debt division. Both sides in the dispute recognize the value of the object of contention (a positive value in the case of disputed waters, and a negative value in the case of disputed debt), and both sides have a strong incentive to invent methods of scuttling negotiations, should the negotiations start to take a turn that looks unfavourable. The primary difference between territorial negotiations and debt negotiations is the relatively leisurely pace at which the negotiations can move in the former case as compared with the latter. The following passage from a book on maritime boundary disputes explains why such issues are better resolved through international arbitration panels rather than through bilateral negotiations. The reader need only substitute the word "debt" for "boundary" in the quote to see the common problem. "Bilateral boundary negotiations tend to be heavily laden with emotional freight. Even when kept secret or private they are likely to become disputatious. Because of their symbolic significance they usually attract the attention of politicians and the public at large more than most other kinds of diplomacy. Not infrequently, therefore, the negotiators of a boundary dispute find they are not the only actors, and that they are required to negotiate with relatively little flexibility in accordance with high-level political directives, which in turn may be perceived as a direct expression of public opinion (or at least colored by an awareness of public sentiment)."[24]

University of Victoria legal scholar Ted McDorman explains why arbitration worked so well in the St. Pierre et Miquelon dispute. These considerations apply equally to the debt division issue: "Factors important in the decision to adjudicate included the frustrating, failed negotiations; the urgency . . . of a resolution; the perceived strength by each country of their legal and political arguments; . . . the negative role the dispute was having on general Canada-France relations; and the realization that an adjudicative-created compromise would be more politically acceptable to a "losing" disputant than a similar, negotiated compromise."[25]

A panel, known as the Court of Arbitration, was established by means of a treaty between Canada and France. Both countries agreed, under Section 10 of the treaty, that "the decision of the Court shall be final and binding." To ensure that neither party would attempt to wiggle out of an unfavourable decision, it was necessary for both parties to enact legislation that ensured in advance that they would comply with the provisions of the treaty. To undo the court's decision would have required special legislative action in either the Parliament of Canada or the French National Assembly.

It is particularly important to note that the court consisted of five members. One of the members (Allan Gotleib) was appointed by the government of Canada, and another (Prosper Weil) was appointed by the government of France. Significantly, the remaining three members of the court represented an absolute majority of its total membership. This meant that the withdrawal of either the Canadian or the French representative (or of both of them) would have had only a limited effect on the legitimacy of the court's findings. In the event, both Gotleib and Weil submitted dissenting opinions; nevertheless, the compromise opinion of the remaining three arbitrators prevailed and was respected by both parties.

The court worked at a slower pace than would be acceptable for a panel charged with the task of dividing the federal debt, but this is a problem that can be easily resolved, as will be shown below. Still, by the standards of the interminable Canada-France boundary dispute, the court produced its findings relatively quickly. Established in March 1989, it announced its decision in June 1992, bringing to a satisfactory conclusion a dispute that had remained unresolved for decades.

In general terms, the model used to resolve the Canada-France boundary dispute will work well if used to adjudicate the division of the federal debt. However, two important changes should be made, which would improve its utility in the context of debt division.

First, the creditor community must have confidence that the three non-Canadian, non-Québécois panelists have the best interests of creditors at heart. The most obvious way of establishing this kind of confidence would be to request that one panelist each be appointed by the governments of the three foreign states in which the largest proportion of federal government bonds are held. This way the panel would include one representative from the United States (where 32 percent of foreign-owned Government of Canada bonds are held), one from Japan (25 percent) and one from the United Kingdom (19 percent).[26] In the event that any of the top three creditor states were unwilling or unable to provide a panelist, the fourth-largest creditor state would be approached, and so on until all three of the positions reserved for foreign panelists had been filled.

Second, the panel must act quickly and decisively. Therefore, an adjudication procedure must be found that allows for rapid decision-making. The history of the role of dispute resolution panels in labour relations indicates that final-offer arbitration is particularly effective in producing fast resolutions. In final-offer arbitration, each party to the dispute submits a complete package of proposals to the panel, in advance of an agreed on deadline. The panel then reviews the two alternate proposals, and chooses either one or the other in its entirety.

Several benefits would arise from the use of the final-offer arbitration technique. First, the job of the panelists would become relatively straightforward. No detailed decisions would be required, merely the approval either of the proposal made by Canada, or of the proposal made by Quebec. This would allow the panel to act in a very timely fashion. Second, the disputing parties would also be forced to act quickly. The court would set a deadline for the submission of the competing proposals. If this deadline was missed by either party, the dispute would immediately be settled by the automatic adoption of the proposal of the other party. As a result, it is unlikely that either side would elect to withhold or delay participation as a means of improving its bargaining position. Third, the nature of the either/or choice being made by the panel would force both parties to present moderate proposals (although it is natural that each side would set terms at least minimally in its own favour). Because final-offer arbitration eliminates much of the distance between the proposals presented by either side, it makes the final choice considerably more palatable to the "loser" than would otherwise have been the case. This feature would be of considerable importance in a situation where each additional percentage point of the debt that is assigned to one party or the other represents six billion dollars.

Binding arbitration would be advantageous to both Quebec and the rest of Canada. But clearly Canada, as the party with its name on the bonds and the treasury bills in the hands of creditors, would benefit even more than Quebec. Because of this asymmetry, it remains possible that Quebec's post-referendum leadership might conclude that the question of Quebec's participation in a deficit adjudication process should itself be treated as a point of negotiation. It is vital that this not be permitted to happen.

This is why it is so important that the panel consist not merely of impartial individuals, but of impartial individuals who are the representatives of the governments of states that are both key creditors and major trading partners. If, in the wake of a pro-secession vote, the government of Quebec were to refuse to participate or to regard itself as bound by the panel's decision, a clear and important message would be sent to the governments of the United States, the United Kingdom, and Japan about Quebec's willingness to undertake its responsibilities as a trade and treaty partner.

In this way, debt division would be intimately connected with Quebec's entry into NAFTA, although the causal connection between the two would run in the direction opposite to the one suggested by Lucien Bouchard when he warned that failure on Canada's part to secure NAFTA entry for Quebec might cause the Quebec government to withhold paying its share of the federal debt. With the causal order between Quebec's repayment and Quebec's entry into NAFTA now reversed, it would be the United States rather than the government of Canada that would become the enforcer of debt repayment provisions,[27] and the government of Quebec could almost certainly be depended on to make full and prompt payments on the share of the debt that had been assigned to it under the arbitration process.

Moreover, the final results of the debt division process would probably be reasonably attractive to the separatists. In practice, the arbitration process would likely result in Quebec's being assigned a somewhat smaller share of the federal debt than would be justified by its current share of the Canadian GDP. This outcome is probable because it would represent the most advantageous terms to Canada's creditors — in other words, the terms most likely to produce full and prompt repayment from both countries. The creditors would want to establish terms under which neither Quebec nor the rest of Canada would be burdened in a manner disproportionate to its ability to pay. For this reason, the creditors would be likely to take into account the fact that most economists have concluded that Quebec's economy would be likely to suffer more direct damage as a result of separation than the combined economies of the other provinces. Quebec's GDP would shrink relative to Canada's; this would reduce Quebec's ability to pay, and it would therefore also shrink the share of the total debt burden that the arbitration panel would want to assign to the new republic.[28]

On the other hand, it is also probable that payment terms would be arranged so that Quebec would make its payments directly to creditors, rather than making payments to Ottawa in the expectation that Ottawa would make final payments to all creditors for the entire amount of a jointly held debt. This outcome is likely because Canada's creditors, and hence the panelists, would take into account the fact that separate direct payment would be more likely to produce full payment than joint responsibility for the entire amount, since it would terminate Quebec's ability to withhold or delay payments to Ottawa for jointly held debt obligations. The desire to avoid assigning "joint and several" liability for the debt will be particularly strong following the unhappy experience with joint liability for the debts of the former Soviet Union.

Finally, the panelists would take into account other factors. For example, they would probably insist that if Quebec is partitioned and a proportion of its population remains a part of Canada at the time of secession, Canada would accept responsibility for a correspondingly larger share of the federal debt, and a share of Quebec's provincial government debt as well. Similarly, if Newfoundland uses the independence of Quebec as an opportunity to terminate the Churchill Falls contract, or if the Cree are successful in asserting their ownership over the James Bay hydro-electric project, Canada would be expected to assume either a large proportion of Hydro-Québec's debt burden or a correspondingly larger share of the total federal debt.[29]

None of this will come to pass, however, unless Parliament enacts the legislation necessary to create and finance such a panel substantially in advance of the date of an actual secession crisis. This planning is needed in order to gain the agreement of the American, British, and Japanese governments to participate in the appointment of panelists, well before they may actually be needed.

So far, one federal government after another has shown a remarkable unwillingness to discuss any contingency plans to deal either with debt division or with any other aspect of secession. Although there are occasional rumblings that federal cabinets over the years have prepared secret contingency plans, no overt actions have ever been taken, or even proposed.[30] One observer has even suggested that, to the extent that successive federal governments have had a strategy to deal with secession, that strategy has been simply to avoid dealing with any of the nuts and bolts of reconstituting the country, on the theory that this will drive up the costs of separation, thereby frightening Quebecers into voting to remain in Canada. He warns that, thanks to this strategy, "all the uncertainty about the constitutional and economic future will immediately hit Quebec and ROC as a sharp rock on the day after a referendum. So transition costs would be very much increased. In fact, it is hard to think of a more effective way of *maximizing* these costs than to refuse to contemplate how to cope with sovereignty until it occurs."[31]

This strategy might have made sense when Quebec secession was a less likely referendum outcome than it is today. As far as the debt is concerned, however, it is time to abandon uncertainty and to lay out real, practical, cost-minimizing rules. Canadians will not soon forgive the prime minister who lets the country wander unprepared into yet another sovereignty referendum.

SCOTT REID

NOTES

1 John Chant, "Dividing the Debt: Avoiding the Burden," in John McCallum, ed., *Closing the Books: Dividing Federal Assets and Debt If Canada Breaks Up* (Toronto: C. D. Howe Institute, 1991), p. 85.
2 Bouchard is quoted in Tu Tranh Ha, "Canada Will 'Beg' for Talks: Bouchard," *The Globe and Mail*, September 28, 1995, pp. A1, A4.
3 Gauthier is quoted in Terrance Wills, "Canada Would Beg for Talks: Bloc," *The Gazette* (Montreal, September 28, 1995, pp. A1, A6.
4 Parizeau is quoted in Philip Authier, "Quebec Could Split in 'Weeks or Months': Parizeau," *The Gazette* (Montreal), October 21, 1995, p. A15.
5 See "Campeau Under Heavy Fire for Hinting at Debt-dodging," *The Gazette* (Montreal), February 8, 1995, pp. A1, A10.
6 Currency analyst Martin Murenbeeld is quoted in Greg Ip, "Turmoil Feared If Vote Is Yes," *The Globe and Mail*, October 30, 1995, p. B1.
7 Bud Jorgensen, "Timing Critical for Debt Rollover," *The Financial Post*, January 13, 1995, p. A5.
8 Deliberate initiation of a full default does not mean that debt payments would not be resumed in the longer term. As Dane Rowlands observes, "The empirical evidence regarding repudiation is unequivocal. There are no modern cases of a country repudiating its foreign debt without provoking international condemnation and being subjected to penalization. . . . The first key lesson from sovereign debt theory is that the threat of repudiation is simply not credible." See Dane Rowlands, "International Aspects of the Division of Debt Under Secession: The Case of Quebec," *Canadian Public Policy*, 23:1 (1997), p. 44. From a purely financial point of view, a policy of deliberate repudiation would in practice amount to a high-cost method of inviting a very intrusive form of international supervision of debt repayment over the succeeding period.
9 See Alan Freeman and Patrick Grady, *Dividing the House: Planning for a Canada Without Quebec* (Toronto: HarperCollins, 1995.), pp. 121–22.
10 Jacques Parizeau "What does Sovereignty Association Mean?" Speech delivered at a joint meeting of the Empire Club of Canada and the Canadian Club, Toronto, December 11, 1990.
11 Until now, the pattern has been for the partisans of separation to make their debt-division scenarios more extreme that the one proposed by Bélanger-Campeau, rather than more moderate. Thus, for example, a 1995 study prepared for the Parti Québécois indicated that Quebec ought to accept only 17.4 percent of the federal debt. See Robert McKenzie, "Sovereign Quebec Debt Should Be 17.4%: Study," in *The Toronto Star*, June 2, 1995, p. A11.
12 The threat of cutting off power in the event of secession has already been raised by the current premier. See Canadian Press, "Separate and Lose Power Deal, Tobin Warns Quebec," November 20, 1996.
13 In his book, *L'accession a la souveraineté et le cas du Québec*, Jacques Brossard cites two other examples. A population-based formula was employed when the Danish territories of

Schleswig and Holstein were annexed by Prussia in 1864. The Prussian Government agreed to assume a share of the Danish crown debt proportionate to the population of the annexed territories as a percentage of the total Danish population. An entirely different method was employed in 1913, following the Balkan Wars. The victorious Balkan states, each of which had just annexed a considerable chunk of formerly Turkish-ruled territory, agreed to assume a portion of the Ottoman debt based upon the fiscal contribution of each of the newly excised territories in the three preceding years to the Ottoman Empire's central treasury. See Jacques Brossard, *L'accession à la souveraineté et le cas du Québec* (Montreal: Les presses de l'université de Montréal), 1976, p. 676.

14 Patrick Grady, *The Economic Consequences of Quebec Sovereignty* (Vancouver: Fraser Institute, 1991), p. 99.

15 As at December 31, 1993, the following countries had signed the Vienna Convention: Algeria, Argentina, Egypt, Estonia, Georgia, Niger, Peru, Yugoslavia, and Ukraine. See United Nations, *Multilateral Treaties Deposited with the Secretary-General: Status as at 31 December 1993*. Section III.13, p. 89.

16 In adopting this position, the Secretariat effectively endorsed what has come to be known as the "American doctrine of state succession," or "the burden and benefit" doctrine. This rule was developed in the late nineteenth century by the United States and Britain, both of which were actively involved in the process of accumulating territory but were anxious to avoid accumulating the associated debts. The burden and benefit doctrine holds that the value of the liabilities being assumed by a successor state should not be disproportionately larger than the value of its assets. See, for example, Herbert Wilkinson, "The American Doctrine of State Succession" in T. T. Poulose (ed.), *Succession in International Law* (New Delhi: Orient Longman, 1974), p. 144; M. H. Hoeflich, "Through a Glass Darkly: Reflections Upon the History of the International Law of Public Debt in Connection with State Succession" *University of Illinois Law Review*, vol. 1 (1982), p. 39. This doctrine never completely superseded the previously dominant rule, under which successor states had assumed an absolute obligation to pay a full proportionate share of the predecessor state's public debt. In the aftermath of the World War I some scholars still supported the doctrine that the debts of the defunct German, Austro-Hungarians, and Ottoman empires should be assumed in whole by their successors. (See, for example, Ernst Feichenfeld, *Public Debts and State Succession* (New York: Macmillan, 1931), pp. 546-570, 624-630.) As Patrick Monahan observes, the result has been that "the ensuing confusion on this issue has persisted throughout the twentieth century, with the result that it is very difficult to state that a customary rule of international law has emerged." (See Patrick Monahan, "Cooler Heads Shall Prevail: Assessing the Costs and Consequences of Quebec Seaparation," Toronto: C. D. Howe Institute, commentary no. 65, January 1995.)

17 For example, see Paul Booth, Barbara Johnston, and Karrin Powys-Lybbe, "Dismantling Confederation: The Divisive Question of the National Debt" in *Closing the Books: Dividing Federal Assets and Debt If Canada Breaks Up* (Toronto: C. D. Howe Institute, 1991), pp. 31-33 and 36-42.

18 Daniel Desjardins and Claude Gendron, "Issues Concerning the Division of Assets and

Debt in State Succession: The Canada - Quebec Debate," in *Closing the Books: Dividing Federal Assets and Debt If Canada Breaks Up.* Toronto: C. D. Howe Institute, 1991, pp. 5-7.

19 *Ibid.*

20 Dan Usher, "A Word in Your Ear, President Clinton," *The Globe and Mail*, January 25, 1995, p. A19.

21 John Chant, "Dividing the Debt: Avoiding the Burden," in John McCallum, ed., *Closing the Books: Dividing Federal Assets and Debt if Canada Breaks Up.* Toronto: C. D. Howe Institute, 1991, p. 89.

22 R. B. Bilder, "International Third Party Dispute Settlement," *Denver Journal of International Law and Politics*, vol. 17, 1989, pp. 477-78.

23 Quoted in G. P. Browne, ed., *Documents on the Confederation of British North America* (Toronto: McClelland and Stewart, 1969), p. 196.

24 D. M. Johnston, *The Theory and History of Ocean Boundary-Making* (Kingston, ON: McGill-Queens University Press, 1988), p. 27.

25 *Ibid.*, p. 57.

26 Canada, Department of Finance, *Debt Operations Report*, Ottawa, September 1994, p. 16.

27 This is the causal connection predicted by Stephen Clarkson in "The United States and Independent Quebec," *Canada Watch*, vol. 3 (March-April 1995), p. 76.

28 See Dane Rowlands, "International Aspects of the Division of Debt Under Secession: The Case of Quebec" *Canadian Public Policy*, 23:1 (1997), p. 46; also Sandra Rubin, "Separate Quebec Would Default," *The Ottawa Citizen*, May 11, 1995, p. A10.

29 Dane Rowlands observes that the final ownership of Quebec's extensive hydro-electric infrastructure would have a significant impact on the province's ability to pay on its own debt obligations, and therefore would be taken into account by any international board of arbitration. See Rowlands, "International Aspects," p. 47.

30 In June 1997, *The Ottawa Citizen* ran a series of articles in which cabinet minutes from the Trudeau era, discussing the need for contingency planning, were discussed. A review of the actual cabinet minutes, which became public documents as a result of access to information requests filed by the author of the articles, reveals that no detailed plans were laid out at that time, and a decision was made to avoid giving credibility to the claims of the separatists by preparing public plans for dealing with the practical aspects of secession. See Jack Aubrey, "Trudeau's Secret Quebec Plan," in *The Ottawa Citizen*, June 16, 1997, pp. A1, A2; Cabinet minutes for January 12, 1977; Cabinet minutes for January 13, 1977.

31 Robert Young, "The Political Economy of Secession: The Case of Quebec" in *Constitutional Political Economy*, 5:2 (1994), p. 236.

CONSERVATIVE
AT HEART

MICHAEL COREN

Most people in the conservative movement, or in politics at large, have at some time or other played the game of definitions and have tried to outline a specific belief system. The great and the not so great have played it. Edmund Burke and Russell Kirk certainly tried; Winston Churchill and Michael Oakeshott did their best; Matthew Arnold and Margaret Thatcher made their contributions. Generally the game of definitions is at best only mildly helpful. And it is also completely inevitable.

Conservatism. The dictionary does not help us very much, particularly as political terms are dynamic and mutable, whereas by their nature literal definitions do not change or, if they do, take generations to do so. *The Concise Oxford Dictionary* defines conservatism as a philosophy "averse to rapid change" and as being "moderate, avoiding extremes." The elegant, eclectic, and eccentric *Brewer's Dictionary of Phrase and Fable* defines a conservative as "one who essentially believes in amending existing institutions cautiously and who opposes doctrinaire changes." Better, but still problematic, is *The Oxford Dictionary of Philosophy*: "Originally in Burke an ideology of caution in departing from the historical roots of a society, or in changing its inherited traditions and institutions. In this 'organic' form it includes allegiance to tradition, community, hierarchy of rank, benevolent paternalism, and properly subservient underclasses. By contrast, conservatism can be taken to imply a laissez-faire ideology of untrammelled individualism that puts the emphasis on personal responsibility, free markets, law and order, and a minimal role for government, with neither community, nor tradition, nor benevolence entering more than marginally. The two strands are not easy to reconcile, either in theory or in practice."

Whether we like it or not, today it is even more difficult to attach definitions to conservatism, and even more imperative. Not because conservatives are less ideological or philosophical than in the past. But, ironically, precisely because they are more ideological and philosophical than in the past. What was often an essentially pragmatic and emotional political creed has become for many people a doctrine and even a dogma. It is difficult, for example, for me to forget the faces of the young Scottish students surrounding their beloved leader, Margaret Thatcher, at a British Conservative party conference in the early 1980s. Brandishing their copies of the works of Friedrich Hayek and Milton Friedman like Maoists with little red books, they screamed their devotion to The Leader and chanted in unison "Privatize the mines, privatize the mines!" A very different picture to that of the creative apathy surrounding past Tory prime ministers such as Stanley Baldwin and Harold Macmillan.

Those young people, and their comrades in Europe and in North America, had embraced a conservatism that has variously been described as libertarianism or neoconservatism. Yet even these terms are inadequate, if not misleading. Because the term *neoconservative* is used in both a constructive and pejorative way, it too has no exact meaning. It signifies different things to different people, different things in different countries. Even more difficult, there are people on the far left as well as on the conservative right who call themselves libertarians. Though few in numbers these days, there do exist libertarian socialist groups, influenced by liberals such as John Stuart Mill as well as anarchists such as Kropotkin

and Bakunin. But it is the libertarian conservatives who are most significant. They stand for a completely free economic market, demanding free
trade, low taxation, and the withdrawal of the state from the economic life
of the country and of its citizens. Many of them then apply this notion to
the non-economic world, desiring the so-called free market to dictate
decisions in the moral, ethical, and social realms.

Thus we are in the midst of linguistic as well as political problems. But
difficulties can be energizing and enlightening. The conservative movement is arguably more thoughtful and intellectually grounded than at
any time in its history. Yet it is this intellectual evolution that has further
divided conservatism. Those who call themselves social conservatives
are often marginalized by others on the right as having been somehow
left behind by this intellectual development. They are thought to be
old-fashioned or reactionary, to be red-necks or religious extremists.
The far from conservative economist John Maynard Keynes said, "I do
not know which makes a man more conservative — to know nothing
but the present, or nothing but the past." I like to think that genuine
social conservatives, unlike some of their rivals, understand the past as
well as the present. They learn from mistakes as well as triumphs. They
are rooted in history, which enables them to comprehend the present
and grasp the future.

There is no explicit and distinct credo around which social conservatives gather, but there are certain principles and unchanging ideas and
ideals that help illuminate social conservatism.

These consist of a belief that the family and the community, rather
than the individual, are the basis of society, and that without strong families and the legal and constitutional defence of the same, society will
disintegrate. A belief that the ideal and natural family is composed of a
married man and woman and their children. A belief that single-parent
families do of course occur and while capable of being vital and valid
units, often involving heroic sacrifice, should not be seen in any way as
an ideal. A belief that same-sex couples do not constitute families
and that when science is exploited to give such people children it is
the wrong and immoral use of science. A belief that marriage can only

be between a man and a woman. A belief that life begins at conception and ends at natural death and that abortion is the taking of the life of an unborn child. A belief that euthanasia is unacceptable, no matter how compassionate some people allegedly and wrongly think it to be. A belief that the state has not only a right but a duty to intervene in some areas of personal life. Censorship of pornography, for example, is a valid expression of government, as is the control of prostitution or of certain forms of hateful speech.

A belief that economic freedom, while desirable, does not necessarily guarantee a good and fair society and is not an end in itself — nor, in a moral vacuum, is it even a means to an end. A belief that any nation-state has a responsibility to guard its borders and that while immigration is essential and valuable it may, must, also be controlled. The needs of the host population as well as the potential citizen must be taken into account, and while compassion must always be a key factor in deciding who is allowed into a country, it is vital that the needs of that nation's economy are taken into account. A state also has the right to guarantee that newcomers are not criminals, that they are prepared to work and observe the manners of the nation. While issues of colour, race, and religion are irrelevant, issues of national commitment and respect for democracy, family, and the rule of law are vital. Countries have identities and must be more than a collection of economically profitable shopping malls. A belief that while the individual has a fundamental right to be free, he has to be free within the limits of an ethical society and that freedom must not infringe on that of others. The freedom, for example, to use illegal drugs or to promote violence is not freedom at all but glorified selfishness. A belief that we do not live in splendid isolation but in far more splendid union with others.

A belief that while not every citizen believes in God, organized religion and the Judeo-Christian concepts that formed modern Europe and North America must be respected and honoured; that we are all products of natural law and directly influenced by its ramifications. A belief that tradition is a binding, unifying, and positive force and that faith, honour, duty, authority, and patriotism are constants. A belief in equality under the law, irrespective of race, gender, or religion. A belief that while human beings are capable of noble, great, and even angelic acts their natures are not perfect and often have to be controlled by the government. A belief that a democratically elected government, supported by an independent judiciary, is the only legitimate body that can form laws and exercise state authority.

Some of these issues have become particularly divisive both within the conservative movement and outside of it. Abortion, for example, is a subject that splits the movement profoundly. Some neoconservatives and many others simply cannot understand what all the fuss is about. They believe that life begins only at birth and that it makes economic sense to control the population. They also see the issue as a digression from matters fiscal. If, as the vast majority of social conservatives believe, abortion is nothing less than the killing of a child, the issue can be nothing other than central and the battle never-ending. To ask a social conservative, a pro-lifer, to bend and adapt on the subject of abortion would be like asking any other man to not mind so much about the beheading of his mother or, more exactly, the genocide of an entire people. It is an issue that cannot be overstated because it is an issue of life and death. In comparison, levels of taxation and notions of free trade do tend to diminish in importance.

This social conservative belief is based on a massive support of evidence, research, and argument. It runs as follows. It is a proven fact that human life begins at conception and there can be no other starting point. Apart from anything else, a baby is genetically complete at conception. The child's heart is beating by the 25th day and three days later its legs, arms, eyes, and ears are already beginning to form. The child's brain has distinctly human features by this period. The first bone cells appear in the sixth week and begin to replace the cartilage of the already complete skeleton. The child's milk teeth begin to form in the following week. By this time its fingers, thumbs, ankles, and toes have also begun to form. By the tenth week all the child's limbs and organs are established and it can turn its head, bend its elbows and wrists, and even make facial gestures such as frowning. The child is also — and this is extremely important — sensitive to touch. This is now quite obviously a human being, even to the layman's eye. By the twelfth week the child can swallow, its fingernails have started to grow, and its ribs and vertebrae have become bone. The child's vocal cords are complete and its reproductive organs are well advanced. Inherited physical features can also be discerned at this stage — the child looks like its father or mother. At sixteen weeks it is half its birth length and its heart pumps at the rate of about 50 pints a day. Eyebrows and eyelashes have begun by the fifth month and the child now turns, kicks, and sucks its thumb. The birth of the child four months later is simply an incident in an already advanced process.

As a pro-life pamphlet puts it, "If it is wrong to kill a child at birth it must be wrong to kill him at 28 weeks, sixteen weeks, twelve weeks, eight weeks, four weeks. Human life is human life is human life. It is entirely arbitrary to pick a moment and say: now he's human, before that he wasn't. Human development is a continuous process, a steady 'becoming,' from conception onwards." This is true for an unborn advocate of abortion as much as it is for an unborn advocate of life.

The issue of homosexuality is another subject that polarizes countries and conservatives within those countries. Many in the conservative movement have been caught up in the essentially liberal and modernistic concept of toleration. They are convinced that a good person is a tolerant person and a very good person is an extremely tolerant person. I tolerate therefore I am.

A tolerance of differing opinions or of a different religion in a kind of open market of ideas is, of course, absolutely essential and an indication of civilization. Indeed, social conservatism regards such tolerance as an essential foundation. But the modern world has reinterpreted tolerance to mean something entirely different: the refusal to pass an opinion and to discern the difference between right and wrong, to indulge in moral equivalence. Ironically, when social conservatives do express their opinions about what is right and wrong, they are attacked and abused by "tolerant" liberals as being "intolerant."

For some neoconservatives the argument over homosexuality goes further. As they believe that every person is primarily an economic unit their sexual activity is really quite irrelevant. Many social conservatives, on the other hand, believe that we are creatures, made with a specific purpose and intended to follow a specific way of life. Homosexuality, while to be tolerated in an open and free society, is not to be encouraged or treated on an equal footing with heterosexuality. Man and woman are more, much more, than the sum of their economic worth. Procreation is not the sole purpose of marriage but it is a crucial one. If homosexuals can be married to each other, why not brothers and sisters, parents and children? It is also naive and disingenuous to argue that if homosexual couples are acknowledged by the state, and by some anti-Christian churches, as being married, this does not alter life for the majority of people. Such an act directly warps the importance and validity of heterosexual marriage. The actions of the individual affect more than the individual who takes the action and the individuals around them. These actions also affect the entire community.

Then we have the issues of pornography and censorship. These are subjects that, like rocks thrown into a conservative pool, send out ripples in all directions. Many conservatives are reluctant to indulge in censorship, believing that in a perfect world the individual should be allowed complete freedom of expression and freedom to read. This was a tenable position at one time but, I believe, is no longer so. As social conservatives themselves are repeatedly told, times do change. A 1914 pacifism in the face of the kaiser's foolishness, for example, would be completely different from a 1939 pacifism in the face of the fuhrer's Nazism. While opponents of censorship delight in mocking the rather absurd banning of books such as *Lady Chatterly's Lover* or even the delightful Tintin cartoons, they fail or refuse to look at the current situation.

Take, for example, the case of Dennis Cooper, a writer highly regarded in some circles. He is championed by many as just the sort of author the state has no right to regulate. Let us take one of his stories, a work entitled "Frisk." Here a man is murdered for sexual kicks, he is humiliated and hit, he is tortured, and his rectum is used for gruesome and grotesque purposes. "He opened his eyes very wide," writes Cooper. "Otherwise he didn't fight me at all. It takes a lot longer to strangle someone than you'd think." The victim is fifteen.

Or, from the same story, an account of the rape, sexual beating, and murder of a boy whose excrement the author has just eaten. The victim's penis is cut in two and he is decapitated. The narrator masturbates over this. Friends arrive. "They kicked the corpse around for a while. This created a pretty hilarious fireworks display of blood."

Or how about a repugnantly graphic story by one Ann Wertheim about incestuous rape. In this elaborately constructed lesbian fantasy, the victim is shown as enjoying herself as she welcomes agonizing penetration, oral sex, and physical violence from her father.

Cooper's and Wertheim's stories appeared in a book entitled *Forbidden Passages*, a collection of banned writings that, paradoxically, is now available in Canada. Of the last piece, one of the compilers of the anthology wrote that when it came into her office "several of us nearly fainted from intense levels of sexual heat." Now imagine if we read of a group of Klansmen describing the beating, torture, and murder of a Black teenager, with graphic detail and description, and then read in an introduction to a collection of banned writings that one of the editorial staff almost fainted over this particular story because of the racist passion in the office. Both involve an innocent, bewildered victim, both involve breaking the moral and the civil law, and both should be anathema to societal standards.

We can at least defeat hate literature, Holocaust denial, and the like with simple fact. But the literary depiction of sadistic pedophilia and the sexual torture of children is not about fact but about a basic immoral stance. This is much harder to control, partly because these things involve intellectual as well as physical masturbation. But none of us, surely, still believes that there is no link between pornography and crime.

The questions often asked are, Where do we draw the line? and, Who is to do the drawing? The answers are not as complex as some would have us believe and need not be extreme or even noticeable to the overwhelming majority of people. We draw lines of limitation every day and give MPs, judges, police officers, and teachers the authority to use ethical pencils. Individual customs officers, overworked and underqualified, are not the most suitable guardians of our literary borders, but there is no reason why a panel of judges should not decide on what is allowed to enter the country. We allow, after all, such a system to control the flow of people into Canada and it is surely axiomatic that one book is capable of much more harm than a single man or woman.

Conservatism is a living ideology and as such it has to be able to adapt and to change, without losing sight and sound of its essentials. It is also about practicality and about practical politics. Its oxygen is reality. It was and is produced by the world and the world's events, unlike other political beliefs, conceived only to shape the world and the world's events. It reacts to reality, as it did, for example, to the summer of 1997. This was not a peculiar season, not an extraordinary season, not an atypical season in Canadian history. We could probably take any few months from the last decade and extract similar events. The summer of 1997 does reveal, however, certain events that illustrate the issues facing and defining contemporary social conservatism.

There was the topless issue, a subject that delighted the headline writers but had a far more significant effect on society at large. After a series of court decisions and appeals it was decided in Ontario that women should be allowed to go about in public with their breasts exposed. Toplessness was now legally permitted on the street as well as on the beach. A group of judges decided that women should be allowed to show their boobs to any boobs who might be interested. This represented a profound change in what society believed to be decent and moral and that very society protested against such change with demonstrations and petitions.

This was also a direct challenge to social conservatives, who see social engineering, the forced and contrived elimination of gender differences, and aggressive changes to existing societal standards as a fundamental attack upon society and community. The argument put forward by the equality fanatics was that because men were permitted to bare their chests, women should be allowed the same right. Women's breasts, however, are directly sexual, the second most erogenous part of a woman's body, and are also more biologically intimate in that they are used for nursing children. Also, only certain types of men would walk along the streets topless, because a thin T-shirt prevents sunburn and may deflect heat. Be they the owners of beer-bellies or perfect pectorals, those men who want to show their upper bodies to the greater world are usually making a deeper, more neurotic point. We should be dissuading them, not persuading others.

The only generally acceptable form of exposure is during nursing, and we should encourage women to feed their children whenever and wherever they want. Breast-feeding represents much of what is best about humanity, such as love, procreation, and family. But the so-called Breast-Walkers' reasoning represents the precise opposite of the nursing scenario, and their behaviour is the contrary of natural. It is full not of care and bonding, but of egotism and perversity.

Which brings us back to the great modern myth of tolerance, the great bullying chimera of the social conservative. Because the legal blessing of toplessness was seen as being tolerant it was welcomed by some as a progressive action. Social conservatism, ever pragmatic, should ask two questions: How many of these people would feel comfortable conducting a conversation with a 70-year-old lady who had her breasts exposed, and how many of them would allow their children to be taught by a bare-breasted woman? Defenders of the decision also argued that few women would take advantage of the ruling anyway. If that was the case, there was no need to alter a fundamental of society. It is true that no emotionally, sexually, and politically mature woman would expose herself in public, but equally true that some politically extreme women are not particularly mature.

The freedom of a small group of people to do what is contrary to the dictates and history of civilized society now overwhelms the freedom of the majority. A restaurant is crowded with families. One woman enters, swinging her exposed breasts. She is indeed free to act in such a manner. And as a consequence, the men and women in that room have to explain to their children, justify to themselves, change their values and virtues, leave the restaurant. This is not liberty but licence.

At around the same time that the courts were making a mountain out of something, well, something much smaller, there came a fine decision by the Supreme Court that the act of lap-dancing was indecent. This made it much easier for the police to ban such activities and arrest those involved. Here was morality meeting the free market, the social conservative meeting his neocon brother. The neocon argued that individuals have the right to do what they want with their own bodies and that the free market is sacred and lap-dancing is merely a form of financial transaction. They also stated that the court had enforced a particular morality when morals are not universal.

The social conservative response is that lap-dancing involves several people. The man paying the money, the woman dancing, the club owner, and the rest of us who make up general society. The man with the cash may, after the court's decision, have his freedom restricted, but not so the dancer. There are very few women who willingly prostitute themselves, but many who do so out of economic desperation. A single mother in near poverty is not acting from her own free will. Nor is she free to choose where she dances. Any club owner knows that if a neighbouring venue offers lap-dancing, he will have to follow suit to maintain his clientele. Men will not patronize a non-touching club if there is a full-contact one down the road. Thus, a dancer no longer has any choice. She was uneasy with stripping, but at least she was not mauled. Before lap-dancing became common she could retain a modicum of dignity by merely dancing or stripping on stage.

As for the wider community, I have yet to hear any convincing argument that our physical, spiritual, ethical, or educational well-being is in any way improved by allowing lap-dancing. I have, however, heard many arguments that permitting such an indulgence eats away at the very core of our society. There is such a thing as collective responsibility.

Then come the arguments concerning the free market. For a market to be genuinely free, the participants must enjoy something like equal rights and privileges. A union stranglehold or a business monopoly prevents true economic liberty. So what of the pimps, pushers, bouncers, and brutal club owners? Indeed, a former lap-dancer said after the

court decision that the clubs will now be free of "the pigs and the pros-
titutes." To assume that a dancer is able to choose her place of work and
her working conditions and is able to keep an equitable share of the
evening's proceeds is laughable.

Those who are so concerned with the free market would do well to
read the arguments of those men in the last century who employed ten-
year-old chimney-sweeps. They said the boys were not being forced into
the work and that the lads were paid and cared for. Because the society
of the time had less refined and sensitive views towards child labour, it
accepted such a defence. Yet when reformers educated that society, the
arguments of the child exploiters suddenly blew away like dirty ashes.

The same will happen if, and when, we educate our society about the
reality of sexual commercialism and its ethical consequences. The state
has a right to limit and control the outer limits of the market so such a
market can be, in the most authentic sense, truly free.

Last comes the issue of morality. We impose something like a universal morality a great deal of the time, precisely because it is considered
universal. Those who argue that the state has no right to decide what is
right and wrong put themselves in a contradictory position. They come
to their conclusions in the first place solely because they themselves
have their own theories of right and wrong and, consequently, impose
them on the state and its decisions. If there is no such entity as universal morality there can be no such thing as conservatism. We cannot
conserve what is not at least largely static in its fundamental ethical
framework. What is extraordinary about the world is not how many
moral codes have existed down the ages but how few there have been.
Agreement on the essentials is almost unanimous.

As all this was going on in Canada in the summer of 1997, Toronto
celebrated Gay Pride Week. Social conservatives have been extraordinarily accepting over the past decade in accommodating extremist
challenges from homosexual groups. This particular celebration of
the homosexual subculture, however, went beyond anything seen in the
past. A police officer, Sergeant Peter Harmsen, announced that he was
disturbed by the men in the Gay Pride parade who marched along the

streets of Canada's largest city with their genitals exposed, with pierced testicles on display, and by those who took part in acts of sado-masochistic sex. In what seemed like an eminently reasonable statement, the officer concluded, "It just seems to be escalating past the point of fair play and common decency. We're certainly concerned. If this type of thing happens next year, we'll stop the parade." But the good sergeant was wrong. In fact the police were not concerned by all these acts of fla-grant lawbreaking. Within 24 hours, a series of statements flowed out from police headquarters. It was announced that Deputy Chief Robert Molyneaux had "no problems with the parade," that the parade would definitely continue, that a debriefing meeting would be held, "but the issue of nude revellers" would not be discussed and, in a statement destined for the quote books, that it was doubtful whether "concerns over some male parade-goers exposing their genitals will even be raised."

That the law was broken was beyond doubt. There was and is a great deal of footage of naked men strolling around in the parade, of acts of indecent exposure, and of bondage and whipping. What was extraordi-nary was how quickly and how vehemently the bureaucrats and high-ranking officers in the police department contradicted Harmsen and how eager they were to excuse the lawbreakers. This support of a special-interest group in turn was contradicted by the police department's reaction to Caribana, the annual West Indian parade through the streets of Toronto. Caribana brings in millions of dollars to the city but was almost cancelled because the police raised objections to the route and to the planning. Someone in the police department stated that Caribana was not "our parade." The West Indian community had to go to great lengths to guarantee that Caribana went ahead. How odd.

Yet Gay Pride organizers seemed willing to make no such changes. One of them, David Dent, said that the "bondage floats" and the nudity were "quite tame" and that he did not find them to be "unacceptable." So now a special-interest group spokesman shapes what is permissible and thus what is the law for the rest of society. Homosexual activists fre-quently try to change the laws to accommodate or protect their own ways of life. That is their right. It is significant, however, that while they want the majority of the population to accept such new laws many homosexual zealots seem intent on mocking and breaking the laws that already accommodate and protect that same majority.

The counter to any such arguments is to scream out accusations of homophobia, a contrived and meaningless word invariably used to silence free debate. But the debate must continue. If a section of society wants to change a country so radically that public sex and genital exhibitionism are standard, let them at least be honest about it. A single person walking along the street without any clothes would be stopped and, if necessary, arrested. Two heterosexuals whipping each other's semi-naked bodies in the middle of a city would, again, be stopped and, if necessary, arrested. The law must apply equally to all, otherwise it is no law at all.

Much of all this concerns how we perceive the nature of state, government, and authority. A healthy fear and mistrust of the state is surely a good thing and something all conservatives should cultivate. But they should also understand the difference between gratuitous state intervention and essential government regulation. Social conservatism accepts the place of the state and sees it not always as a last resort but often as a constructive regulator and intervener. Consider a group of people playing a team sport. They are given complete freedom, in that there is no referee, no uniforms, and no rules. They foul each other, hurt each other, have no idea what is going on, and end up fighting. They are truly free but are not truly happy. What should have been a magnificent sport became an ugly mess. Then consider the team sport in which there are too many rules and the referee is officious and intrusive. The sport becomes a slow, muddy annoyance. The participants are neither free nor happy.

There is, however, a middle way. The rules can be applied intelligently and fairly. The referee can be accountable and understanding, the players are responsible and, knowing that the referee understands the game, can observe the rules. The result is the game as it should be played, with the maximum enjoyment for the maximum number of players. The truly offensive and violent players are taken off. The participants are free in the real sense and happy in a meaningful sense.

The modern state is feared and despised for good reason. It indulges in ludicrous interventions into our daily lives and often seems intent on extending its own power simply for the sake of power itself. But a greater accountability, a change in the electoral process, and a more actively political population could change this, without requiring the disappearance of the state itself. For example, there are currently attempts being made in North America to make it a crime for parents to spank their children. An absurd and offensive example of state interference, often initiated by people who do not have any children. But the state already makes it illegal for parents to physically assault their children, which is surely a good thing. It is the nature of the state and the extent of its power, not its very existence, that have to be questioned.

Let us take the case of the late eighteenth-century social conservative and economic interventionist William Wilberforce, a man who understood and appreciated the dynamic between citizen and state. After this politician's conversion to Christianity he gave himself two goals. He dedicated his life to the abolition of slavery, and to the reformation of the manners of the English people. By slavery, Wilberforce was referring to the wretched kidnapping, sale, and slaughter of Africans by the European powers, a trade that injected fortunes into the economies of Britain, France, Spain, Holland, and other nations. By manners he meant morality.

It could be argued that slavery would have eventually come to an end because human labour was not as efficient as machinery and the free market would have dictated that the slave trade was unprofitable. This is what some Tory MPs and slave owners argued in the 1790s. But Wilberforce argued that this was most unlikely. He was right. He forced an end to European slavery half a century before Abraham Lincoln's declaration and the American Civil War. Slavery still continues in some places to this day. So slavery did not end due to market forces, and we have seen that the free market can be awfully slow in doing what it does. More than this, however, is the essential humanity of conservatism. It is a politics that demands social action. Slavery could only be abolished by the determined intrusion of the state into the lives of individuals, businesses, communities, and even foreign governments. The Royal Navy was obliged to attack foreign slave traders and sometimes kill them. Instead of free trade there was fire trade. If you want to be free, we have to fire.

But while Wilberforce spent decades calling for state action against slavery, he also called for the state to withdraw from the life of the Christian church and to leave religious nonconformists alone. He argued that the Church of England, the national church, should withdraw from national life and that non-Anglican Christians should be allowed full participation in national affairs, without fear of financial penalty or social stigma. He understood when the state should interfere and when the state should leave alone.

Similarly with the reformation of the country's manners. What we think of as Victorian progress, which ironically enabled the free market and economic expansion to occur, only came about after the transformation of England from its eighteenth-century decadence. Wilberforce the social conservative was an integral part of this process. He preached to individuals and groups, but he also lobbied for the government to control the sale of alcohol and to enforce standards in family life.

Another great social conservative, the British journalist and broadcaster Malcolm Muggeridge, once said that "without moral order, a society can have no real order at any level." Now this is interesting. Because many of those who call themselves conservatives and who preach freedom seem to be unaware of this surely self-evident fact. The liberty of the swimmer to float out to sea is actually better known as drowning. There is no example in history of authentic progress without authentic order. Nations and empires were only economically and culturally productive when they were relatively ordered societies, with a suitably strong government. Further, when the moral order of those societies began to decay, economic and political collapse quickly followed. The Roman Empire is only one example of this. First came moral disintegration, then political catastrophe, then what we now think of as the Dark Ages.

Many social conservatives believe that a new dark age may be upon us unless we rethink our ways. The state is being used to end human life rather than to save it. It is being used to open our borders to damaging and obscene literature rather than guarding them against such material. Its legal arm appears to be intent on dismantling the civilized order rather than safeguarding it. G. K. Chesterton said that "all conservatism is based upon the idea that if you leave things alone you leave them as they are. But you do not. If you leave a thing alone you leave it to a torrent of change."

Which is why those in the social conservative movement are intent, in the spirit of true conservatism, on changing much and restoring more. They come not so much to innovate as to renovate. And they must do it now, before it is too late.

CONSCIENCE WILL HAVE ITS REVENGE: NATURAL LAW AND SOCIAL COLLAPSE

J. BUDZISZEWSKI

Things are getting worse very quickly now. The list of what we are required to approve is growing ever longer. Consider just the domain of sexual practice. First we were to approve sex before marriage, then without marriage, now against marriage. First with one, then with a series, now with a crowd. First with the other sex, then with the same. First between adults, then between children, then between adults and children. The last item has not been added yet, but will be soon: you can tell from the change in language, just as you can tell the approach of winter from the change in the colour of leaves. As any sin passes from being tempting, to being tolerated, to being approved, its name is first euphemized, then avoided, then forgotten. A colleague tells me that some of his fellow legal scholars call child molestation "intergenerational intimacy": that's euphemism. A good-hearted editor once tried to talk me out of using the term "sodomy": that's avoidance. My students don't know the word "fornication" at all: that's forgetfulness.

The pattern is repeated in the house of death. First we were to approve of killing unborn babies, then babies in process of birth; next came newborns with physical defects, now newborns in perfect health. Nobel prize laureate James Watson proposes that parents of newborns be granted a grace period during which they may have their babies killed,[1] and in 1994 a committee of the American Medical Association proposed harvesting organs from some sick babies even before they die.[2] First we were to approve of suicide, then to approve of assisting it. Now we are to approve of a *requirement* to assist it, for Ernest van den Haag says that it is "unwarranted" for doctors not to kill patients who seek death.[3] First we were to approve of killing the sick and unconscious, then of killing the conscious and consenting. Now we are to approve of killing the conscious and *protesting*, for in the United States, doctors starved and dehydrated stroke patient Marjorie Nighbert to death despite her pleading "I'm hungry," "I'm thirsty," "Please feed me," and "I want food."[4] Such cases are only to be expected when food and water are now often classified as optional treatments rather than humane care; we have not long to go before joining the Netherlands, where involuntary euthanasia is common. Dutch physician and author Bert Keizer has described his response when a nursing home resident choked on her food: he shot her full of morphine and waited for her to die.[5] Such a deed by a doctor in the land that resisted the Nazis.

Why do things get worse so fast? Of course we have names for the process, like "collapse," "decay," and "slippery slope." By conjuring images — a stricken house, a gangrenous limb, a sliding talus — they make us feel we understand. Now, I am no enemy to word-pictures, but a civilization is not really a house, a limb, or a heap of rocks; it cannot literally fall in, rot, or skid out from underfoot. Images can only illustrate an explanation; they cannot substitute for one. So why *do* things get worse so fast? It would be well to know, in case the process can be arrested.

The usual explanation is that conscience is weakened by neglect. Once a wrong is done, the next wrong comes more easily. On this view conscience is mainly a restraint, a resistance, a passive barrier. It doesn't so much drive us on as hold us back, and when persistently attacked, the restraining wall gets thinner and thinner and finally disappears. Often this explanation is combined with another: that conscience comes from culture, that it is built up in us from outside. In this view the heart is mal-leable. We don't clearly know what is right and wrong, and when our teachers change the lessons, our consciences change their contents. What once we deemed wrong, we deem right; what once we deemed right, we deem wrong.

There is something to these explanations, but neither can account for the sheer dynamism of wickedness — for the fact that we aren't gently wafted into the abyss but violently propel ourselves into it. Nor, as I will show, can either one account for the peculiar quality of our present moral confusion.

I suggest a different explanation. Conscience is not a passive barrier but an active force; though it can hold us back, it can also drive us on. Moreover, conscience comes not from without but from within: though culture can trim the fringes, the core cannot be changed. The reason things get worse so fast must somehow lie not in the weakness of con-science but in its strength, not in its shapelessness but in its shape.

～

Whether paradoxical or not, the view of conscience I defend is nothing new; its pedigree is ancient. In one of the tragedies of Sophocles, the woman Antigone seeks to give her dead brother a proper burial, but is forbidden by the king because her brother was an enemy of the state. She replies to the tyrant that there is another law higher than the state's, and that she will follow it because of its divine authority. Not even the king may require anyone to violate it. Moreover, it requires not only for-bearance from evil but active pursuit of the good: in this case, doing the honours for her brother.

Antigone's claim that this higher law has divine authority can easily be misunderstood, because the Greeks did not have a tradition of verbal revelation. The mythical hero Perseus had never climbed any Mount Sinai; the fabled god Zeus had never announced any Ten Command-ments. So, although the law of which Antigone speaks somehow has divine authority, she has not learned it by reading something like a

Bible, with moral rules delivered by the gods. Instead she seems to be speaking of principles that everyone with a normal mind knows by means of conscience. She seems to be speaking of a law written on the heart — of what philosophers call the natural law.

Now by contrast with the pagan Greeks, Jews and Christians do have a tradition of verbal revelation. Moses did climb the mountain, God did announce the commandments. One might think, then, that Jews and Christians wouldn't have a natural-law tradition because they wouldn't need it. But just the opposite is true. The idea of a law written on the heart is far stronger and more consistent among Jews, and especially Christians, than it was among the pagans. In fact, the very phrase "law written on the heart" is biblical: it comes from the New Testament book of Romans. Judaism calls the natural law the Noahide Commandments because of a rabbinical legend that God had given certain general rules to all the descendants of Noah — that is, all human beings — long before he made His special covenant with the descendants of Abraham. In similar fashion, Christianity distinguishes between "general revelation," which every human being receives, and "special revelation," which is transmitted by witnesses and recorded only in the Bible. General revelation makes us aware of God's existence and requirements so that we can't help knowing that we have a problem with sin. Special revelation goes further by telling us how to solve that problem.

The natural law is unconsciously presupposed — even when consciously denied — by modern secular thinkers, too. We can see the presupposition at work whenever we listen in on ethical debate. Consider, for example, the secular ethic called utilitarianism, which holds that the morally right action is always the one that brings about the greatest possible total happiness. Arguments against utilitarianism by other secularists often proceed by showing that the doctrine yields conclusions contrary to our most deeply held moral intuitions. For instance, it isn't hard to imagine circumstances in which murdering an innocent man might make all the others much happier than they were before. Utilitarianism, seeking the greatest possible total happiness, would require us to murder the fellow; nevertheless we don't, because we perceive that murder is plain wrong. So instead of discarding the man, we discard the theory. Here is the point: such an argument against utilitarianism stakes everything on a *pre*-philosophical intuition about the heinousness of murder. Unless there is a law written on the heart, it is hard to imagine where this intuition comes from.

The best short summary of the traditional, natural-law understanding of conscience was given by the medieval thinker Thomas Aquinas when he said that the core principles of the moral law are the same for all "both as to rectitude and as to knowledge" — in other words, that they are not only right for all but known to all.[6] To be sure, not every moral principle is part of the core, but all moral principles are at least derived from it, if not by pure deduction (killing is wrong and poison kills, so poisoning is wrong), then with the help of prudence (wrongdoers should be punished, but the appropriate punishment depends on circumstances). Our knowledge of *derived* principles may be weakened by neglect and erased by culture, but our knowledge of core principles is ineffaceable. These are the laws we *can't not know*.

Ranged against this view are two others. One simply denies that the core principles are right for all; the other admits they are right for all, but denies they are known to all. The former, of course, is relativism. I call the latter *mere* moral realism — with emphasis on "mere" because natural law is realistic, too, but more so.

Not much need be said here about relativism. It is not an explanation of our decline, but a symptom of it. The reason it cannot be an explanation is that it finds nothing to explain. To the question "Why do things get worse so fast?", it can only return "They don't get worse, only different."

Mere moral realism is a much more plausible opponent, because by admitting the moral law it acknowledges the problem. Things *are* getting worse quickly — plainly because there *isn't* anything we "can't not know." *Everything* in conscience can be weakened by neglect and erased by culture. Now if mere moral realists are right, then although the problem of moral decline may begin in volition, it dwells in cognition: it may begin as a defect of will, but ends as a defect of knowledge. We may have started by neglecting what we knew, but we have now gone so far that we really don't know it any more. What is the result? That our contemporary ignorance of right and wrong is genuine. We *really don't* know the truth, but we are honestly searching for it — trying to see on a foggy night — doing the best that we can. In a sense, we are blameless for our deeds, for we don't know any better.

All this sounds persuasive, yet it is precisely what the older tradition, the natural-law tradition, denies. We *do* know better; we are *not* doing the best we can. The problem of moral decline is volitional, not cognitive; it has little to do with knowledge. By and large we do know right from wrong, but wish we didn't. We only make believe we are searching for truth — so that we can do wrong, condone wrong, or suppress our remorse for having done wrong in the past.

If the traditional view is true, then our decline is owed not to moral ignorance but to moral suppression. We aren't untutored, but "in denial." We don't lack moral knowledge; we hold it down.

⁓

Offhand it seems as though believing in a law we "can't not know" would make it harder, not easier, to explain why things are so quickly getting worse. If the moral law really is carved on the heart, wouldn't it be hard to ignore? On the other hand, if it is merely pencilled in as the mere moral realists say — well!

But this is merely picture thinking again. Carving and pencilling are but metaphors, and more than metaphors are necessary to show why the suppression of conscience is more violent and explosive than its mere weakening would be. First let us consider a few facts that ought to arouse our suspicion — facts about the precise kind of moral confusion we suffer, or say we suffer.

Consider this tissue of contradictions: Most who call abortion wrong call it killing. Most who call it killing say it kills a baby. Most who call it killing a baby think it should be allowed. Most who think it should be allowed think it should be restricted. More and more people favour restrictions. Yet more and more people have had or have been involved in abortions.

Or this one: Most adults are worried about teenage sex. Yet rather than telling kids to wait until marriage, most tell kids to wait until they are "older," as they are. Most say that premarital sex between consenting adults is a normal expression of natural desires. Yet hardly any are comfortable telling anyone, especially their own children, how many people they have slept with themselves.

Or this one: Accessories to suicide often write about the act; they produce page after page to show why it is right. Yet a large part of what they write about is guilt. Author George E. Delury, jailed for poisoning and suffocating his wife, says his guilt feelings were so strong they were "almost physical."[7]

As to the first example, if abortion kills a baby then it ought to be banned to everyone; why allow it? But if it doesn't kill a baby it is hard to see why we should be uneasy about it at all; why restrict it? We restrict what we allow because we know it is wrong but don't want to give it up; we feed our hearts scraps in hopes of hushing them, as cooks in the American south once quieted their kitchen puppies.

As to the second example, sexual promiscuity has exactly the same bad consequences among adults as it has among teenagers. But if it is just an innocent pleasure, then why not talk it up? Swinging is no longer a novelty; the sexual revolution is now gray with age. If shame persists, the only possible explanation is that guilt persists as well.

The third example speaks for itself. Delury calls the very strength of his feelings a proof that they did *not* express "moral" guilt, merely the "dissonance" resulting from violation of a primate instinctual block.[8] We might paraphrase his theory, "the stronger the guilt, the less it matters."

Clearly, whatever our problem may be, it isn't that conscience is weak. We may be confused, but we aren't confused *that* way. It isn't that we don't know the truth, but that we tell ourselves something different.

If the law written on the heart can be repressed, then we cannot count on it to *restrain* us from doing wrong; that much is obvious. I have made the more paradoxical claim that repressing it hurls us into *further* wrong. Holding conscience down doesn't deprive it of its force; it merely distorts and redirects that force. We are speaking of something less like the erosion of an earthen dike so that it fails to hold the water back, than like the compression of a powerful spring so that it buckles to the side.

Here is how it works. Guilt and guilt feelings are not the same thing; men and women can be guilty without having guilt feelings, and they can have guilt feelings without being guilty. True guilt, however, always produces certain objective needs, which make their own demand for satisfaction irrespective of the state of the feelings. These needs include confession, atonement, reconciliation, and justification.

Now when guilt is acknowledged, the guilty deed can be repented so that these four needs can be genuinely satisfied. But when guilt is not acknowledged, they can only be displaced. That is what generates the impulse to further wrong. Taking the four needs one by one, let's see how this happens.

The need to *confess* arises from transgression against what we know, at some level, to be truth. I have already commented on the tendency of accessories to suicide to write about their acts. Besides George Delury, who killed his wife, we may mention Timothy E. Quill, who prescribed lethal pills for his patient,[9] and Andrew Solomon, who participated in the death of his mother. Solomon, for instance, admits explicitly that "the act of speaking or writing about your involvement is, inevitably, a plea for absolution."[10] Many readers will remember the full-page signature advertisements feminists took out in the early days of the abortion movement, telling the world that they had killed their own unborn children. The practitioners of sodomy feel the confessional impulse, too: "coming out" is the central rite of their movement. At first it seems baffling that the sacrament of confession can be inverted to serve the

ends of advocacy. Only by recognizing the power of suppressed conscience can this paradox be understood.

The need to *atone* arises from the knowledge of a debt that must
somehow be paid. One would think such knowledge would always lead
directly to repentance, but the counsellors whom I have interviewed tell
a different story. One woman learned during her pregnancy that her husband had been unfaithful to her. He wanted the child, so to punish him
for betrayal she had an abortion. The trauma of killing was even greater
than the trauma of his treachery, because this time she was to blame.
What was her response? She aborted the next child, too; in her words,
"I wanted to be able to hate myself more for what I did to the first baby."
By trying to atone without repenting, she was driven to repeat the sin.

The need for *reconciliation* arises from the fact that guilt cuts us off from
God and man. Without repentance, intimacy must be simulated precisely
by sharing with others in the guilty act. Leo Tolstoy knew this. In *Anna
Karenina* there comes a time when the lovers' mutual guiltiness is their
only remaining bond. But the phenomenon is hardly restricted to cases
of marital infidelity. Andrew Solomon says that he, his brothers, and his
father are united by the "weird legacy" of their implication in his mother's
death, and quotes a nurse who participated in her own mother's death as
telling him "I know some people will have trouble with my saying this
but it was the most intimate time I've ever had with anyone."[11] Herbert
Hendin comments, "The feeling that participation in death permits an
intimacy that they are otherwise unable to achieve permeates euthanasia
stories and draws patients and doctors to euthanasia."[12] And no wonder.
Violation of a basic human bond is so terrible that the burdened conscience must instantly establish an abnormal one to compensate; the
very gravity of the transgression invests the new bond with a sense of
profound significance. Naturally some will find it attractive.

The reconciliation need has a public dimension, too. Isolated from
the community of moral judgment, transgressors strive to gather a substitute around themselves. They don't sin privately; they recruit. The
more ambitious among them go further. Refusing to go to the mountain
they require the mountain to come to them: society must be trans-

formed so that it no longer stands in awful judgment. So it is that they change the laws, infiltrate the schools, and create intrusive social-welfare bureaucracies.

Finally we come to the need for *justification*, which requires more detailed attention.

Unhooked from justice, justification becomes rationalization, which is a more dangerous game than it seems. The problem is that the ordinances written on the heart all hang together. They depend on each other in such a way that we cannot suppress one except by rearranging all the others. A few cases will be sufficient to show how this happens.

I begin with sexual promiscuity. The official line is that modern people don't take sex outside marriage seriously any longer; mere moral realists say this is because we no longer realize the wrong of it. I maintain that we do know it is wrong but pretend that we don't. Of course one must be careful to distinguish between the core laws of sex, the ones we can't not know, and the derived ones, which we certainly can fail to know. For example, though true and reasonable, the superiority of monogamous to polygamous marriage is probably not part of the core. On the other hand, no human society has ever held that the sexual powers may be exercised by anyone with anyone, and the recognized norm is a durable and culturally protected covenant between man and woman with the intention of procreation. Casual shack-ups and one-night stands don't qualify.

Because we can't not know that sex belongs with marriage, when we separate them we cover our guilty knowledge with rationalizations. In any particular culture, particular rationalizations may be just as strongly protected as marriage; the difference is that while the rationalizations vary from culture to culture, the core does not. At least in our culture, such sexual self-deceptions are more common among women than men. I don't think this is because the female conscience is stronger (or weaker) than the male. However, sex outside marriage exposes the woman to greater risk, so whereas the man must fool only his conscience, she must fool both her conscience and her self-interest. If she does insist on doing wrong, she has twice as much reason to rationalize.

One common rationalization is to say "No" while acting "Yes" in order to tell oneself afterward "I didn't go along." A rape crisis counsellor says that many of the women who call her do so not to report that they *have* been raped, but to ask *whether* they were raped.[13] If they have to ask, of course, they probably haven't been; they are merely dealing with their ambivalence by throwing the blame for their decisions on their partners. But this is a serious matter. Denial leads to the further wrong of false witness.

Another tactic is inventing private definitions of marriage. Quite a few people "think of themselves as married" although they have no covenant at all; some even fortify the delusion with "moving-in cere-monies" featuring happy words without promises. Unfortunately, people who "think of themselves as married" not only refuse the obligations of real marriage but demand all of its cultural privileges; because ratio-nalization is so much work, they require other people to support them in it. Such demands make the cultural protection of real marriage more difficult.

Yet another ruse is to admit that sex belongs with marriage but fudge the nature of the connection. By this reasoning I tell myself that sex is okay because I am *going* to marry my partner, because I *want* my partner to marry me, or because I have to find out if we *could* be happy married. An even more dangerous fudge is to divide the form of marriage from its substance — to say "we don't need promises because we're in love." The implication, of course, is that those who *do* need promises love impurely; that those who don't marry are more truly married than those who do.[14]

This last rationalization is even more difficult to maintain than most. Love, after all, is a permanent and unqualified commitment to the true good of the other person, and the native tongue of commitment is precisely promises. To work, therefore, this ruse requires another: having deceived oneself about the nature of marriage, one must now deceive oneself about the nature of love. The usual way of doing so is to mix up love with the romantic feelings that characteristically accompany it, and call *them* "intimacy." If only we have these feelings, we tell ourselves, we may have sex. That is to say, we may have sex — if we feel like it.

Here is where things really become interesting, because if the criterion of being as-good-as-married is sexual feelings, then obviously nobody who has sexual feelings may be prevented from marrying. So homosexuals must also be able to "marry"; their unions, too, should have cultural protection. At this point suppressed conscience strikes another blow, reminding us that marriage is linked with procreation. But now we are in a box. We cannot say "therefore homosexuals cannot marry," because that would strike against the whole teetering structure of rationalizations. Therefore we decree that having been *made* marriageable, homosexuals must be *made* procreative; the barren field must seem to bloom. There is, after all, artificial insemination. And there is adoption. So it comes to pass that children are given as a right to those from whom they were once protected as a duty. The normalization of perversion is complete.

When ordinary rationalization fails, people revert to other modes of suppression. We often see this when a young woman becomes pregnant. Suddenly her conscience discovers itself; though she was not ashamed to lift her skirts, she is suddenly ashamed to show her swelling belly. What can she do? Well, she can have an abortion; she can revert to the mode of suppression called getting rid of the evidence. Once again conscience multiplies transgressions. But she finds that the new transgression is no solution to the old one; in fact now she has something even more difficult to rationalize.

Think what is necessary to justify abortion.[15] Because we can't not know that it is wrong to deliberately kill human beings, there are only four options. We must deny that the act is deliberate, deny that it kills, deny that its victims are human, or deny that wrong must not be done. The last option is literally nonsense. That something must not be done is what it *means* for it to be wrong; to deny that wrong must not be done is merely to say "wrong is not wrong," or "what must not be done may be done." The first option is hardly promising either. Abortion does not just happen; it must be performed. Its proponents not only admit there is a "choice," they boast of it. As to the second option, if it was ever promising, it is no longer. Millions of women have viewed sonograms of their babies kicking, sucking their thumbs, and turning somersaults; even most feminists have given up calling the baby a "blood clot" or describing abortion as the "extraction of menses."

The only option left is number three: to deny the humanity of the victims. It is at this point that the machinery slips out of control. For the only way to make option three work is to ignore biological nature, which tells us that from conception onward the child is as human as you or I (does anyone imagine that a dog is growing in there?) — and invent another criterion of humanity, one which makes it a matter of degree. Some of us must turn out more human, others less. This is a dicey business even for abortionists. It needs hardly to be said that no one has been able to come up with a criterion that makes babies in the womb less human but leaves everyone else as he was; the teeth of the moral gears are too finely set for that.

Consider, for instance, the criteria of "personhood" and "deliberative rationality." According to the former, one is more or less human according to whether he is more or less a person; according to the latter, he is more or less a person according to whether he is more or less able to act with mature and thoughtful purpose. Unborn babies turn out to be killable because they cannot act maturely; they are less than fully persons, and so less than fully human. In fact, they *must* be killed when the interests of those who are more fully human require it. Therefore, not only may their mothers abort, but it would be wrong to stop the mothers from doing so. But look where else this drives us. Doesn't maturity also fall short among children, teenagers, and many adults? Then aren't they also less than fully persons — and if less than fully persons, then less than fully humans? Clearly so, hence they too must yield to the interests of the more fully human; all that remains is to sort us all out.

So conscience has its revenge. We can't not know the preciousness of human life — therefore, if we tell ourselves that humanity is a matter of degree, we can't help holding those who are more human more precious than those who are less. The urge to justify abortion drives us inexorably to a system of moral castes more pitiless than anything the East has devised. Of course we can fiddle with the grading criteria: consciousness, self-awareness, and contribution to society have been proposed; racial purity has been tried. No such tinkering avails to change the character of our deeds. If we will a caste system, then we shall have one; if we will that some shall have their way, then in time there shall be a nobility of Those Who Have Their Way. All that our fiddling with the criteria achieves is a rearrangement of the castes.

Need we wonder why, then, having started on our babies, we now want to kill our grandparents? Sin ramifies. It is fertile, fissiparous, and parasitic, always in search of new kingdoms to corrupt. It breeds. But just as a virus cannot reproduce except by commandeering the machinery of a cell, sin cannot reproduce except by taking over the machinery of conscience. Not a gear, not a wheel is destroyed, but they are all set turning in different directions than their wont. Evil must rationalize, and that is its weakness. But it can, and that is its strength.

We've seen that although conscience works in everyone, it doesn't restrain everyone. In all of us some of the time, in some of us all of the time, its fearsome energy merely "multiplies transgressions." Bent backwards by denial, it is more likely to catalyze moral collapse than hold it back.

But conscience is not the only expression of the natural law in human nature. Thomas Aquinas defined law as a form of discipline that compels through fear of punishment.[16] In the case of human law, punishment means suffering the civil consequences of violation; in the case of natural law it means suffering the natural consequences of violation. If I cut myself, I bleed. If I get drunk, I have a hangover. If I sleep with many women, I lose the power to care for anyone, and sow pregnancies, pain, and suspicion.

Unfortunately, the disciplinary effect of natural consequences is diminished in at least two ways. These two diminishers are the main reason why the discipline takes so long, so that the best that can be hoped for in most cultures is a pendulum swing between moral laxity and moral strictness.

The first diminisher is a simple time lag: not every consequence of violating the natural law strikes immediately. Some results make themselves felt only after several generations, and by that time people are so deeply sunk in denial that even more pain is necessary to bring them to their senses. A good example of a long-term consequence is the increase of venereal disease. When I was a boy we all knew about syphilis and gonorrhea, but because of penicillin they were supposed to be on the way out. Today the two horrors are becoming antibiotic-resistant, and AIDS, herpes, chlamydia, genital warts, human papilloma virus, and more than a dozen other sexually transmitted diseases, most of them formerly rare, are ravaging the population. Other long-term consequences of violating the laws of sex are poverty, because single women have no one to help them raise their children; crime, because boys grow into adolescence without a father's influence; and child abuse, because although spouses tend to greet babies with joy, live-ins tend to greet them with jealousy and resentment. Each generation is less able to maintain families than the one before. Truly the iniquities of the fathers — and mothers — are visited upon the children and the children's children to the third and fourth generation.

The second diminisher comes from us: "Dreaming of systems so perfect that no one will need to be good,"[17] we exert our ingenuity to *escape* from the natural consequences of breaking the natural law. Not all social practices have this effect. For instance, threatening drunk drivers with legal penalties supplements the discipline of natural consequences rather than undermining it. Nor is the effect always intended. We don't devise social insurance programs in order to encourage improvidence, though they do have this result. It isn't even always wrong. It would be abominable to refuse treatment to a lifelong smoker with emphysema, even though he may have been buoyed in his habit by the confidence that the doctors would save him. But to act with the *purpose* of compensating for immorality is always wrong, as when we set up secondary school clinics to dispense pills and condoms to teenagers.

Here is an axiom: We cannot alter human nature, physical, emotional, or spiritual. A corollary is that no matter how cleverly devised, our contrivances never do succeed in cancelling out the natural consequences of breaking the natural law. At best they delay them, and for several reasons they can even make them worse. In the first place they alter incentives: People with ready access to pills and condoms see less reason to be abstinent. In the second place they encourage wishful thinking: Most people grossly exaggerate their effectiveness in preventing disease and pregnancy and completely ignore the risks. In the third place they reverse the force of example: Before long the practice of abstinence erodes even among people who *don't* take precautions. Finally they transform thought: Members of the contraceptive culture think liberty from the natural consequences of their decisions is somehow owed to them.

There comes a time when even the law shares their view. In a 1992 case which reauthorized the private use of lethal violence against life in the womb, the United States Supreme Court *admitted* that its original abortion ruling might have been wrong, but upheld it anyway. As it explained, "For two decades of economic and social developments, people have organized their intimate relationships and made choices that define their views of themselves and their places in society in reliance on the availability of abortion in the event that contraception should fail. . . . An entire generation has come of age free to assume [this] concept of liberty[.]"[18] To put the thought more simply, what we did has separated sex from responsibility for resulting life for so long that to change the rules on people now would be unfair.

Naught avails; our efforts to thwart the law of natural consequences merely make the penalty more crushing when it comes. The only question is whether our culture will be able to survive the return stroke of the piston.

To survive what is bearing down on us, we must learn four hard lessons.

First, to acknowledge the natural law as a true and universal morality written on the heart.

Second, to be on guard against our own attempts to overwrite it with new laws that are really rationalizations for wrong.

Third, to fear the natural consequences of its violation, recognizing their inexorability.

Fourth, to forbear from all further attempts to compensate for immorality, returning on the path that brought us to this place.

Unfortunately, the condition of human beings since before recorded history is that we don't want to learn hard lessons. We would rather remain in denial. What power can break through such a barrier?

The sorts of measures that conservatives propound may offer some help at the margins: recovering a historical sense, so that we can learn from the catastrophes of the past, and recovering a sense of posterity, so that we do not burden our sons and daughters with the detritus of our pride. In the end, though, I doubt that any power is great enough, short of the grace of the Lawgiver; unless we love Him more than the culture, the culture will not be worth loving.

NOTES

1 "Children from the Laboratory,"*AMA Prism*, chap. 3, p. 2, May 1973, cited in J. C. Willke, *Abortion Questions and Answers* (Cincinnati: Hayes Publishing, 1985), p. 207.

2 Under pressure, it reversed itself in 1995, but even then gave only scientific, not ethical, reasons for doing so.

3 "Make Mine Hemlock," *The National Review* 47:10 (July 12, 1995), pp. 60-62.

4 Wesley J. Smith, *Forced Exit: The Slippery Slope from Assisted Suicide to Legalized Murder* (New York: Times Books/Random House, 1997), pp. 217-19.

5 *Dancing with Mr. D: Notes on Life and Death* (New York: Nan A. Talese/Doubleday, 1997), pp. 17, 19.

6 *Summa Theologica* I-II, Q. 94., Art. 4.

7 *But What If She Wants to Die? A Husband's Diary* (Seacaucus, NJ: Birch Lane, 1997), p. 316.

8 *Ibid.*, pp. 317-18.

9 "Death and Dignity: A Case of Individualized Decision Making," *New England Journal of Medicine* 324 (1991), pp. 691-94, and *Death and Dignity: Making Choices and Taking Charge* (New York: Norton, 1993).

10 "A Death of One's Own," *New Yorker* (May 22, 1995), pp. 54-69.

11 *Ibid.*

12 Herbert Hendin, M.D., *Seduced by Death: Doctors, Patients, and the Dutch Cure* (New York: W. W. Norton, 1997), p. 222.

13 William D. Gairdner, *The War Against the Family: A Parent Speaks Out on the Political, Economic, and Social Policies That Threaten Us All* (Toronto, ON: Stoddart, 1992), p. 560, citing an August 1991 article in *Chatelaine*.

14 See, for example, Anthony Giddens's promotion of what he calls the "pure relationship" in *The Transformation of Intimacy: Sexuality, Eroticism, and Love in Modern Societies* (Stanford: Stanford University Press, 1992), p. 138.

15 At this point several paragraphs are taken from my article "What We Can't Not Know," *Human Life Review* 22:4 (fall, 1996), pp. 85-94.

16 *Summa Theologica* I-II, Q. 95, Art. 1.

17 T. S. Eliot, *The Rock.*

18 *Planned Parenthood v. Casey*, 505 U.S. 833 (1992).

CONTRIBUTORS

JANET AJZENSTAT, Ph.D., teaches in the department of political science at McMaster University. She recently edited (with Peter J. Smith) a collection of essays on the Canadian founding, *Canada's Origins: Liberal, Tory, or Republican?*, and is now working with a group of scholars on a new edition of Canada's founding legislative debates.

J. BUDZISZEWSKI, Ph.D., teaches at the departments of government and philosophy at the University of Texas at Austin. He is a frequent contributor to *First Things*, a monthly journal of religion and public life, and has written four books, most recently *Written on the Heart: The Case for Natural Law*.

ALLAN CARLSON, Ph.D., is president of the Howard Center for the Family, Religion & Society in Rockford, Illinois. Carlson holds a doctorate in modern European history from Ohio University. His books include *The Swedish Experiment in Family Politics* and *From Cottage to Work Station: The Family's Search for Social Harmony in the Industrial Age*. From 1988 to 1993, he was a member of the National Commission on Children.

MICHAEL COREN is the author of internationally acclaimed biographies of G. K. Chesterton, H. G. Wells, and Sir Arthur Conan Doyle. He is a prolific journalist on both sides of the Atlantic. He writes a weekly column for *The Financial Post* and Sun newspapers in Canada, and hosts *The Michael Coren Show* on CFRB Radio in Toronto.

TOM FLANAGAN, Ph.D., received his doctorate in political science from Duke University. He has taught political science at the University of Calgary since 1968. He was also director of research for the Reform Party of Canada in 1991-92. Flanagan is the author of *Waiting for the Wave*, an analysis of Preston Manning's populist politics.

WILLIAM D. GAIRDNER, Ph.D., is a former professor of English literature, a successful businessman and an Olympic athlete. He has published five books, including the major bestsellers *The Trouble with Canada, War Against the Family*, and *On Higher Ground*. He is currently at work on a book about democracy.

STEPHEN HARPER received his M.A. in economics from the University of Calgary. He was the Reform MP for Calgary West from 1993 to 1996, and is now vice-president and president-elect of the National Citizens' Coalition.

MARK HOLMES, Ph.D., holds degrees from the Universities of Cambridge, New Brunswick, and Chicago. He has been a teacher, principal, secondary and postsecondary administrator, and professor of educational policy. He is married to a teacher and has four children and thirteen grandchildren, whom he enjoys together with writing and the outdoors near Warkworth, Ontario.

F. L. MORTON, Ph.D., is a professor of political science at the University of Calgary. He earned his doctorate at the University of Toronto in 1981. His publications consist of four books and more than 50 articles in constitutional law and judicial politics. In 1995 he was the recipient of the Bora Laskin Fellowship in Human Rights Research.

SCOTT REID is the author of *Canada Remapped: How the Partition of Quebec Will Reshape the Nation* and *Lament for a Notion: The Life and Death of Canada's Bilingual Dream*. From 1994 to 1997 he was the Reform party's senior researcher. Currently he is visiting scholar at the Centre for Canadian

Studies, University of Western Sydney, Australia.

PETER STOCKLAND is a columnist and member of the editorial board of *The Calgary Herald* and is the former editor of *The Calgary Sun*. He has worked as a reporter and columnist for newspapers in British Columbia, Alberta, and Ontario, in the process covering Parliament Hill for seven years. He was the Quebec bureau chief for *The Toronto Sun*.

MICHAEL A. WALKER, Ph.D., is the executive director and one of the founders of the Fraser Institute. He has written or edited 40 books on economic topics, and his articles have appeared in professional journals in Canada, the U.S., and Europe. His directorships include the Mont Pelerin Society, the Milton and Rose D. Friedman Foundation, and the Max Bell Foundation.